THE
Royal Exchange
THEATRE COMPANY

AN ILLUSTRATED RECORD

Edited and written by
DAVID FRASER

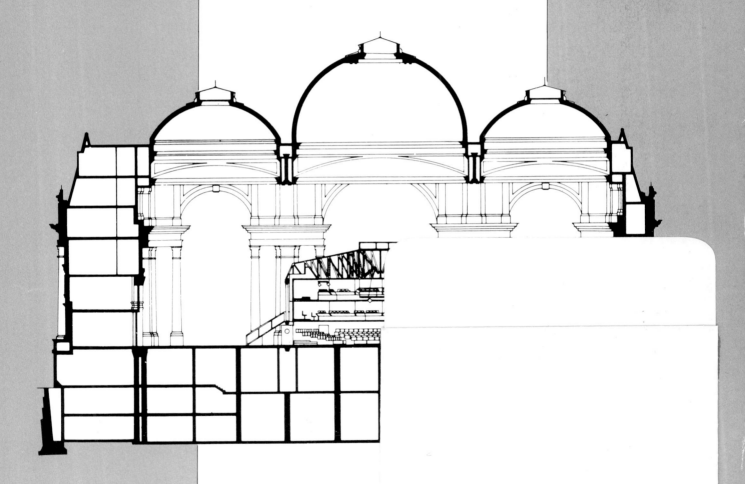

Design
ROGER SC
Typeset and
HOLBROOK PRINTING C

SUPPORTED BY
·A·G·M·A·
ASSOCIATION OF
GREATER MANCHESTER
AUTHORITIES.

An unusual role to play

The Mobil Playwriting Competition with the Royal Exchange Theatre has established a number of promising new dramatists. Many of their winning and commended plays have since gone into production.

We shall be joining forces again when Mobil Touring Theatre takes the Royal Exchange's production of Bernard Shaw's play 'Arms and the Man' on a nationwide tour.

Mobil Touring Theatre is now in its fourth year. It enables productions of the highest quality to tour regional theatres.

It may seem an unusual role for an oil company to play but it reflects a broad commitment to the arts which includes sponsorship of concerts, exhibitions and gallery guides.

CONTENTS

All photographs by **Kevin Cummins** except where otherwise stated.
Editorial Assistants: **Margot Field, Alexandra Greenman, Lynne Walker**. The help of **Bradshaw, Gass & Hope** of Bolton (for information and photographs relating to the Royal Exchange building) and of **Richard Negri, Casper Wrede, Malcolm Brown, Rosalind Knight** and **Avril Elgar** is gratefully acknowledged.

Published by the Royal Exchange Theatre Company Ltd
St Ann's Square, Manchester M2 7DH
© Royal Exchange Theatre Company 1988

ISBN 0 9512017 0 0

THANK YOU ROYAL EXCHANGE

THE ROYAL EXCHANGE THEATRE WAS OUR FIRST ARTS CLIENT WAY BACK IN 1976.

We soon learnt that the needs of arts organisations differed radically from those of our other clients... so we developed a specialist unit to cater specifically for marketing 'the arts.'

This unique section of The Advertising Unit has now grown to act for probably the biggest arts portfolio of any advertising agency in the country.

Today our clients include: Arts About Manchester, B.B.C., Bradford Alhambra, Contact Theatre, Liverpool Playhouse, Northern Ballet Theatre, Oldham Coliseum, Octagon Theatre, Rambert Dance, Royal Liverpool Philharmonic Orchestra, Sheffield Crucible, Sunderland Empire, Theatr Clwyd, Welsh National Opera, Wigan Pier, York Theatre Royal and, of course, Royal Exchange Theatre
— *to name but a few.*

The Advertising Unit

WE'VE PIONEERED THE ART OF SERVING THE ARTS

The Advertising Unit Limited, 35 Dale Street, Manchester M1 2HF. Telephone Denise Hitchin on: 061-236 8002

The biggest room in the world

A short history of The Royal Exchange adapted from the book by Robert Scott

The usual reason given in local history books for the building of Manchester's first Exchange in 1729 is that trade had grown to such a pitch in the town by the start of the century that somewhere was needed for "chapmen to meet in and transact their business." But why did Sir Oswald Mosley (who was to become Lord of the Manor in 1734, but already in the 1720s was doing the job for his elderly aunt Lady Anne Bland, the titular Lady of the Manor) spend his own money on building a meeting house? Presumably for profit – to stimulate trade, which would increase the number of stall holders and so swell the rent roll.

Yet for that purpose, extending the market place would have been enough. Why a meeting house? A splendidly eccentric doctor called Stukeley, writing of Manchester in 1724, spotted something that Sir Oswald capitalised on. He said of Mancunians: "Like the Athenians, they are much inclined to hear and tell news."

Athenians had the "Agora" – and Mancunians had their market place. But Mancunians also had rain, and what Sir Oswald did was build a covered place of assembly where men could gossip.

Dr Stukeley's Manchester was very busy – he called it "The largest, most rich, populous and busy village in England." Sadly, there is probably less of the 18th century town left today than in any equivalent city in the world. There are only three buildings of any note left in the centre that the doctor would have recognised; the shell of the cathedral is much as it was, St Ann's Church had been built just twelve years before he made his visit, and the third building is the Old Wellington Inn in the Shambles. Nothing else. Market Street was a narrow lane. Corn still grew in St Ann's Square. Deansgate too was a lane that ended at Quay Street. There were about 15,000 inhabitants, but only about 75 children in the whole town attended school.

What local government there was, the Court Leet, was conducted in a large two-storied building next to the Shambles, called the Booths. The policing of the town was in the hands of a borough reeve and two constables, all of whom were elected. The flying coach to London took 4½ days. The post office was in a side room of the main pub, the Bull's Head Inn, and the postage on a three page letter to London was about 9d. The roads were truly terrible; inside the town they were narrow and filthy and stank, on the roads out of town the dung gave way to ankle-deep mud in the winter and bone-breaking ruts in the summer.

And yet Manchester was increasingly important. By the beginning of the century Manchester goods were famous in London and even on the Continent. Inevitably the hub of the town was the market place. Manchester's right to hold a market, granted by the Lord of the Manor in 1301, was important to its emergence as the centre of the district – the grant forbade the creation of any other market within a radius of 6½ miles.

The title is more a claim than a fact. The Manchester Royal Exchange is certainly not the biggest room in the world today. It probably never was. But that wasn't the most extravagant claim – it was even referred to as "the eighth wonder of the world" and "the hub of the universe". The claim was made at two moments in the building's life: first in 1874 when it was about the size it is today, and again in 1921 when it was twice as big – one and a half acres of parquet floor.

But no one has ever contested the fact that it was the greatest place of assembly for traders that the world has ever seen.

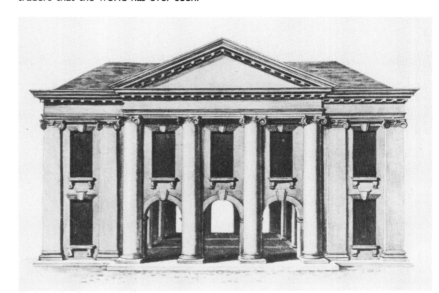

The First Exchange 1729-1790

The market place was also the meeting-place. All the early public buildings were close by, the coffee shops were either in the market place or just set back from it. This was the obvious site for the Exchange, which was built where Marks and Spencer's is today on the Market Street-Corporation Street corner.

According to an early sketch of the building in a 1740 map of the town, it was rather handsome. The ground floor was open, with a large room above. One can easily imagine the advertising blurb: "... on street level an elegant, pillared concourse where the business men of the town may meet to talk and exchange news. Fully protected from the elements. Upstairs a fine public room where the ladies of the town may visit and gentlemen may privately conduct their business."

Second Exchange (first portion) 1809
View taken from Market Place

Of course, it never worked out like that. The lanes leading to the market-place were small and filthy. Animals, including pigs and cows, roamed the streets, and one suspects that elegance and spaciousness were not much in evidence on market day.

It seems, indeed, that the Exchange never really worked in the way intended. A visitor to the town said it was a failure – "instead of affording a convenient walk for the merchants, it is crowded with butchers' stalls and blocks up the road." Nevertheless, the Exchange became the first really popular public building in the town. Frequent references to it in the Court Leet records and the Constable's Accounts show the colourful and varied existence it enjoyed.

Regiments were constantly passing through Manchester, either on their way to a European battle-ground, or simply as an outward manifestation of a new and nervous Hanoverian monarch. If they spent a night in the town they were often billeted at the Exchange. Visiting soldiers meant revels; revels meant broken windows, and the Constable's accounts reveal that one man, at least, must have rubbed his hands in glee at the approach of every regiment. There were frequent entries reading "To Luke Ashley, glazier, for repairing of windows at the Exchange, 3s 6d." He made a fortune!

The inheritors of the Exchange, the new Royal Exchange Theatre Company, when they first hatched their exotic scheme to build a theatre in the Victorian vastness of the Great Hall felt apprehension at all the solemn gentlemen turning in their graves at the very idea of theatricals being performed in their cherished solemn home. What the theatre company did not know at the time was that they were, in fact, returning the Exchange to a frequent use of the eighteenth century – musical and dramatic performances.

In fact, it was the home of Manchester's first recorded theatrical performance, in 1743, and a playbill still preserved shows that the entertainment consisted of Farquhar's *The Recruiting Officer* followed by a pantomime entitled *Harlequin's Vagaries*. Pit seats cost 1s 6d and admission to the gallery was 1s, by no means low prices for those days.

It is believed that the famous actor Charles Macklin appeared at the Exchange in 1750, and a reference in the same year to a performance of *Macbeth* sheds a curious light on the problems facing actors and managers in those days.

Strolling players found it hard to get permission to present plays, but music was entirely respectable. The advertisement in Whitworth's *Manchester Magazine* refers to *Macbeth* – "with all the original music, songs and dances." Clearly the public wanted Shakespeare and got Shakespeare, but the performance was permitted only if the equivalent of the "watch committee" could pretend it was an evening of madrigals.

The Exchange was the scene of a Grand Ball in 1760 to celebrate the coronation of George III. A great procession took place through the town, which was specially illuminated to mark the occasion. This must indeed have been spectacular, because there is reference at the time to only two lights in the whole town, one on the Cross in the Market Place and one on the Old Bridge connecting Manchester with Salford. There were over 700 at the ball and a commentator later observed that the room was considerably more crowded than was elegant.

When the streets of Manchester were widened in 1771 – an improvement which meant the demolition of the Booths – the Exchange became busier than ever. The Court Leet met regularly there and there are frequent references to entertainments, lectures and demonstrations.

Many of the early textile inventions were shown for the first time in the Exchange. One can imagine John Kay, Richard Arkwright, Samuel Crompton and the rest making their way up the stairs with models of their inven-

Poster for The Recruiting Officer *at the Exchange in 1743*

tions, hoping to arouse the interest of some enterprising businessman but anxious to avoid the hostility of the working men.

One announcement gives a glimpse into the sharp practices of those days. A Mr Stevens, advertising in 1773 his lecture on "Heads and Headdresses" at the Exchange, hoped that the ladies and gentlemen would buy tickets in advance, since otherwise they would be severely inconvenienced by delays while their gold was weighed. Apparently the clipping of gold coins was so common that when it was offered in payment it became necessary to check their weight.

In September of the same year there was a gala performance by Breslaw and his Italian Opera Company to raise money for the build-

Second Exchange after enlargement 1849
View taken from corner of St Ann's Square

ing of the Infirmary in Piccadilly. It appears almost certain that, until the first theatre was built in Marsden Street in 1762, the Exchange was the only building in the town capable of presenting plays.

But these were special events, usually at night and always on the upper floor of the building. Downstairs, amongst the stalls spilling into the market place, there would be plenty of free, if often brutal, entertainment to be had from the drunk in the stocks, or from the rogue in the pillory.

Behind St Ann's Churchyard there is still an attractive covered walkway called St Ann's Passage, linking the Square with King Street. Above it is an inscription which includes the words "The Old Exchange". Apparently there was a large room over the passage which was used for dances and meetings, and, as the Exchange proper became more disreputable, it was used as an alternative place of assembly.

At the other end of the Square, where Exchange is now, there was a solid row of houses including the old Coffee House. The only connection between St Ann's Square and the Exchange was a pitch-black alleyway called Dark Entry, which had a right-angled turn in the middle and was a notorious spot for muggings. It is said that before going down the passage you should stop and listen. If you heard footsteps coming towards you, then you waited; if not, you ran through as fast as possible.

With the coming of the Industrial Revolution, Manchester grew with fantastic speed towards the end of the 18th century and the Exchange, from being simply dirty, became sordid. Its demolition in 1792 was described as a great benefit to the neighbourhood.

Nathan Crompton, who was the Borough Reeve of that year, erected on the site of the Exchange a monument with a clock on top. The clock never worked, the purpose of the monument puzzled the townspeople, and it became known as Crompton's Folly.

As the area continued to decay, the site of the Exchange became "the resort of the ne'er do wells and the won't-works of the town", and earned itself the name of Penniless Hill. Twelve years after the first Exchange was pulled down, a public meeting was called on 8 October, 1804, in Spencer's Tavern, to discuss the inadequacies of the fast-growing town, which now had a population of 90,000 compared with 9,000 in 1729.

After discussion, the meeting agreed that "the erection of a handsome building in the Market Place for the purposes of a commercial coffee room and tavern was highly desirable, and would afford great accommodation to the merchants and manufacturers of this town and neighbourhood."

A committee of 21 was formed with members drawn from a wide range of Manchester life. The chairman, George Phillips, had been Borough Reeve the previous year, and the Borough Reeve-elect, William Fox, was made treasurer. There were manufacturers and dealers, a banker, an architect and a solicitor. Rather more surprisingly, the committee also included a silk handkerchief maker who lived on the corner of King Street and Cross Street, a silversmith, and a drysalter who appears to have been the owner of Strangeways.

The committee tried hard to erase all possible connection with the former Exchange. They called the new project The Commercial Building, and not until well after it was opened in 1809 did it become formally known as The Exchange, though to most people it was probably never known as anything else.

The former site was ruled out because of the filth and the tramps, but land belonging to Lord Ducie at the other side of Market Street (within the site of the present building) was thought suitable, and there was no difficulty in persuading him to grant a lease.

The committee quickly did their sums and calculated they needed £20,000. They issued

Third Exchange 1874
View taken from Corporation Street

400 shares at £50 each, and were able to close the list in a few hours.

A competition to design the new building was won by a Chester architect, Thomas Harrison, who persuaded the committee that they would be best served by a copy of Lloyds Coffee House in London. There were some difficulties (mostly about buying out sitting tenants) before the work could be begun, but the corner stone was laid on 21 July, 1806.

According to the Manchester Mercury report, behind the inscription was placed a Wedgwood vase containing newly minted coins and medals of Nelson and Pitt. But when a major extension took place 40 years later, although the vase was found still there, all it contained was one halfpenny piece. An investigation cleared the workmen who unearthed the vase and left suspicion lying squarely on the workmen of 1806. Incidentally the plate bearing the inscription can still be seen in the Central Library.

The membership subscription for the new Exchange was fixed at two guineas for a man either living in Manchester or having his business there, one guinea for anyone else. The committee, it appears, had misgivings about whether Manchester merchants, being notoriously tight-fisted, would be willing to pay to

Interior of the Exchange in 1877 with portraits of well-known members

do something they were already doing gratis – namely, meeting their contacts.

They need not have worried. The building opened on 2 January, 1809, with 1,543 paid-up members, and within five weeks the committee was instructing the architect to prepare plans for an extension. But what did the subscribers get for their two guineas, beyond a sense of their own importance? The building was certainly handsome, two storied, semi-circular at one end. The main rooms on the ground floor were the newsroom and the bar.

The newsroom, which was open from seven in the morning until ten at night, was the facility most used by the subscribers. Several copies of all the London newspapers were available and there were also provincial newspapers – Manchester by this time had five weekly papers.

The ground floor included rooms to let, and the first two went to a tailor and a hatter. Later the Post Office moved in – at a reduced rent, for this was a most convenient facility as the markets of members moved further and further abroad. (Eventually it was felt that the Post Office had become too identified with the Exchange, and in 1847 the Town Council

Visit of HM Queen Victoria in 1851

insisted on its removal to new premises in Brown Street.)

Upstairs was a large dining room which could seat 300 with room for an orchestra if required. The main kitchens were in the basement, but next to the dining room was "a kitchen fitted up for making gravy and dishing up the viands."

The two principal employees were the Porter and the Barman. The image created by the Porter was felt to be so important that his dress was the subject of detailed discussion by the full committee. They decided to fit him out, at their expense, with "a lace-cocked hat, a staff with a silver head, on which shall be engraved the Manchester Arms and the words Manchester Exchange, a dark blue cloak-coat with gold lace at the collar and with twist at the button holes."

The first Barman was sacked and replaced by a manager. Within four years he was given the title of Master of the Exchange, and never served behind the bar again.

hile the subscribers of the new Exchange flourished, the majority of Mancunians were suffering hardship and oppression in the industrial revolution. Fortunes were being made while the average weekly wage of an operative was 10 shillings, and the price of a loaf was 1s 2d. Angry workers wrecked machines, burned mills, and in 1812 there was a riot that nearly ended in the destruction of the new Exchange. In April the Prince Regent (later George IV) took on the duties of Head of State from his extremely sick father. There was great excitement about the Ministers he would choose. Reactionary, hard-line men like Castlereagh and Addington were widely expected to be replaced; instead, they were retained.

The bosses were triumphant, and 154 of them petitioned the authorities to convene a public meeting to express support and congratulations to the Prince. With some trepidation the Borough Reeve agreed and a meeting was called for 8 April in the Exchange dining room at 11 am.

It was an extremely provocative step and within a few hours a protest, headed "Now or Never", was on the streets in handbills and posters. It called on citizens to assemble at the Exchange and express their "detestation of the conduct of those men who have brought this country to its present distressed state, and are entailing misery on thousands of our industrious mechanics." The Exchange committee, now greatly alarmed, cancelled the meeting on the rather specious grounds that the staircase to the dining room would not be able to stand the weight of all the people.

But it was too late. An angry crowd assembled; the 154 gentlemen did not. The mob invaded the newsroom, broke windows, smashed pictures and furniture, while a splinter group headed for St Ann's Square to hold a public protest meeting. Only the arrival of the militia saved the Exchange.

In the aftermath of the trouble the founder of the Manchester Guardian, John Edward Taylor, was falsely accused of having written the "Now or Never" message. His denunciation of his accuser was so strong that he was sued for libel. But Taylor won, a victory which established his public reputation, and nine years later the Guardian began under his editorship.

During the quarter of a century after the Peterloo incident in 1819, in Manchester and its surrounding towns, wealth came to an entirely new group of men. Manchester had been able to produce not only the new inventions and the management to exploit them, but it also produced the men and the ideas to develop the society that resulted from this industrial explosion.

The robustness of early Exchange members, who both fought for reform and made their fortunes was remarkable. To see them in their natural habitat, the place to visit was the Exchange. With exports growing at a tremendous rate, it was said that in the Manchester Exchange there was a more detailed knowledge of every corner of the earth than in any other room in the world. In 1847 a major extension, which more than doubled the facilities, was started. It was completed in 1849.

In mid-September, 1851, there came official news that the Queen and the Prince Consort would visit Manchester on October 10, giving the city less than a month for preparation. A hasty meeting between the mayor, John Potter (son of the first mayor) and corporation with the Exchange Committee agreed that the Exchange was the only building in the city suitable for the presentation of the Loyal Address to Her Majesty.

Everything went well, and after his ringing presentation of the Loyal Address the mayor went on his knees to be dubbed Sir John at

Looking up Market Street, with a view of the Exchange Tower, c 1899

the foot of a specially-constructed throne. His knighthood was not the only honour handed out by a well-pleased Queen. Within a month the Home Secretary, Sir George Grey, sent confirmation that it was the Queen's pleasure that the building should be known henceforth as the Manchester Royal Exchange.

O ther changes were coming. In 1859 the Royal Exchange Committee became the proprietors of the Manchester Royal Exchange. New company laws had been introduced in Parliament four years previously, enabling private firms to shed their ultimate legal responsibilities and become public companies with limited liabilities. The character of the Exchange itself was changing too.

As the business became more intense, the furniture was pushed to the sides of the room, the bar was moved out, and left in the middle was a big open space where the serious talking could be done standing up.

Then in 1863 the elderly, amiable Master, Francis Wrigley, was forced after 20 years' service to retire. He was no longer suitable. What the proprietors needed was a tough, efficient administrator and they got him in Mr

Edwin Simpson. Little did the members dream what was in store.

Not only could Edwin Simpson have been more unlike his kindly predecessor; he also had a quite different sort of contract of employment. Instead of Wrigley's annual salary of £500, he asked for and received £250 and a percentage of turnover. Turnover meant membership, and he set about the matter with what must have been alarming vigour.

Simpson quickly realised that many people coming on 'Change were not members. He rooted out the defaulters, demanded subscriptions, and where he could prove his case he demanded arrears as well. The members were incensed. Simpson continued his battle by persuading the proprietors to display the names of defaulters on a list on the pillars, and if they still held out, to take them to the County Court.

He also decided to introduce a ticket system which further outraged the members. On the first day that tickets were inspected, over £2,000 was taken at the doors in new subscriptions. Membership still stood at two guineas and in the first year of his appointment, Edwin Simpson raised the membership by 1,121. No wonder he wanted a percentage arrangement!

It was clear that the twice-extended Exchange was far too small, especially with all the new members, and in 1865 it was decided to replace the building with a new one.

Faced by an uncooperative local authority and a membership that refused to provide money, the proprietors took on the less daunting obstacle of Westminster. In 1866 they made themselves into a limited company, then applied for and obtained an Act of Parliament that would give them the planning permission and borrowing powers they had been so far denied.

The third Exchange was built in two stages, and the old building was not demolished until the first half was completed in October, 1871. Exactly three years later in October 1874 the whole project was complete. It was monumental: a "room" measuring 206 feet by 96 feet with a massive dome 125 feet above the centre – almost exactly ten times the size of the 1806 building. It was by far the largest

View of the extension being constructed, taken from Cross Street 1916

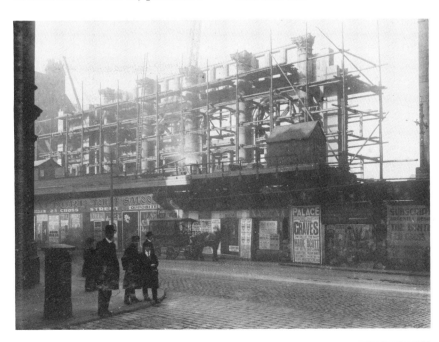

single commercial room in the world.

The building was not, and never had been, exclusively devoted to cotton. Cotton was, of course, the key, but as well as the original members, the manufacturers and merchants, there were their salesmen, the middlemen (the importers of raw cotton and the yarn agents) and the finishers (the firms who dyed, bleached or printed the manufactured cloth). As technology developed, the engineers and machinery suppliers needed access to the manufacturers and, with the export trade expanding, shippers, bankers and insurance companies jostled with each other for Members' custom. And as the wealth of the members grew, so even wine merchants and jewellers joined to find new buyers. The Exchange was a business community.

The broadening of the Exchange membership became even more marked after the opening of the Manchester Ship Canal in the 1890s and the numbers began to climb again. Lack of space was a perpetual problem, made more irritating to the members by the knowledge that they were the sufferers while the directors were reaping handsome dividends from the ever-increasing subscriptions. In 1906 the directors, under pressure, announced a proposal to buy more land, build a £500,000 extension, and meanwhile raise the subscription from three to six guineas to pay for the improvements.

As in 1865, the subscribers were incensed. They formed the Manchester Royal Exchange Subscribers' Association, which, within two years, enrolled 6,000 of the 9,000 members. Then they put forward their own plans, which were that the directors should sell the Exchange to the council, buy the now-vacant infirmary site in Piccadilly, build a new Exchange, and still keep the subscription at three guineas.

The directors said to the subscribers in effect: "Very well, you do it. We will sell the Exchange to you, and you can put up the new building." But there were no takers, the whole matter drifted on for seven years with much bad feeling and many rows. Eventually the Board had once more to seek an Act of Parliament, and was given the go-ahead on 4 July 1913, by which time membership had topped 10,000.

Announcing in August, 1913, that Parliament had given the go-ahead for the extended Manchester Royal Exchange, the chairman of the board said it would open by the end of 1916 "unless something unforeseen happens." Something did happen, World War I, and it was not until October 1921 that the new building was ready.

The Exchange did not have a particularly distinguished war. Membership dropped by about 2,000, but the directors managed to pay a fairly good dividend each year. The end of the war was commemorated by the first visit to the Exchange by an incumbent American President, President Wilson, who was wildly cheered when he appeared on the gallery.

The new building was of course sensational – 1.7 acres with six instead of three domes, and around the now doubled hall were 10 floors which included 250 offices, 38 shops, six restaurants and a Post Office.

It was by far the largest place of assembly for traders of any kind in the world, and in 1921 Lancashire's dominance still seemed total. It was calculated that there were 130 million spindles in the world, and members of the Manchester Royal Exchange controlled 60 million of them.

View of the domes under construction, looking towards Albert Square 1920

But trade troubles were increasing, and 1921 was the worst year for cotton since the famine 60 years before. So it was not surprising that the commentators were a little cautious when King George V and Queen Mary came to open the new building on 8 October.

It was a splendid occasion, with a seated audience of over 15,000 assembled on the "Floor", including the Lord Mayors and Mayors of 70 northern cities and boroughs, but His Majesty too sounded notes of caution and concern in his speech, with hopes that trade would pick up.

For a few years the Exchange was busier than ever but by 1926 exports had been halved and the cotton industry's downward slide was irreversible. The Exchange itself was never in a desperate state in the '30s because it did not depend completely on cotton and the subscription continued to rise, but the directors' search for other uses for the building showed an unmistakable need for more income.

The second week of February 1935 was an upsetting time for the older members. On the Tuesday the directors announced that they were letting the Floor for the annual dance of the Manchester and District Farmers' Association. As if that were not bad enough, on Friday there suddenly appeared on the Floor five glass stands advertising shirts and ties.

Members took strong exception to this, and without actually smashing the glass shook the stands hard enough for all the displayed items to collapse in a heap. As a further protest they lit up their pipes and cigarettes, very much against the rules. The directors took the point and the stands were removed.

Then Hitler intervened. In the first of the three great air raids on Manchester, the Exchange was hit. What exactly happened has never been quite clear, but the bombs struck the building at about 7pm on 22 December 1940, and by dawn the original half of the building was more or less destroyed.

Although it was 13 years before the building became fully operational again, the inconvenience to members was slight. The bombs had cut the building in half so neatly that only the building of a wall was needed to make the remaining half usable. The members returned after an uncomfortable 16 weeks in the Houldsworth Hall on Deansgate.

The completed extension of the Royal Exchange in 1921

Work did not start on the rebuilding of the shattered half until 1948, by which time it was quite apparent that the threequarters of an acre of Hall that remained was quite enough for the 4,000 members who were left. The Exchange was the first building in Manchester to be rebuilt with Government money, and there were strong protests about using funds for what one critic described as "nothing more than a glorified gambling den" instead of on housing.

The only reason the Exchange had priority was that it had been decided to put in six storeys of offices where the bombed half had been, and to let two floors to Government departments. Happily the main walls had been left standing, and the office development was completed within the old exterior.

Boots the Chemist returned in 1950 and on 12 November 1953 Princess Margaret re-opened the completed building.

The brief textile boom just after the war was over by the late 1950s. On reopening in 1955 the Exchange membership had risen to around 6,000; by 1960 it was 2,062. In December of that year the corporation gave planning permission to remove the great domes, to reduce the size of the Hall to half, and to build two blocks of offices on the remainder. The work never started because a fortnight later, on 20 December, Messrs Jack Cotton and Charles Clore put in a £2,400,000 bid for the Royal Exchange Company Ltd.

Why should anyone want to buy a company that was in such trouble? The answer was the building itself. Ironically, the bombs had saved it; although the Hall was no longer a going concern, all the offices and shops brought in handsome rents. The land value, with prices rising, was reason enough.

There was a brief resistance by the Board, but the £3 offer for every £1 share was one shareholders could not refuse. Most of the Manchester directors of the company resigned and although the new owners assured the members that the Exchange Floor would go on for ever, it was only eight years before it was agreed that enough was enough.

The development of the telephone and telex, the growth of man-made fibres and their much more stable prices compared with the up-and-down world of raw cotton prices, and the fact that a handful of companies contained all the elements of the trade under one huge umbrella, meant that the social side of the Exchange became all that was left.

So on 2 July 1968, the Master announced that with only 660 members left the company could no longer pay its way.

There was no ceremonial ending, and the few remaining members agreed to continue to meet in a room in the rebuilt part of the premises. The company, which had been absorbed within the Cotton/Clore empire, sold its one and only asset – the building – to the Prudential Assurance Company a fortnight before the Hall closed.

On 31 December 1968 trading ceased, the doors were closed and the Hall was silent.

To its new owners the Exchange was simply a block of shops and offices with a good yield of rents, but as an investment property it had a yawning absurdity – the Hall, three-quarters of an acre of pillared Victorian splendour, big enough to hold Manchester Cathedral. But it was to hold a very different building.

High 'Change in the hectic days of the mid-twenties before the slump

The bombed building on the morning of 23 December 1940

View from the centre of the building looking towards Market Street and showing the old arcade wall of the Exchange Hall and the perimeter offices over, partly demolished. Taken during reconstruction 1948

THE DEVELOPMENT OF THE COMPANY

If ever there was a group project, this is it. The Royal Exchange Theatre Company has its origins in several other theatre companies but all were run by members of a group, one that has evolved and stuck together despite all difficulties and conflicts for well over thirty years.

Amongst the many trained at the influential Old Vic Theatre School by Michel Saint-Denis, George Devine and Glen Byam Shaw between 1947 and 1952 were a group which included a Finnish director Casper Wrede, a designer of Italian extraction Richard Negri, and an anglicised American actor James Maxwell. When they graduated a number of this group of actors, directors and designers wanted to stay together because they shared similar aims and ambitions. The first opportunity for them to work together arose when two of the group, Richard Negri and Frank Dunlop, formed a new company in 1954 – in Manchester.

The Piccolo Theatre Company launched the first of its two short seasons in March that year in the Chorlton Theatre Club in Wilbraham Road. Richard Negri, who had just spent two seasons as designer at Oldham Coliseum, and Frank Dunlop, the veteran of the company at 27, assembled the Piccolo Players almost entirely from ex-Old Vic students. Among them were Eric Thompson, George Hall (later Head of the Acting Course at the Central School), Dilys Hamlett, Avril Elgar, Lee Montague, Priscilla Morgan, June Brown and Rosalind Knight. Patrick Wymark and James Maxwell were to join the company for its second season, and other actors included Bernard Cribbins, Phyllida Law, Mike Morgan, Ann Morrish and Kenneth Watson.

The whole company worked night and day to prepare the theatre (which, since its demise as Chorlton Repertory Theatre, had housed amateurs) for its opening: decorating, scrubbing, hanging an awning of undertakers' shroud material (because it was cheap) painted with nearly a mile of black stripes, raising the seating for 200, installing a refreshment bar and cloakroom, and building a new forestage beyond the proscenium. Significantly, Richard Negri was already thinking about the intimacy of theatrical space. One newspaper reported his views: "We want to break down this awful barrier between the actors and the audience. The stage shouldn't be just another form of TV – a light square in a darkened room – but part of the auditorium. We want to make the audience feel that they are really part of the play."

Above politics (the premises were on the top floor of the local Conservative Club's large building!), the company had little money – all of its members received only £5 a week – but it did have the patronage of several distinguished members of the profession including Peggy Ashcroft, Angela Baddeley, Sir Lewis Casson and Dame Sybil Thorndike in addition to the group's Old Vic School mentors. Peggy Ashcroft gave her blessing to the venture in a speech from the stage on the opening night, 17 March 1954: "This is a page of theatre history in the making. ... They are going to give us all kinds of plays. I hope to God they have enough money to do a lot of them."

Certainly there were all kinds of plays – Frank Dunlop's opening production, *The Women Have Their Way* by the Spanish brothers Serafin and Joaquin Quintero, was followed by *Arsenic and Old Lace*, *The Taming of the Shrew, She Stoops to Conquer, Guilty* (an adaptation of *Thérèse Raquin*) and Molière's *Don Juan*, but money was always a problem. The most successful play of first March-June season – a serious, experimental production of the melodrama *Maria Marten, or The Murder in the Red Barn* directed by Richard Negri with music by George Hall – was even revived for an extra week before touring to the Arts Theatre in Cambridge. Artistically, however, the season was adjudged a success and Piccolo managed to attract an Arts Council grant of £500 and 800 one-guinea guarantors for the next one. For the players' return in October George Devine, with Jocelyn Herbert

Richard Negri with his model of the Piccolo Theatre auditorium
Photo Manchester Evening News

Eric Thompson and Avril Elgar in *The Taming of the Shrew*
Photo Peter Selby

designing, produced the Goldoni comedy *The Mistress of the Inn* and Patrick Wymark performed Chekhov's *Swan Song* as a curtain raiser. Its choice might have been prophetic: the company was to survive for only five more productions – a *Playboy of the Western World* "touched with magic", Beaumarchais' *The Barber of Seville* with music by John McGregor, *Twelfth Night, Treasure Island* and *Dial M for Murder*.

By the time Frederick Knott's thriller was staged, however, the writing was on the wall. The Piccolo Theatre Company had failed to find sufficient support from the local community. Although they had achieved a reputation for imaginative and intelligent productions, the choice of repertoire was too adventurous for suburban Manchester. The company were forced to close in January 1955, a mere ten months after they had opened.

While Piccolo may be regarded as peripheral to the eventual development of the Royal Exchange – even though it introduced some of the group to Manchester – the next formal venture, the 59 Theatre Company, was undoubtedly of crucial importance, bringing Michael Elliott into the fold.

When Casper Wrede left the Old Vic School he spent a couple of years as a professional producer for the Oxford University Dramatic Society. It was there that Michael Elliott, then an undergraduate, met the group through writing a rave review in a university magazine of a production by Casper Wrede (of whom he had never heard) of a new play by Michael Meyer (*The Ortolan*) which contained another student called Maggie Smith. When he left Oxford Elliott became Casper's assistant for an OUDS production on the Edinburgh Fringe in 1954, in which James Maxwell played Marlowe's *Edward II*. That professional relationship was cemented when both joined the BBC Television Drama Department; they ended up doing five co-productions of classics together.

Then in 1959 Casper Wrede formed the 59 Theatre Company to produce an ambitious season of plays drawing on the talents of many of the group at the Lyric Opera House, Hammersmith. Backed entirely by private money, it was one of the first attempts in Great Britain to do what later became commonplace – stage a season of major European classics. At that time the National Theatre did not exist, the Old Vic was almost completely devoted to Shakespeare, the Royal Court was concerned mainly with new English writing, and the Royal Shakespeare Company was confined to Stratford and the Bard. That trail-blazing season introduced a remarkable programme of foreign masterpieces which were virtually unknown in this country – *Danton's Death*, *Brand*, *Creditors* – and for a few brief months, the 59 Theatre Company rivalled the best companies in Britain.

Patrick Wymark and Dilys Hamlett in *Danton's Death*
Photo: Ivor Sharp

BBC studio recording of Michael Elliott's production of *Brand*
Photo BBC

The directors were James H Lawrie, the businessman who put up, and lost, all the capital needed, and Casper Wrede who was assisted on the artistic side by Michael Elliott. They were joined by Malcolm Pride and Richard Negri who designed the five plays, Richard Pilbrow who lit them, George Hall who composed the music and David Collison who designed the sound. The casts included many actors who were to become famous, on television as well as the stage, and several whose names were to crop up repeatedly over the years as members of the group. Amongst the company were Patrick McGoohan, Fulton Mackay, Patrick Wymark, Peter Sallis, Frank Windsor, Harold Lang, John Turner, James Maxwell, Dilys Hamlett, Avril Elgar, Olive McFarland, Michael Gough, Lyndon Brook, Alan Dobie, Jack MacGowran, Rupert Davies, Patrick Allen and two who were to become rather better known as writers, Ronald Harwood and P.J. Kavanagh.

Casper Wrede's production of Büchner's *Danton's Death* opened the season on 27 January, 1959. A brave choice which received mixed reactions, it was the first English staging of the play. James Maxwell translated and adapted it, producing a version that was later also seen on BBC Television. Patrick Wymark played Danton, Harold Lang was Robespierre and Patrick

McGoohan St Just. The next production which played throughout March was a double-bill of Strindberg's *Creditors*, which starred the Swedish actress Mai Zetterling as Tekla, and *The Cheats of Scapin* by Thomas Otway (from the Molière comedy). The former, directed by Wrede and translated by Michael Meyer, was a considerable success but the latter, a production by Peter Dews, was the company's only artistic failure.

It was followed, however, on 8 April by Michael Elliott's first professional stage production, the supposedly unstageable *Brand*, which was, according to Harold Hobson in the *Sunday Times* "a revelation". John Elsom later wrote that: "*Brand* was a startling and unlikely success. Ibsen had written it as a long dramatic poem, to be read rather than staged: but Michael Meyer's adaptation, substantially cutting the original, brought out its theatrical qualities. Patrick McGoohan's Brand was a haunting performance, throwing aside normal heroic rhetoric in favour of an intense down-to-earth fervour, inspired but prosiac, a modern fanatic. His hero captured the imagination of British audiences." Kenneth Tynan, writing in *The Observer* noted: "Michael Elliott has directed it with imagination and a real understanding of its qualities. In this he is considerably aided by Richard Negri who, with bold simplicity and ingenuity, has evoked in a small space the ghostly splendours of mountain and fjord and of darkness and light." Fifteen years later at the time the Royal Exchange opened, Richard Pilbrow, who designed the lighting, recalled: "From the Hammersmith Broadway, the spectator was ensnared, captured and transported into a world of the spirit, and of inspiration that seemed to live inseparably amongst the fjords and mountains of Norway. The stage was five miles deep, six thousand feet high and yet the actors played – or lived – in a solidly real space that gave their presence a captivating reality which made an obscure, almost Victorian, text have an immediacy and truth that was galvanizing ..."

Casper Wrede's hope of developing new work was limited to the premiere of *The Rough and Ready Lot*, a play by Alun Owen about four soliders of fortune (played by Jack MacGowran, Patrick Allen, Alan Dobie and Rupert Davies) in a Spanish American republic shortly after the American Civil War. When its run finished at the end of June so did the 59 Theatre Company – apart from hosting a Cambridge ADC May week production of *Love's Labours*, a new musical by Clive Swift, Richard Cottrell, Corin Redgrave and John Wood. Financially the six-month season had been disastrous but its impact was enormous. The venture was a watershed: it established the names of many involved and it pointed the way forward for the group.

There followed, however, a period of nearly ten years in which they mainly all pursued their individual careers. Several shows bore their stamp – Michael Elliott's magical *As You Like It* at Stratford and London in 1961/62 in which Vanessa Redgrave played Rosalind, the whole of the last season of the Old Vic Theatre Company in 1962/63 before the National Theatre took over, and Elliott's productions of *Little Eyolf* in the Assembly Hall at the 1963 Edinburgh Festival and *Miss Julie*, with Maggie Smith and Albert Finney, for the National at the Chichester Festival and London in 1965/66. At the Old Vic Michael Elliott, as artistic director, reassembled many of the 59 Company. He and Casper Wrede directed the shows – Michael Meyer's new translation of *Peer Gynt* with Leo McKern in the title role, *Othello, The Merchant of Venice* and *Measure for Measure* – except for one, Sir Tyrone Guthrie's memorable return with *The Alchemist*. Litz Pisk and George Hall were responsible for all movement and music. Richard Negri and Malcolm Pride again designed most of the productions, Richard Pilbrow and David Collison created all light and sound. Many of the same names appeared in the casts, but the group was growing. Trevor Peacock, for instance, was an actor in that company.

Manchester then came back into the picture. In 1959 Braham Murray had been a schoolboy member of the audience which was overwhelmed by *Brand* and had resolved one day to work with Michael Elliott. By the end of 1965 at the age of only 22 Murray had been appointed artistic director of Century Theatre which was then about to move into the new University Theatre in Manchester, while continuing to make full use of its mobile theatre [which for the past 20 years has been stationary at Keswick] for touring to towns throughout the North West. During his two years in charge of Century Theatre Braham Murray transformed it into a company receiving national attention. He directed 16 productions for them including the premiere of Joe Orton's revised version of *Loot* (the success of which helped to establish its status), Michael Meyer's *The Ortolan*, the premiere of Gerard McLarnon's *The Saviour, The Philanderer, See How They Run, Macbeth, The Importance of Being Earnest*, a double bill of Ionesco's *The Chairs* and Pinter's *The Dumb Waiter, Waiting for Godot* (with Anton Rodgers, Wolfe Morris, Derek Fowlds and Trevor Peacock in the cast), *Long Day's Journey Into Night* (in which Helen Mirren made her professional debut as the maid), *Charley's Aunt* and *Romeo and Juliet*, the last two with Tom Courtenay. Dilys Hamlett was a regular visitor, James Maxwell played Shylock in *The Merchant of Venice* and, in the autumn of 1967, Michael Elliott agreed to come to Manchester to direct Tom Courtenay in *The Playboy of the Western World*.

It was a fateful moment. Michael Elliott explained at the time: "I greatly admire the work that Braham has done in the North and I am also attracted by the idea of working in the University Theatre itself. The proscenium arch theatre no longer interests me, and the highly adaptable stage of this theatre is very exciting. I've always wanted to work with Tom Courtenay, and although, of course, we could easily stage *Playboy* in the West End, we both prefer to stage it in Manchester to a fresh audience and free those pressures which constantly cripple one's work in London." He, Casper Wrede and others of the group had been feeling for some time that London was not the right environment in which to evolve their kind of theatre. Around the time that *Playboy* was running, they conceived the idea of forming a new company to operate intermittently at the University Theatre knowing that the relationship between Century Theatre, the running of which Braham was soon to relinquish, and the University Drama Department was breaking down. Professor Hugh Hunt invited them to apply and they became part-time professional tenants of the 295-seat theatre.

Although the company was formed on 12 February 1968, the news was not made public until early April. It was called the 69 Theatre Company to echo the 59 Theatre Company. The original (and unpaid) Artistic Directors were Casper Wrede, Michael Elliott, Richard Pilbrow (who was later to resign because of the success of his own expanding company, Theatre Projects) and Braham Murray. The core of the multiple directorship, which has given the company continuity and consistency in the quality of its work during the past twenty years, was in place. Jack Good, whose connections with members of the group stretched back to OUDS in the early fifties and known to a wider audience as an actor and producer of *Six Five Special* and other television

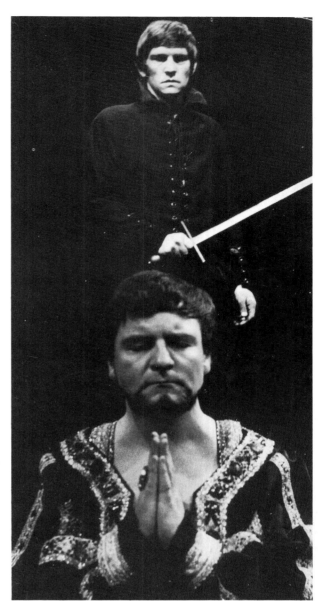

Tom Courtenay and Glyn Owen in *Hamlet*

pop shows, was also a director for a period before returning to live in America. James Maxwell, who soon became an Artistic Director in all but name, was officially appointed in 1973 and Richard Negri the following year.

In 1968 there were only three 'live' theatres in Manchester – compared with fifteen at the beginning of the century – but no money from the City was forthcoming for the new company. That did not deter them, however. With Laurence Harbottle as Chairman and friend, and Robert Scott as Administrator (initially the only member of the company permanently resident in Manchester), they set about raising funds. A generous grant of £15,000 from the Arts Council and some support from North West Arts was sufficient to begin operating.

Stockbroker Peter Henriques, who was to be enormously influential in ensuring that the company stayed in Manchester, created what was called "The Council" of the 69 Theatre Company. It had absolutely no powers but some of the most able and highly placed Mancunians served on it. Its function was to encourage the Artistic Directors with their personal support and to try to raise money to make the whole operation possible. In fact, when the company's finances had inevitably become disastrous later on, only the personal bank guarantees of Henriques and other members of the Council saved the '69' from bankruptcy. In the first few months of the company's existence some £10,000 of private money – including substantial contributions from Tom Courtenay and Richard Burton – had been raised to ensure that the books balanced in the opening season.

Mia Farrow and Ralph Bates in *Mary Rose*
Photo Photocall (Manchester)

Besides fund-raising and grants, there were three other important sources of money – box office income, London transfers and, for a while, BBC Television (with which there was an association of a loose kind to record some productions). The box office was immediately successful, partly because of the attraction of stars like Tom Courtenay, Wendy Hiller and Vanessa Redgrave. Transfers, in addition to providing much needed income, were also attractive to many of the distinguished actors who, when in Manchester, were paid a top weekly salary of only £40. It must be said, however, that famous names were chosen not merely because they were international stars: they were engaged because they were the best in the country available for that particular role and because their own ideals and attitudes coincided with those of the directors. That is an artistic policy which has continued to the present.

At the University Theatre the 69 Theatre Company presented nineteen productions over four years. Many of the actors were ex-students of the Central School, whose Acting Course was by then directed by George Hall. Richard Pilbrow and David Collison still worked with the group, until the pressure of their London commitments made it impossible, and Michael Williams, the company's production manager, and Ian Gibson respectively took over the design of most of the lighting and sound.

The two opening productions, *Hamlet* and *When We Dead Awaken* were premiered not in Manchester but in Edinburgh. Both were staged in the Assembly Hall at the 1968 Edinburgh International Festival. The first, with Tom Courtenay in the title role and directed by Casper Wrede, was also the first to open in Manchester – on 12 September 1968. The second, with Wendy Hiller as the lady traveller and Alexander Knox as the sculptor Rubek, was directed by Michael Elliott, the acknowledged master of Ibsen. Between its Festival performances and its Manchester premiere in October, Elliott directed the production for television, a recording which the BBC broadcast on 12 February 1970, the company's second anniversary.

Although Courtenay's Hamlet was coolly received by the majority of the critics (Harold Hobson in the *Sunday Times* was a notable exception), its success with audiences was never in doubt: *Hamlet* sold out completely in both cities and established a box office trend. *When We Dead Awaken* was not so popular but it paved the way in production values. Broadcaster Brian Redhead, who was for a time a member of the Royal Exchange Theatre Company's board, later recalled, "The production was so compelling that it was one of those evenings when you could not bear to be talked to in the interval for fear of breaking the spell, and you drove home older, wiser, richer in experience."

There followed a series of productions in which the high standards of the 69 Theatre Company's work was beyond doubt. Six of them, mostly those directed by Braham Murray, transferred to London. They were *She Stoops to Conquer* (with Tom Courtenay and Juliet Mills) which Theatre Projects presented for six months at the Garrick, *Charley's Aunt* (again with Tom Courtenay), *Journey's End* (with James Maxwell) which was Eric Thompson's directorial debut and brought Peter Egan the *Plays & Players* Award as the Most Promising Actor in 1972, *Mary Rose* in which Mia Farrow made her British stage debut, and two musicals, *Erb* and *Catch My Soul. Erb,* based on a novel by William Pett Ridge about a cockney railway carman who became a trade union pioneer, was Trevor Peacock's first musical. Jack Good's rock Othello *Catch My Soul* was perhaps the company's most enduring success. Directed by Braham Murray, it first transferred to the Round House and then to the Prince of Wales Theatre. The show was recorded by Polydor and televised by London Weekend Television for Aquarius. [A couple of years later Jack Good produced a film version directed by Patrick McGoohan, but only Lance LeGault remained from 69's production].

The musicals were not the only premieres. Braham Murray and several of the team which had staged *Hang Down Your Head and Die* (the phenomenal Oxford E.T.C. success which had gone on to the West End and Broadway) produced *Have You Seen Manchester?* Gerard McLarnon wrote *The Trial of Joan of Arc* for Dilys Hamlett to play the eponymous heroine, and Ronald Harwood, several of whose television plays had already been directed by Casper Wrede, produced his first stage work for the company, *Country Matters.* Arguably the most memorable premiere, however, was James Maxwell's adaptation of the George Eliot novel *Daniel Deronda* which reunited director Michael Elliott with Vanessa Redgrave. It was later shown on television, and Elliott also directed *She Stoops To Conquer* (he had rehearsed the production for its London transfer because Braham Murray was not available) for the BBC. Tom Courtenay, Juliet Mills and Trevor Peacock were again in the cast, but Sir Ralph Richardson and Thora Hird were other star names added to it. Michael Elliott also directed two other outstanding 69 productions, both designed by Richard Negri – *The Tempest*, in which James Maxwell played Prospero, and *Peer Gynt* with Tom Courtenay – and a concert performance with the Hallé of *Beatrice and Benedick* by Berlioz in which Vanessa Redgrave and Paul Scofield took the speaking roles.

Marvellous though it was, the size and location of the University Theatre was by no means ideal for the company. Too far from the city centre and with a name which frightened away some of the potential audience by its "intellectual" associations, the theatre had a seating capacity which often proved inadequate. And, crucially, it was only available for a few scattered weeks of the year in between productions by the University's own drama, language and literature departments and student societies. Productions were therefore separately planned and rehearsals were almost invariably held in London. It quickly became obvious that if the group was ever to become *totally* committed to Manchester and '69' a major regional theatre company, then nothing less than a new theatre in the heart of the city was required.

Alexander Knox and Wendy Hiller in *When We Dead Awaken*
Photo John Madden

PRODUCTIONS AT THE UNIVERSITY THEATRE

HAMLET
by William Shakespeare
with Tom Courtenay, Anna Calder-Marshall, Glyn Owen,
Dilys Hamlett, Trevor Peacock, John Nettles,
Russell Hunter
directed by Casper Wrede
First performance 19 August 1968 at the Edinburgh
International Festival
First Manchester performance 12 September 1968

WHEN WE DEAD AWAKEN
by Henrik Ibsen
with Wendy Hiller, Alexander Knox, Brian Cox
directed by Michael Elliott
First performance 26 August 1968 at the Edinburgh
International Festival
First Manchester performance 22 October 1968

HAVE YOU SEEN MANCHESTER?
by David Wright (Premiere)
with Trevor Peacock, Bridget Turner, Julian Chagrin,
David Wood
directed by Braham Murray
First performance 18 December 1968

DANIEL DERONDA
adapted from the novel by George Eliot
by James Maxwell (Premiere)
with Vanessa Redgrave
directed by Michael Elliott
First performance 9 January 1969

SHE STOOPS TO CONQUER
by Oliver Goldsmith
with Tom Courtenay, Juliet Mills, James Cossins,
Trevor Peacock, Rosalind Knight
directed by Braham Murray
First performance 2 April 1969
Transferred to the Garrick Theatre, London 7 May 1969

THE TRIAL OF JOAN OF ARC
by Gerard McLarnon (Premiere)
with Dilys Hamlett
directed by Braham Murray
First performance 13 May 1969

THE TEMPEST
by William Shakespeare
with James Maxwell, John Bennett, George Howe,
Michael Feast
directed by Michael Elliott
First performance 10 September 1969

COUNTRY MATTERS
by Ronald Harwood (Premiere)
with Graham Crowden, John Wood, Leonard Sachs,
Dilys Hamlett
directed by Casper Wrede
First performance 16 October 1969

ERB
a musical by Trevor Peacock (Premiere)
with Trevor Peacock, Bridget Turner, Deborah Grant,
Nickolas Grace, Peter Childs, Dudley Jones
directed by Braham Murray
First performance 22 December 1969
Transferred to the Strand Theatre, London 7 April 1970

THE GLASS MENAGERIE
by Tennessee Williams
with Valerie Taylor, David Horovitch, Nigel Terry
directed by Robert Cheesmond
First performance 25 March 1970

THE OWL AND THE PUSSYCAT WENT TO SEE ...
by David Wood
with Neil Fitzwilliam, Caryl Little
directed by David Wood
First performance 6 May 1970

A MIDSUMMER NIGHT'S DREAM
by William Shakespeare
with Brian Cox, Susan Carpenter, Malcolm Rennie, Richard
Durden, John Cording, Delia Lindsay, Zoe Wanamaker
directed by Braham Murray
First performance 3 September 1970

CATCH MY SOUL
the Rock Othello by Jack Good (British Premiere)
Music by Ray Pohlman
with Jack Good, Lance LeGault, P J Proby, Angharad Rees
directed by Michael Elliott and Braham Murray
First performance 14 October 1970
Toured to Birmingham and Oxford; transferred to The Round
House, London 21 December 1970 and later to the Prince of
Wales Theatre 17 February 1971

PEER GYNT
by Henrik Ibsen
with Tom Courtenay, Avril Elgar, Wolfe Morris,
Fulton Mackay
directed by Michael Elliott
First performance 21 December 1970

GREEN JULIA
by Paul Ableman
with Jonathan Lynn, Giles Block
directed by George Mully
First performance 19 May 1971
Toured to Bury St Edmonds and Oxford June 1971

CHARLEY'S AUNT
by Brandon Thomas
with Tom Courtenay, James Cossins, Wolfe Morris, Dilys
Hamlett, Joanna McCallum, Celia Bannerman
directed by Braham Murray
First performance 30 August 1971
Toured to Newcastle, Oxford, Liverpool and Hull; transferred to
the Apollo Theatre, London 6 December 1971

JOURNEY'S END
by R C Sherriff
with James Maxwell, Peter Egan, Harold Goodwin
directed by Eric Thompson
First performance 29 September 1971
Toured to Nottingham, Swansea and Harlow; transferred to the
Mermaid Theatre, London 18 May 1972 and later to the
Cambridge Theatre 20 July 1972

MARY ROSE
by J M Barrie
with Mia Farrow, Ralph Bates, Carmel McSharry
directed by Braham Murray
First performance 2 May 1972
Toured to Brighton; transferred to the Shaw Theatre, London
13 July 1972

GUYS AND DOLLS
Music and lyrics by Frank Loesser,
book by Jo Swerling and Abe Burrows based
on Damon Runyon
with Trevor Peacock, John Labanowski, Michael Feast,
Heather Page, Zoe Wanamaker
directed by George Hall
First performance 26 September 1972
Final performance 28 October 1972

PRODUCTIONS IN THE TENT AT THE ROYAL EXCHANGE

ARMS AND THE MAN
by George Bernard Shaw
with Tom Courtenay, Jenny Agutter, Brian Cox
directed by James Maxwell
First performance 16 May 1973
Toured to Sheffield, Nottingham, York and Brighton June 1973

ENDGAME
by Samuel Beckett
with Wolfe Morris, Trevor Peacock
directed by Braham Murray
First performance 7 June 1973
Toured to Lincoln and Nottingham; transferred to the Shaw
Theatre, London 12 July 1973

THE FAMILY REUNION
by T S Eliot
with Edward Fox, Marian Spencer, Nora Swinburne,
Esmond Knight, Avril Elgar, Constance Chapman
directed by Michael Elliott
First performance 4 October 1973

TIME AND THE CONWAYS
by J B Priestley
with Dilys Hamlett, Christopher Gable, Susan Penhaligon,
Marion Lines, Michael Culver
directed by Braham Murray
First performance 20 December 1973
Final performance 19 January 1974

PRODUCTIONS IN MANCHESTER CATHEDRAL

HOLLY FROM THE BONGS
A Nativity Opera by Alan Garner and
Gordon Crosse (Premiere)
with children from five Salford schools
directed by David Terence
First performance 9 December 1974

A MAN FOR ALL SEASONS
by Robert Bolt
with James Maxwell, Bob Hoskins, Martin Potter,
Olive McFarland
directed by Casper Wrede
First performance 21 January 1975

THE COCKTAIL PARTY
by T S Eliot
with Polly James, Freddie Jones, Brian Cox
directed by Michael Elliott and Richard Negri
First performance 15 October 1975

MUCH ADO ABOUT NOTHING
by William Shakespeare
with Kenneth Haigh, Susan Tracy, Bryan Pringle
directed by Braham Murray
First performance 28 January 1976
Final performance 21 February 1976

THE BUILDING OF THE THEATRE

On the day in July 1968 that the Master of the Royal Exchange announced the closure of its Great Hall, rehearsals for the 69 Theatre Company's debut production of *Hamlet* had just started in London. The two events were not, of course, connected but both were later to assume greater importance – in the history of the Royal Exchange Theatre Company. Without the Royal Exchange building it is doubtful that the company would have remained in Manchester, and without the development of the 69 Theatre Company the city might never have become the home of *any major* repertory theatre.

When Prudential Assurance became owners of the Royal Exchange that December, they began to consider proposals for the Hall. A science museum, a covered market and an indoor sports stadium were all mooted but nothing came of the suggestions. Meanwhile, the artistic directors of the 69 Theatre Company, having made the decision to build a new theatre, began a plan. Richard Negri started models for a 7-800 seat theatre and the Town Hall was lobbied for a site and £1¼ million – but to no avail. With no money at all, hope faded and the directors agreed to withdraw from the bridgehead they had created. Then, legend has it, one day in June 1971, while lying in his bath, Peter Henriques remembered the huge empty hall of the Royal Exchange. But he thought of the building only in terms of a temporary solution.

Several of them went to see it. In Michael Elliott's words: "Of course nothing could prepare us, as nothing does the newcomer now, for what we saw. It was chilly, it was very dirty, and it was very empty. But in only a few minutes we knew. *Here* anything was possible." Richard Negri remembers well his first sight of the three-quarters of an acre of parquet flooring under its 120 foot high domes: "I knew what the previous few years and my unconscious thoughts of the relationship between the audience and the stage had all been about." It instinctively triggered memories of the cavernous Xanadu in *Citizen Kane* and he wrote "rosebud" with his finger in the dust. The word Negri chose was not so fanciful: it may not be overtly apparent but all the rhythms in the theatre's structure are based on a rose.

At last things began to move. The Prudential was approached, and they offered a short five-year lease. But gradually it dawned on the directors that perhaps the Royal Exchange *was* the building where their dreams could be realised. Building inside a building would solve several problems, the biggest one being lack of money. The hall could provide the largest foyer in the world – space inconceivable in a new theatre on the budget that the company envisaged. By building comparatively cheaply inside a monumental edifice and by boldly responding to the original architecture, the theatre could link the past and the future with an auditorium for the *present* day.

Negotiations with the Prudential became protracted as a 25 year lease and a guarantee of the £16,000 annual rental by Manchester City Council was sought. In September 1971, when the 69 Theatre Company finally knew they could get the Royal Exchange if they wanted it, what was later referred to as "the 30" met in Michael Elliott's London flat – a group of thirty directors, writers, designers, actors, actresses, choreographers, composers and their solicitor and Chairman Laurence Harbottle – to decide if they should *commit* to building and running a theatre in Manchester. Of course, they did.

A year was spent thinking and talking about the concept of the new auditorium and Richard Negri prepared entirely new models for the Exchange before consultants were appointed for the project and some thirty architects were interviewed. By July 1972 everyone felt that the scheme could proceed. A Trust was created to raise the capital and Peter Henriques formed an Appeal Committee. A young, little-known firm of architects Levitt, Bernstein, Associates was appointed after several rounds of interviews and Richard Negri began to make dozens of models and thousands of sketches. The project was finally launched on 9 November 1972 with support promised from the Arts Council and the City Council. The theatre was initially costed at £400,000 but by the time it opened four years later the sum had riseń to £1.2 million.

In May 1973 Manchester staged a festival to celebrate the birth of Greater Manchester and the company was asked to

An artist's impression of the theatre, used in fund-raising for the building.

provide a temporary theatre in the Exchange and plays for the Festival. It was a fortunate offer because it gave the company the chance to experiment with the Hall. The temporary 430-seat theatre, designed by Laurie Dennett, was constructed within a month for £8,000. Built from scaffolding, old boards, discarded seats (from the refurbished Usher Hall in Edinburgh) arranged in a key-hole shape, and a roof of old canvas floor-cloths from Covent Garden, the structure was draped in fabric donated by Tootals. It was a colossal success. Intended to last for three weeks, the "tent" theatre stayed up ten months. The opening production of Shaw's comedy *Arms and the Man* (16 May-2 June) was followed by Beckett's *Endgame*. Both productions went on tour and the latter became 69's seventh and final transfer to London. In October Edward Fox made his debut with the company in *The Family Reunion* and over the Christmas period Priestley's *Time and the Conways* was given its first major revival since its premiere in 1937. In addition Ballet Rambert performed there and a huge number of late night performances and poetry readings – by Dame Edith Evans, Michael Flanders, Anna Calder-Marshall, Gerald Harper, Eleanor Bron, Frank Muir and Geraldine McEwan amongst others – were held. Concerts by many musicians ranging from Imrat Khan to Elisabeth Söderström and Thomas Allen were heard. Overall the 142 performances of plays and other events played to a capacity of 86%. The "tent" was dismantled in February, 1974 after insurance was finally refused, but the designers had learned a great deal from its use.

By then the project was unstoppable – financially, publicly, politically. What was to become the most successful theatre building appeal in the country was rapidly filling its coffers. The first of several fund-raising functions – a star-studded dinner, with Albert Finney in the chair, at the Hotel Piccadilly in Manchester in May 1973 – raised £36,000, and not long before building commenced, the Royal Exchange was transformed into a giant fairground for one Saturday which raised over £2,000 and attracted 7,000 people into the Hall.

Later in 1974 and throughout the following year *Rogues and Vagabonds*, an entertainment devised by Michael Meyer tracing in an informal and amusing way the development of actors and acting up to the time of Henry Irving, was presented by the company in a large number of venues around the North West to raise both funds and the profile of the project. Among those who took part, in addition to Michael Meyer who introduced each show, were Michael Flanders, Kenneth Haigh, Billie Whitelaw, Polly James, Robert Powell, Michael York, Anna Calder-Marshall, Edward Fox, Esmond Knight, Frank Muir, Wendy Hiller, James Maxwell, Freddie Jones, Brian Cox and Clive Francis. A Gala Night of *Rogues and Vagabonds* at the Old Vic in London on 8 June 1975 – in which Dame Edith Evans, Tom Courtenay and Albert Finney joined several of those already mentioned – raised over £6,000. Esmond Knight also devised and presented a one-man show to raise funds – *Agincourt, The Archer's Tale* – throughout the same period.

Robert Scott, still at that time the company's administrator, was spending a great deal of time on fundraising activities as Appeal organiser for the Trust, and the Board, Trustees and members of the Appeal Committee were lobbying all their contacts. Naturally, the largest contributions came from the Arts Council, which gave £300,000, and the local authorities. The Greater Manchester Council, which had pledged support as soon as it was created in 1973, committed £200,000 before the theatre opened and was eventually to add a further £75,000. Manchester City Council's grant towards the cost was £100,000. But a major proportion of the money came from generous national and North West firms and from thousands of individuals.

Granada headed the list with a magnificent £30,000 but more than twenty firms and individuals made donations in excess of £2,000 each. The Trustees received a handsome contribution from the Prince of Wales and many household names from films, the stage and television gave freely. American dollars were received from Rod Steiger, Canadian dollars from Christopher Plummer, and Swiss francs from James Mason, not to mention pounds from Sir Ralph Richardson, Albert Finney, Sir Michael Redgrave, Peter Sellers, Sean Connery, Peter O'Toole, Edward Fox, Celia Johnson, Peter Barkworth, Alec McCowen, Brian Rix, Michael Hordern, Edward Woodward, Richard Briers, Leo McKern, Alan Bates, Ian McKellen, Sir Richard Attenborough, Donald Pleasance, Anthony Hopkins, Dames Peggy Ashcroft,

The temporary 'tent' theatre under construction. *Photo* Sophie Marshall

Edith Evans and Wendy Hiller, Dave Allen, Joyce Grenfell, Harry Secombe, Ronnie Corbett, Frankie Howerd and a host of others. Over £250,000 had been raised from private donations by the time the opening season began and a very successful Theatre Lottery, which the Trust set up and operated from 1977, contributed most of the outstanding money needed to pay for the inflation-hit capital costs.

Not everything went so smoothly as the building appeal. The first body blow was the premature death in January 1974 of the Appeal Chairman, Peter Henriques. He had worked tirelessly for the project and his efforts on behalf of the company were the key to the Appeal's success. But gallantly the Appeal Committee, under the joint chairmanship of Lord Hewlett and Bernard Terry, shouldered the extra burden. Two memorials now exist to mark his invaluable contribution: the Peter Henriques Trust Fund for the commissioning of new work for the theatre, and the Peter Q. Henriques Room, the functions suite overlooking the foyer which was renamed when it ceased to be a full-time restaurant.

Another major blow was the realisation that the floor of the Royal Exchange would not take the combined weight of theatre and full audience. Richard Negri's original conception had been for a drum-like auditorium free-standing in the centre of the Hall. The solution to the problem was to suspend the structure from the four massive columns which carry the central dome, but the extra design work required added to the delay in the start of building. A further contibutory factor was the availability of tubular steel. The need to limit the load on the brick columns dictated a choice of materials that was practical as well as aesthetic. Specially toughened glass panels became more preponderant than in the original plans, for instance. However it was the requirement of light but immensely strong *tubular* steel which created great problems. Precisely the same steel was used in the construction of North Sea oil rigs and in 1975 there was a shortage. It took the intervention of the Chairman of British Steel to reduce delivery from 18 months to six weeks and to avert what Richard Negri

Guests at the fund-raising banquet in May 1973 include Geoffrey Keen, Braham Murray, Edward Woodward, Robert Powell, Frank Windsor, Albert Finney, Ronald Harwood, Coral Atkins, Polly James, Michael Meyer, Alfred Burke, Rosalind Knight, Patrick Allen, Eleanor Bron, Rupert Davies, Clive Francis and Trevor Peacock.

The theatre during construction:
above November 1975. *Photo* Picture Coverage Ltd.
below January 1976. *Photo* Elsam, Mann & Cooper

and Levitt Bernstein Associates would have found disastrous – a Royal Exchange Theatre built with much thicker *square* steel trusses!

While this drama was being played out backstage the 69 Theatre Company had taken to the boards elsewhere. Without a home during the building of the new theatre, the company were rescued by the Dean and Chapter of Manchester Cathedral. Between December 1974 and February 1976 four productions were mounted in the nave of the Cathedral, once again before capacity audiences. The first *Holly from the Bongs* (the 'Bongs' being a wood near the Cheshire village of Goostrey) was a new nativity opera, with music by Gordon Crosse and a text by the children's author Alan Garner, performed by children from five Salford schools. It was broadcast by Granada Television. Casper Wrede then returned to stage direction with *A Man For All Seasons* in which James Maxwell had considerable success as Sir Thomas More and Bob Hoskins played the protean Common Man. The production's designer Laurie Dennett also designed a temporary raised seating structure which was to serve the remaining two shows as well – a second T S Eliot play *The Cocktail Party* directed by Michael Elliott and Richard Negri (in October 1975) and Braham Murray's *Much Ado About Nothing* with Susan Tracy and Kenneth Haigh playing Beatrice and Benedick. By the time the last production of the season – a season in which all five artistic directors had fittingly had a hand – was staged in early 1976, the company had changed its name to the Royal Exchange Theatre Company.

Work on the Royal Exchange Theatre itself was also progressing well. It had started on 14 April 1975 with Project Manager Michael Williams providing the bridge between the designer and the consultants, between the Trustees and the contractor. In December that year the opening date was set and the first photographs of the partially completed framework began to appear in the press. Intense excitement grew into euphoria when building work was completed on 12 August 1976 and the first audience was present for an acoustic test. Two days later the public – many thousands of them – were admitted to view the theatre for the first time.

The Royal Exchange Theatre – the fruition of an impulse that had been germinating for two decades in the British theatre –

was finally opened by Lord Olivier on Wednesday 15 September, 1976. Prior to the first performance of Braham Murray's production of *The Rivals*, Olivier walked on stage before a hushed audience and stated that the occasion was "one of the greatest joys I have known." Standing alone in the spotlight he recited the words of an anonymous 19th century poet which were first spoken at the opening of the Exchange in 1809, and then, his voice suddenly gathering power, he cried: "I declare this theatre . . . OPEN!" A second opening night took place the following evening, presided over by Dame Wendy Hiller: the British premiere of *The Prince of Homburg* by Heinrich von Kleist directed by Casper Wrede.

Critical acclaim for the building was immediate. The theatre was awarded the 1976 Manchester Society of Architects President's Award and the British Tourist Authority 'Come To Britain' Award. The following year it gained the coveted Gold Medal of the Royal Institute of British Architects. Professional theatre-goers waxed lyrical. "Today the light beams upon an amazing visual thrill; between the cerulean and the earthbound hangs a dream realised, a poem of steel and glass, a hovering counterpoint of stress and balance gripped in, launched from, the towering marble of another age. It is Manchester's new Royal Exchange Theatre" wrote J W Lambert in the *Sunday Times*. The architectural correspondent of the *Financial Times* noted: "This amazingly ingenious structure spreads like an inverted cat's cradle of steel under the great central dome . . . here is a tour-de-force of theatrical engineering and architectural inspiration."

THEATRE & TECHNICAL INFORMATION

Transparent theatre-in-the-round based on a seven-sided figure with raked seating for 400 at ground level and two galleries above each seating 150 in rows two deep. Galleries suspended by 25mm diameter rods from 14 roof trusses bearing on 4 tubular steel frames anchored to pillars supporting main hall. 40 moveable seats around edge of acting area, so maximum seating 740. One stage level bank of seats moveable to give thrust effect. Great Hall approx. 180' by 100' under three giant domes supported by 60' marble pillars. Theatre structure 70' in diameter, 40' high. 70 toughened glass panels (totalling 400 sq.m in overall area) form continuous band around the steel structure to form the 'walls' of the module.

Stage: 'in-the-round', approx 8m diameter. Stage area can be increased to a maximum of 15.25m diameter with the loss of some seating. Stage floor solid wood block parquet. No seat further than 9m from stage. 8 entrances to stage. Height 10.98m minimum clearance 5.49m, maximum 7.32m. Get-in up 27 steps St Ann's Square public entrance, 2 sets of doors, 1.3m x 2.35m and 1.7m x 2.1m. Passenger lift for small items at stage door.

Lighting: Board Rank Strand Galaxy c/w Theatre Playback 100 x 10 amp circuits and 20 x 20 amp circuits over 3 phases. Supply for temporary lighting board 60 amp over 3 phases. Basic rig of 100 spots, 80 fresnels, Rank Strand/CCT.

Acoustics: variable by three tiers of louvres near roof and use of 15 double doors (7-8 second reverberation time in Hall).

Sound: Desk Neve 24/8/2, situated on second gallery with LX and SM controls, open acoustically. Sound system comprises sound desk, racks housing jackfield and power amplifiers, speaker lines around theatre, microphone tielines around theatre. Additional moveable amp-racks, JBL and Electrovoice Pro-Ac Speakers.

Stage Management: Prompt corner second gallery with LX and FX – 15 way cue lights – show relay/tannoy to dressing rooms.

Dressing Rooms: 4 x singles, 2 x foursome, 1 x sixsome, 1 x sevensome. 2 rehearsal rooms.

Views of those involved in
THE CREATION
OF THE THEATRE

EXCHANGE EXPERIENCE
BY MICHAEL ELLIOTT

As I understand it, architecture is only expressed with purpose in real estate. We are at an end (and it *is* the end) of a theatre building boom. I don't know what our descendants will make of it, but it seems to me that the vast majority of the theatres we have built in this country since the war have proved partial or total failures because of a confusion or absence of purpose. When a building is bad it is almost always more the fault of the client than the architect, or the society that wants and allows such growths. It is in every way artistically a confusing time, and the theatre is as confused as it has ever been. We know the Greeks had something we have lost. We know we don't want to copy Elizabethan and eighteenth-century models exactly, we are dissatisfied with our Victorian heritage of theatres, splendid as some of them are, but what *do* we want? Every new theatre at least coyly slips a forestage in front of the proscenium, like a Victorian lady showing her ankle, but dare we, should we, go all the way?

The Royal Exchange Theatre was not built because the City of Manchester had decided that it must, like all self-respecting modern authorities, boast a civic theatre. The City, and the Greater Manchester Council, had to be persuaded. I am just one, and not the most important one, of a group that have kept together and grown over more than 20 years. In 1968 we formed the 69 Theatre Company to operate at the Manchester University Theatre – one of the best buildings we had encountered. Despite constant impending collapse, the company staged an ambitious series of plays (some seen in London later) at this tiny out-of-the-way spot. We tried to get a new theatre built in Manchester and failed. And then, at the moment of despair, we found the Royal Exchange. We launched an appeal, and created for the Manchester Festival of 1973 the temporary tent theatre inside the Exchange hall which taught us, and Manchester, so much.

Richard Negri, whose child this theatre is, conceived – not an aesthetic idea – but an experience, and an envelope that would not only make possible, but enforce that experience on both the actor and the audience. We had our purpose, and the theatre was to be the exclusive, committed, point-of-no-return expression of it, even beyond our understanding. Richard Negri made many models over the years. What we thought in our naivety to be the final one, was our brief. Only then did we interview architects. We interviewed 30. We made a short list of four, and then, after they had survived four gruelling sessions, we appointed Levitt Bernstein Associates as architects. Afterwards, with them, we chose the consultants, with equal care. We entered then on the actual design process. Richard Negri and the architects encountered new realities, one after another. They absorbed and digested them, often very painfully, but through never-flagging inspiration and patience always making virtues of them. The difficulties did not make the concept slowly evaporate, as so often happens, they simply forced it to evolve.

But in the end, for £1.2 million, a theatre was built. If it had been on a free-standing site and designed to fulfil the same major purpose – a regional theatre for the North-West – it would have cost £4-5 million at today's prices. It was great luck that we found, and obtained, this extraordinary vast hall of the old Royal Cotton Exchange, and could put within it a theatre module (that's the word we use) of uncompromisingly modern design. The experience of seeing the building as you enter cannot be prepared for, or photographed. It is a place, and places, like people, need to be met – three-quarters of an acre of polished golden parquet floor to wander in; three blue domes that float over the module; a glass lantern of a theatre that is lit from within, and seen everywhere from without; a reverberation time of seven seconds in the main hall, which with a totally sealed auditorium is irrelevant, but when the two are partially connected by opening the theatre envelope produces a truly variable acoustic.

Why are we in the round? Because we believe that theatre is a happening, and that what happens among people has more effect than what happens the other side of a peep-hole. Why are we in Manchester? Because we want the theatre to be rooted in a community, and serve it, not open the doors to the endless anonymous mass that is London. We are an arts centre. Apart from the main play repertoire, we already have classical, pop, jazz and folk concerts, poetry recitals, one-man-shows, children's shows and lectures. We have two restaurants. We have a special fund for commissioning new work.

Architecture, as I said, is only expressed with purpose in real estate. Our purpose has long been growing. The building is one expression of it. What comes to occupy the building over the years, allowed, encouraged, and insisted upon by the architecture itself will reveal to us, as much as to others, what its real depth and nature is.

From *The Architectural Review*, December, 1976

REALISING MY EXPERIMENTS
BY RICHARD NEGRI

During the ten years I spent with the Theatre Department at Wimbledon School of Art, I had the unique opportunity to experiment with different formations of tiered auditoria in a free space, and as a consequence to develop particular concepts of theatre. These innovations were only possible because of the close relationship which was gradually built up amongst staff and students and I remember those times with much affection and gratitude.

When the opportunity came, through the Royal Exchange project, to actually realise these experiments, the prospect was both exciting and daunting. For almost three years there has had to be continued discussion amongst all those involved, demanding great patience, understanding and discipline. Our achievement in getting the theatre built is largely due to the sensitivity, skill and determination with which all the people, who have had to create the concrete result, have worked.

We live in an age where the relationship to function is of paramount importance in the design of everything, and simplicity is an absolute necessity in order to achieve it. One could say the theatre has been conceived with one simple function in mind, namely to please people – those who perform in it, those who operate it, those who run it, and most of all those whom we hope will come to enjoy it. If it proves itself in the performance of this function, those of us who have worked together on it will be very content.

From *The Stage,* 9 September 1976

THE ARCHITECTURAL CHALLENGE
BY DAVID LEVITT, MALCOLM BROWN, AXEL BURROUGH
(Partners in the Firm of Levitt Bernstein Associates)

The beginning for us was a small paper and wire model sitting in the middle of the table with Richard Negri striding round it talking about the form of a rose. How, we wondered, would we ever bring this man down to earth? Fortunately, we never did.

By the time we and the team of consultants had been appointed, Richard Negri and the other Artistic Directors of the 69 Theatre Company had developed their earlier work in the Manchester University Theatre, the temporary theatre in the Exchange and elsewhere, into the idea of a free-standing concentric auditorium under the main dome of the hall. Richard Negri tansmits his ideas as a series of delicate and sometimes elusive images. Over a period of time he used these images to convey the essential simplicity of a theatre which was to have a completely new relationship between the actors and the audience, both inside and outside the auditorium itself. Of conviction as well as necessity there was never the intention of building flexibility into the relationship between acting area and the audience, as in many other new theatres. The statement therefore is extremely direct. Except for the sophisticated lighting and sound systems almost all the actors' traditional aids have been swept away, for instance, the entrances upstage, the proscenium itself and the possibilities of any formal stage sets.

For us as architects in the beginning there were many problems: The most challenging was how to build a large 700 seat auditorium in the centre of the hall without destroying its character and the vast sense of space. The domed roof provided a protective umbrella so that in theory a simple structure to support 700 seats was all that was needed. However, due to its size, the hall has a colossal echo and as this had to be reduced for speech it became clear that the theatre must become a separate acoustic entity.

Another problem was the question of support for the structure itself. Climbing up the broad flight of stairs and arriving on the floor of the hall it is easy to forget the layers of shopping and basements beneath it. No further loads could be placed on the floor itself. The four vast brick piers supporting the main dome alone were capable of taking the weight of the theatre. The limitations set by this became the most influential factor in determining the final structural form of the auditorium and have assisted rather than hindered the development of the design. As the only points of support appeared to be along the outside of the hall and the theatre was to be in the centre, some form of bridge was required if the whole hall was not to be divided into two. Once the principle was established it was possible to think in terms of suspending the theatre above the floor like a huge "acoustic dish cover" leaving the floor entirely clear of structural supports. By suspending two seven-sided galleries each with two rows of seats above the floor, it has been possible to create an

A view of the Royal Exchange's domes taken through the theatre under construction, November 1975. *Photo* Picture Coverage Ltd.

intimate space in which no member of the audience is more than 35 feet from the centre of the stage.

Next, the weight of the structure became an important consideration. Although not conforming with Building Regulations the authorities agreed that a lightweight steel structure could be permitted, provided that no combustible materials would be used and provided that the entire audience could leave before a fire could affect the structure. To reduce the weight of the building still further an allowance has been made for the whole structure to deflect downwards when the galleries are full of people. This accounts for the mechanical appearance of many of the details since every component must either pivot or slide to permit this movement. In its final form, half the audience sitting on tiered platforms and the stage itself, are the only parts of the theatre which rest on the floor. The remainder of the audience is seated on two galleries which are suspended from the roof on thin steel rods. The whole weight of the theatre's acoustic shell, together with the two suspended galleries weighing 150 tons, is transferred onto two main girders. The extreme ends of these girders, made up from a consignment of steel tubes, once destined for a North Sea Gas line, rest on four small bronze bearings inside the brick piers at each corner.

Before beginning the design of the auditorium it had first been necessary to find a place for all the back stage and public facilities in the theatre without encroaching on the hall itself. Whereas the intention throughout has been to give the auditorium a lightness and a character precisely opposite to that of the building which houses it, in all the other public areas the intention was to preserve the character of the old building unaltered.

For the restaurant, rehearsal rooms, workshops, dressing rooms and all the other parts of the theatre to fit into the areas available, space has been at a premium. It is perhaps a reflection on the original scale of the Royal Exchange that, for instance, the whole theatre workshop now resides in what were formerly the Members' lavatories. In another part of the hall, two small, wooden cubicles which once housed representatives of the Cotton Exchange have been turned into entrance lobbies for new lavatories which in turn occupy an area previously only used for public telephone boxes.

It is now 3½ years since the first discussion around that small model. The constructional pyrotechnics are over, the nuts, bolts, tubes and rivets are fitted into place. We believe that the essential qualities of the original model are still there in the new theatre. We hope in use that it will fulfil the hopes of those who have pinned their faith in it for so many years.

From the Royal Gala programme of *The Rivals* for the visit of HRH Princess Alexandra, 18 September 1976

THE DESIGN TEAM FOR THE THEATRE

Theatre conceived by **Richard Negri**
Architects **Levitt Bernstein Associates**
Designed by
Levitt Bernstein Associates
in collaboration with **Richard Negri**
Consulting Engineers **Ove Arup and Partners**
Quantity Surveyors
Monk Dunstone Mahon and Sceares
Mechanical & Electrical Services
Max Fordham and Partners
Theatre Services **Theatre Projects Consultants**
Acoustics **D.K. Jones**
Original Sound System **Ian Gibson**
Project Manager **Michael Williams**
Main Contractors **J. Jarvis & Sons Limited**

THE THEATRE
THREE ARTICLES BY CASPER WREDE

It would be futile to engage in a discussion of the state of the British theatre. The field is too wide and contains artistic, financial and personal conditions so fluid and paradoxical that merely to fix the premises for a reasonable argument would require far more space than the limited number of words I have at my disposal. However, the basis of your enquiry seems to be that the self-supporting actor's and manager's theatre no longer can advance the artistic aspirations of the day. If so, we have to concern ourselves with the creation of Art Theatres and as the scene is full of more or less qualified practitioners advocating their remedies, I hope you will allow me to present mine.

The real trouble with the new breeze in the theatre is that it doesn't blow hard enough. Our innovators half-heartedly cling to the house they have themselves almost succeeded in tearing down.

How can one talk of new approaches to acting and presentation and yet work in premises built for Kean and Irving? Where is the sense in rehearsing subtleties of intimate personal relations, when the gallery is ninety feet away? (Even the lions of West End hanker for the small house these days.) One must have scenery to hide the backstage. But is it not sheer hypocrisy to make a virtue of abstract or standing sets when the passing of cheap labour alone is to blame? And how can one demand more freely flowing organically constructed writing for a playhouse that Ibsen himself longed to be done with. Even the most ingenious conceptions of Brecht sigh and creak on the boards of a proscenium stage.

The invaluable work at the Royal Court time and again breaks itself against the limitations of its stage and shows up unfavourably in comparison with the established and conventional skill of a first rate West End performance. At Stratford East they have developed an extraordinarily elaborate technique of banging about, almost like a ritual to scare away the ghosts of yesteryear. And even Stratford on Avon has succumbed to the time honoured example of the Comédie Française, when invoking 'the speaking of the verse' and 'pictorial presentation'. Presumably that appalling stage, rebuilt with monotonous regularity, has once again defeated the swiftness and passion of the author it was created to serve.

We need a playhouse suited to the times. Not a converted or convertible multi-purpose bastard aimed at instruction in manners of the past, but an unequivocal, contemporary playhouse, designed by modern men, making use of modern materials and equipment, endowed with our standards of comfort and sense of beauty; we need a playhouse wholly different from the draughty, gilded miniature opera houses we now reluctantly frequent.

The conventional theatre is an unsatisfactory financial proposition, cumbersome and overstaffed. The waste of space alone justifies the tearing down of at least a third of London's theatres. The so-called good seats are too expensive and the cheaper ones not worth their price. Backstage and scenery building continue, with precious full rationalisations, exactly as they began some two hundred years ago. These anachronisms, and many more, are the background of the manager's dilemma. And there is no answer to them short of complete reorganisation.

The actor's problem of having to project, with increasing accuracy, psychologically truthful behaviour is one that few have overcome and even they are constantly in danger of appearing hollow. The least one can demand of a theatre is that it should facilitate communication between actor and audience. And this failure has cost the theatre more potential customers than any competition from new mass media.

Worst of all fares the playwright, who has the choice between placing himself in the shadow of Chekhov, Ibsen and Shaw by accepting the conventions of realism and the picture frame, or appearing more or less successfully to 'experiment' simply because there isn't a theatre that can offer an unselfconscious solution to the problems of presenting his play. It is not surprising that half our young dramatists have been forced into naturalism in order to remain true to their heroic awareness of society; while the other half have retreated to an esoteric world from whence they keep us posted with oracular readings from the inwards. In either case the forging of style and construction has had to be abandoned, leaving the producer to choose his means from the stale relics of theatrical history.

We need a stage that can conjure places and make time relative to the demands of drama. Other ages have had their illusions, only we have none and are contented. We need a new stage on which to wake our dreams and awake ourselves within the dream.

But if we want that stage we'll have to build it ourselves.

New Wine into Old Bottles
from The London Magazine July 1960

Neither the 59, nor the 69 Theatre Company, produced much memorable new work. The task facing us – as we saw it – was the building of a new theatre, which would not only free us from the conventions of the past but, which itself would force us on to unbroken ground. Once in use, the writers would appear to whom this theatre was as necessary as it was to us! The truth of this rather naive faith will now be put to the test.

Meanwhile, it is true to say that we have resisted all but the very best of the contemporary drama. This we have done, not because in itself we prefer the old to the new, but because we have thought that the imprisonment of the individual into his most trivial and irrefutably subjective world – which stems from the denial of common values – is a passing phase to which we do not feel committed. We have also rejected the intellectualization of the theatre – as in Brecht – and the domination of the stage by politics.

All those trends, seem to me, to result from a tortured – or unconscious – involvement with the fast disappearing world of our predecessors. What is new, to me, in much of the theatre today is its lack of vitality, the vicariousness of its excitement and the absence of individual aspiration to greater consciousness of life. And when I read that Peter Brook's latest production concerns itself with the slow starving to death of an African tribe whose culture no longer serves to support them in a changing world, it strikes me how remote the connection is with the lives of the starving millions of the third world and how close the parallel to aspects of our political, intellectual and artistic life.

To me, the heart of the theatre lies in its capacity for probing the world through the individual and thereby reveal the individual to the world. But, for this we need – as an intermediary – the poet of action. The 59 Theatre Company began its life with what is arguably the first large scale, poetical, modern play, *Danton's Death* by Georg Büchner.

It is a nightmare play in which the characters act out their own deaths, the death of civilization through violence: 'like reading history by lightning,' someone has said. Tonight's play is arguably the last great poetical play of that tradition, which first flowered in Spain and in England in the Renaissance. It is a dream play with a double theme: the re-birth of an individual and of a nation. This too is German and has frequently been the object of both suspicion and abuse. In my view it deserves neither but I must ask you to bear with those assertions of national feeling, which Napoleon provoked in the German heart – no less than Hitler in the British. *The Prince of Homburg* was written in 1810 just 25 years before *Danton's Death*. It foreshadows the whole movement of the modern theatre and even points beyond it!

Two duties face us. The first turns us out towards our audiences. It is the demand for entertainment and embraces all the moods and humours of the stage. We respond to it. It is our living. The second turns us in towards ourselves. It is the call to find a voice for that which is personal to us. We must obey it. It is our life.

September 1976 writing in the programme for
The Prince of Homburg

A living theatre reflects the world, past, present and future. It has to select of course. And so do audiences. It is the more heartening therefore to see the growing number of theatre-goers who are prepared to buy season tickets and share with us the entire experience our repertoire has to offer. This willingness to open oneself to the unlooked for event, to entertain the unfamiliar view, to hear out the antagonistic voice and to be able to criticise without condemning – is the most admirable feature of British life. Without it there could be no theatre such as the Royal Exchange. We acknowledge with gratitude the breadth of humanity and spirit of adventure of our Manchester audiences.

The storehouse of world drama is the living memory of human struggle through the ages. And our theatre is the live museum in which, seated around the stage, we can share in two and a half thousand years of the essence of life lived through by our forebears as they presented it to themselves in order to come to terms with themselves and the world around them. But what of ourselves and our own time? In the early years we had come to feel more and more strongly the need to present new plays. And for a long time we almost totally failed to find writers whose work we could perform with conviction. The advent of Mobil as sponsor made possible the two play competitions which have so remarkably expanded our repertoire and revitalised our hopes for the future.

The last twelve years have gone to establishing the Royal Exchange Theatre as a necessary force in our cultural life. This has been more difficult and taken longer than we had hoped. And the years have taken their toll among us. At the heart of every season has been the battle for continued existence and for the improved terms which would allow us to take the next step in our development with some confidence. This struggle is unending. More than once the future looked black but, so far, there has been no night without a dawn: new ideas, new projects, new talents, new plays.

3 October 1988

Lord Olivier declaring the theatre open. *Photo* Manchester Evening News.

FACTS & FIGURES

At the height of its cotton trading days in the 1920's, 9,000 traders used to assemble on the floor of the Great Hall of the Royal Exchange between 2.15pm and 3.15pm (High 'change) every Tuesday and Friday. A written contract never changed hands; business was sealed with a handshake or a nod of the head. Women were only admitted to full membership of the Exchange in 1946.

Now more than 15,000 people pass through the foyer of the Royal Exchange Theatre each week — a grand total of 9,500,000 in the theatre's lifetime.

Each season well over 200,000 people buy tickets for the major theatre productions. Since the theatre opened in 1976 ticket sales have exceeded £8,200,000.

927,000 of the total audience of 2,452,000 people have purchased programmes. 950,000 ice-creams have been eaten either before performances or during intervals. Members of the audience and other visitors to the theatre have, between them, consumed over 20 tons of coffee and drunk more than 100,000 gallons of beer.

230 lotteries have been run in Manchester by the Royal Exchange Theatre Trust, selling 8 million tickets and raising in the region of £700,000 for the theatre.

Almost 1400 characters have been portrayed on the Royal Exchange stage by more than 850 performers – 530 actors and 321 actresses. Of these several have appeared repeatedly, some in more than ten productions. Frequent visitors have included Tom Courtenay, Trevor Peacock, Lindsay Duncan, Avril Elgar, Robert Lindsay, Gabrielle Drake, Enn Reitel, Dilys Hamlett, Rosalind Knight, Geoffrey Bateman, John Bardon, Gary Waldhorn, Jonathan Hackett, Tim McInnerny and Eleanor Bron. However the actor with the most appearances is Ian Hastings who has been associated with 33 productions – a total of 1,177 stage performances!

The actors have worn over 3,000 costumes, made in wardrobe and used over 1,200 props, constructed in the workshop.

The main floor area of the hall within which the theatre is situated comprises ¾ acre of parquet flooring (some 65,000 separate blocks of maple wood) and that is only half its original size. The parquet is continued on the stage, which is at the same floor level as the hall and, with all the seats in place, is approximately 26 feet in diameter. The height of the theatre is 36 feet, and the weight of the entire structure is about 100 tons.

The Royal Exchange was the first theatre in Britain to have a purpose-built 'in-the-round' auditorium. The foyer is believed to be the largest of any theatre in the world. The central dome carries the inscription "He who seeks to gain eternal treasure must use no guile in weight or measure".

Up to the end of 1988, the company had mounted 114 major productions, of which 26 were world premieres, 6 British premieres and 2 European premieres. 23 of the productions were also seen outside Manchester, 17 of them in London.

It costs around £2.5 million per year to run the Royal Exchange Theatre Company. Income comes from four main sources: grants, box office income, self generated income and private support. The Royal Exchange is a subsidised theatre company and as such receives annual revenue grants from the Government through the Arts Council and from the Association of Greater Manchester Authorities, amounting to £1.2 million in total. A further £1.2 million of income is generated, mostly from the sale of tickets (nett box office income £900,000), sponsorship and fundraising (£50,000) and catering (£70,000).

A CHRONOLOGY OF THE ROYAL EXCHANGE THEATRE COMPANY

1976

Construction of the building, which had commenced on 14 April 1975, went on all the time up to 12 August, the day on which an invited audience was first present in the module for an acoustic test; fitting and other work continued thereafter. On 8 June the repertoire for the Royal Exchange's opening season was announced by James Maxwell and season tickets went on sale. On 9 August the box office opened for the first time for public booking. 7,000 people came to view the building during an open day on 14 August. The first performance in the theatre – a preview of **The Prince of Homburg** – took place on 8 September. The restaurant opened the following day.

The Theatre was officially opened by Lord Olivier on Wednesday 15 September prior to the opening performance of Sheridan's **The Rivals.** A second opening night, introduced by Dame Wendy Hiller, was held on Thursday 16 September when **The Prince of Homburg** received its British premiere. A Gala Performance of **The Rivals** attended by HRH Princess Alexandra took place on Saturday 18 September. The performance, which was followed by a candlelight gala buffet and celebration ball, was sponsored by the National Westminster Bank. Proceeds were divided between the building appeal and the Peter Henriques Memorial Trust.

1976 The Actors and Artistic Directors for the opening productions of The Royal Exchange Theatre Company.

1976 Michael Elliott and Lord Olivier at the opening of the theatre.
Photo: Manchester Evening News

The first musical event – a late night concert featuring Alan Price – was on 17 September and the first spoken recital, also a late-night event, was given by Paul Scofield and Joy Parker on 21 September.

The Theatre was awarded the Manchester Society of Architects President's Award and the British Tourist Authority's 'Come to Britain' Trophy. Michael Williams was appointed an Associate Artistic Director in December.

The opening productions of **The Rivals, The Prince of Homburg, Zack** (the Harold Brighouse comedy – revived and brought back into the general repertory by the company – which was directed by Eric Thompson, the first guest director) and **What The Butler Saw** played to an average of 86.51% capacity. The first Christmas show (one of only four productions staged by the company to be aimed at children) was a new version of **Dick Whittington** devised by Derek Griffiths and presented only in daytime performances.

1977

Albert Finney played for three months in **Uncle Vanya** (a production in which Leo McKern also gave his first Royal Exchange performance and rehearsals of which were taped by BBC Radio 4 for a programme, *In Rehearsal*, broadcast on 17 August) and **Present Laughter**. Finney also made his debut as a singer in concert on 1 May, with his own lyrics set to music by Denis King. The concert, like a Gala Performance of **Present Laughter** on 31 March, was in aid of the Theatre Building Appeal.

In September the Royal Exchange Theatre Trust began to operate a series of lotteries to raise money to pay off the outstanding capital costs of building the theatre.

On 25 February Timothy Mason (who, in December 1975, had followed Robert Scott as Administrator of the Company) left. He was succeeded by Michael Williams as General Manager. Williams had joined the 69 Theatre Company as Production Manager in 1969 and had acted as Project Manager for the building of the Royal Exchange Theatre. He was also lighting designer for many productions.

Michael Williams

On 1 March it was announced that Sir Alec Guinness was unable to appear in the scheduled production of **The Ordeal of Gilbert Pinfold** due to ill health. It was replaced by **The Adventures of Huckleberry Finn** and Guinness by Michael Hordern when **Pinfold** – the first new play specially commissioned by the company – was finally premiered in September.

The first totally new work to be premiered was the musical by Trevor Peacock **Leaping Ginger**. Other productions included the European premiere of **The Golden Country** by the Japanese Shusaku Endo and the first Shakespearean production in the theatre, **Twelfth Night**. Overall the productions played to 82.87%, with **Uncle Vanya, Present Laughter**, and **Twelfth Night** selling out.

Two foreign tours were made. The first, in May, was a visit to the International Festival of Arena Theatre in Münster, West Germany, with Tom Courtenay and Leo McKern in **Crime and Punishment**; the second was a European tour of **The Winter's Tale** funded by the British Council, playing 14 theatres in seven countries during September and October. Performances sold out in all the countries visited and in Romania and Hungary extra performances had to be put on.

Ronald Harwood's **A Family,** the first original straight play presented by the company, was also the first production to transfer to London. With a cast including Paul Scofield, Irene Handl and Harry Andrews, the production toured to Birmingham, Leeds and Brighton before spending three months at the Theatre Royal, Haymarket.

On 27 April Sir Hugh Casson presented the theatre with the 1977 Royal Institute of Architects Award.

On 1 October the Musicians of the Royal Exchange, under the directorship of pianist Anthony Goldstone, gave their debut concert.

Notable productions included the Yiddish dramatist S. Anski's **The Dybbuk** and Vanessa Redgrave in **The Lady From The Sea.** Robert Lindsay made his Royal Exchange debut in a revival of the very popular **Leaping Ginger** and David Storey's **Sisters** was premiered. The average seating capacity was 82.61% with especially high figures being recorded for **The Lady From The Sea** (95%), **A Family** (90%) and **Leaping Ginger** (92%). A long running series of contemporary one-act plays, performed in the theatre in lunchtime, early evening or late-night performances, opened with Peter Flannery's **Last Resort** (17,19 & 20 January).

The Royal Exchange undertook its first season at London's Round House, guaranteed by the National Westminster Bank, from 14 February to 7 July. Three productions, all of which had previously been seen in Manchester, were staged: Michael Hordern in **The Ordeal of Gilbert Pinfold,** Edward Fox in **The Family Reunion** and Vanessa Redgrave in **The Lady From The Sea.** For the season Richard Negri, the inspiration behind the Manchester theatre, completely re-designed the auditorium of the Round House so as to recreate as closely as possible the in-the-round Royal Exchange. The new auditorium and the highly successful season of plays was welcomed and praised by press and public alike, showing the huge potential that existed for co-operation between a major regional company and a London venue. **The Family Reunion** later transferred (on 19 June) to the Vaudeville Theatre in the West End.

Another production – the British premiere of Neil Simon's **Last of the Red Hot Lovers** – also transferred to London, to the Criterion Theatre, in November for a six-month run.

1979 Tom Courtenay and Gabrielle Drake at the opening of the new bar and cafe. *Photo* Spencer.

The same month, on 11 November, the Musicians of the Royal Exchange made their London debut at the Round House.

On 24 October Tom Courtenay opened the new and extended Cafe-bar in the theatre. A completely new bar area, the design of which (by Camilla Bunt) was based on the theatre module, was created and the old area previously shared by cafe and bar was refurbished as the cafe.

In audience terms the third season was the most successful to date with several productions including **The Schoolmistress, The Family Reunion, Last of the Red Hot Lovers** and **The Three Musketeers!** selling out. The last named, a musical adaptation of the Dumas novel, was a world premiere. Hofmannsthal's **The Deep Man** was given its British premiere and **The Cherry Orchard** and **The Lower Depths** played in repertoire, the first such venture since the theatre's opening productions. The overall capacity for the year was 79.83%

Ronald Harwood's **The Dresser,** with Tom Courtenay and Freddie Jones, received its world premiere on 6 March. Michael Elliott's production transferred on 30 April to the Queen's Theatre in London for a long run.

Vanessa Redgrave won the Evening Standard Drama Award as Best Actress for her performance as Ellida in **The Lady from the Sea** the previous year.

In April Braham Murray visited Milwaukee Repertory Theatre in Wisconsin at the invitation of its directors to discuss the

1979 The Round House auditorium designed by Richard Negri for the Royal Exchange's first London season. *Photo* Donald Cooper

possibility of close links between the two companies.

In July the artistic directors launched a campaign to make the grant-giving bodies and the public more aware of the financial difficulties involved in running a theatre of national standards and maintaining the quality of productions. Gregory Hersov joined the company as an assistant director at the beginning of the 1980/81 season.

Besides **The Dresser**, other notable productions included the premiere of Gerard McLarnon's **Blood Black & Gold, Love on the Dole** (which was broadcast on BBC Radio 4 on 19 July), the British premiere of the farce **Have You Anything to Declare?** Helen Mirren and Bob Hoskins in **The Duchess of Malfi**, and **Waiting For Godot** with Max Wall and Trevor Peacock. 96% capacity figures were recorded for **The Dresser** and **The Duchess of Malfi** but the average for the year was 82.92%

1980 The cast of *The Duchess of Malfi*

1981

The Dresser finished its 266-performance West End run on 17 January, ending a period of just under two years during which Royal Exchange productions had been running continuously in London. The transfer attracted four major awards – two for Tom Courtenay as Best Actor and two for Ronald Harwood for Best New Play – from the Evening Standard and Drama magazine. **The Dresser** later transferred to Broadway, again with Tom Courtenay but with Paul Rogers taking over the role of 'Sir'. It opened at the Brooks Atkinson Theatre on 9 November (for six months). The play, both stars and Michael Elliott received ecstatic reviews from the New York critics.

The second Round House season of Royal Exchange productions took place between 1 April and 1 August. The plays were **The Duchess of Malfi, Have You Anything to Declare?, Waiting For Godot** and **The Misanthrope**. For the first, Helen Mirren won the Best Stage Actress Award from the Variety Club of Great Britain.

The Friends of the Royal Exchange, with Tom Courtenay as Patron, was launched in June.

In October the Royal Exchange and the Milwaukee Repertory Company embarked on an Anglo-American exchange project. Braham Murray directed his Royal Exchange production of **Have You Anything to Declare?** in Milwaukee with Dilys Hamlett reprising her Manchester role. The rest of the cast, which included the playwright Larry Shue, was American.

On 31 October the Craft Centre opened in the foyer as a retail outlet for the work of Britain's finest craftsmen. Its construction was jointly funded by North West Arts and the Crafts Council.

In November the box office was computerised, and the same month, on the 19th, the first selling exhibition to be held at the Royal Exchange opened: Dazzle, the annual jewellery exhibition.

The year's repertoire, which included Casper Wrede's production of **Rosmersholm** in which Espen Skjønberg made his British debut, **Measure for Measure, Doctor Faustus** with Ben Kingsley in the title role, **Heartbreak House** and the premiere of James Maxwell's adaptation of **Treasure Island**, played to an overall capacity of 80.90%.

1982

The Dresser closed on Broadway on 1 May and the company's other trans-Atlantic connection, the Milwaukee exchange, also finished following the production of **Detective Story** (directed by Milwaukee's artistic director John Dillon and starring the American actor Daniel Mooney) in May and June.

The Royal Exchange won the race to stage the British premiere of Schnitzler's famous play **La Ronde** (known as **The Round Dance** in Charles Osborne's translation) – on 1 January, the day copyright ceased.

On 13 June Diana Rigg, Albert Finney, Frank Muir and Michael Meyer appeared at the Palace Theatre in the latter's entertainment **He and She**. The evening was in aid of the Royal Exchange's new 400-seat in-the-round mobile theatre which was then under construction. Designed by Alan Broadhurst of the Manchester firm of structural engineers Broadhurst and Goodwin, it was a replica of the stage level of the Royal Exchange Theatre.

Andy Capp, the musical by Alan Price and Trevor Peacock, received its world premiere on 29 June. The sell-out production was extended in Manchester and transferred to the Aldwych Theatre in London on 28 September.

Other productions included **The Beaux' Stratagem**, the first Greek play to be presented by the company **Philoctetes**, the European premiere of Larry Shue's comedy **The Nerd, One Flew Over the Cuckoo's Nest** (Gregory Hersov's first major production) and Ronald Harwood's **After the Lions** with Dorothy Tutin as Sarah Bernhardt. Four plays sold out and the average seating capacity was 86.65%

Dazzle, the annual jewellery exhibition
Photo John Peters

1983

Andy Capp, still running in London, won the Plays & Players Award for Best New Musical.

Festival '83, a festival of contemporary drama, was staged in the mobile theatre (known at the time as the Young Exchange Theatre) which was erected inside the Corn Exchange, from 19 April until 11 June. The Royal Exchange presented three plays **Cock-Ups, Street Captives** and the premiere of **Masterpieces** by Sarah Daniels, and there were four visiting productions – The People Show's **The Cabaret**, Black Theatre Co-Operative in **The Nine Night**, Paines Plough in Tony Marchant's **Welcome Home** and the National Theatre of Brent's **The Messiah** – as well as concerts, playreadings and workshops.

Masterpieces transferred to London's Royal Court Theatre Upstairs from 11 October to 5 November and subsequently moved into the Royal Court's main auditorium on 5 January the following year. Sarah Daniels won the Plays & Players Award for Most Promising Playwright.

Laurence Harbottle

Alex Bernstein

Laurence Harbottle, Chairman of the company since 1968, resigned and was succeeded on 20 October by Alex Bernstein, Chairman of the Granada Group. Maggie Whitlum was appointed Administrator in April and Sophie Marshall became an Associate Artistic Director in December.

Notable productions included Casper Wrede's Mandelstam adaptation **Hope Against Hope,** Sir Kenneth Macmillan's drama directorial debut with Edward Fox and Jill Bennett in **The Dance of Death,** Robert Lindsay's **Hamlet** ("The ideal Hamlet for the Eighties" according to the Daily Mail) and Michael Elliott's final production, a spellbinding **Moby Dick.** The seating capacity for the year averaged 70.85%.

1984

With funding from the Arts Council, the first national tour in the mobile theatre took place between 9 April and 9 June. The sell-out tour of **Hamlet,** with Robert Lindsay in the title role, opened at Lowton High School near Leigh and finished with three weeks on the roof of the Barbican Centre in London.

Michael Elliott, one of the company's founding artistic directors and to many the inspiration behind it, died on 31 May. A memorial service was held in Manchester Cathedral on 6 June, and on 15 July many leading members of the profession who had worked with Michael Elliott took part in a celebration of his life in the theatre. It was hosted by Frank Muir and among those who entertained the invited audience were Albert Finney, Tom Courtenay, Leo McKern, Edward Fox, Freddie Jones, James Maxwell, Avril Elgar, Joanna David, Robert Lindsay, Dilys Hamlett, Brian Cox, his father-in-law Esmond Knight and the pianist Stephen Bishop-Kovacevich.

Michael Elliott

Michael Elliott's last production **Moby Dick** won two awards including the Manchester Society of Architects President's Award for its staging. Elliott was posthumously awarded the Horniman Award for outstanding services to theatre.

Tom Courtenay won the Golden Globe for Best Screen Actor and was nominated for an Oscar for the role of Norman in Peter Yates's film of **The Dresser,** the part he had created at the Royal Exchange four years previously.

On 18 October the first Mobil Playwriting Competition, with £21,000 in prizes, was launched at a press conference at the Savoy Hotel in London.

During the Spring a functions suite named The Peter Henriques Room, was created occupying the former restaurant overlooking the foyer.

A public conference – **The Arts: Haughty Culture?** – was held in the theatre on 12 October to discuss the implications of the Arts Council's proposed strategy *The Glory of the Garden* and the abolition of the Metropolitan Counties. In November the directors had a major row with the Arts Council over the company's funding.

Gregory Hersov was appointed an Associate Artistic Director in June and joined the other directors Casper Wrede, Braham Murray and James Maxwell for a season of plays (including **Cymbeline, Great Expectations** and **The Admirable Crichton)** in which every production was directed by all four and a permanent ensemble of actors was cast.

Other productions included the first major revival of **Jumpers** (with Tom Courtenay and Julie Walters appearing in Nicholas Hytner's directorial debut at the Royal Exchange) and the company's only 'non-original' musical **Carousel.** The overall capacity achieved was 83.69% with very high box office figures for **The Plough and the Stars** (92%), **Jumpers** (98%) and **The Prime of Miss Jean Brodie** (89%). Season ticket sales topped 6,000 for the first time.

1985 the curtain call for *Three Sisters*
Photo Spoken Image

1985

The first Mobil Playwriting Competition closed, with 2,000 entries, on 31 August. Earlier in the year the competition had attracted one of the first Business Sponsorship Incentive Scheme Awards: a cheque for £20,000 was presented, on 29 March, by Lord Gowrie to Willy Russell, who accepted it on the theatre's behalf. The money was used to promote the competition further. At the prize ceremony in the theatre on 6 December two first prizes of £7,500 were won by Robin Glendinning for **Mumbo Jumbo** and Tony Perrin for **War Pictures** and four other prizes were awarded.

1986 A demonstration of pyrotechnics at the Open Day
Photo Mike Frisbee

On 19 April the theatre began to operate its costume hire business from two units located in the Corn Exchange.

In April Michael Williams resigned after 17 years with the company and administrative responsibility passed to Maggie Whitlum. Nicholas Hytner joined the company as an Associate Director at the beginning of the 1985/86 season. In October the theatre's first development director was appointed to raise much needed additional income.

Michael Frayn's translation of Chekhov's **Three Sisters** was premiered; Casper Wrede, who had commissioned it, directed a strong cast which included Espen Skjønberg as Dr Chebutykin. Skjønberg won the 'Drama' magazine award as Best Supporting Actor, a rare accolade for a performance which was not seen in London.

Two shows written by Trevor Peacock were premiered – the musical **Class K** and the Christmas entertainment **Jack and the**

1986 James Maxwell, Casper Wrede and Braham Murray cutting the 10th anniversary cake

Giant. Peacock also received considerable acclaim for his performance as Willy Loman in **Death of a Salesman.** The other premiere was another musical – **Who's A Lucky Boy?** – conceived by Alan Price, Braham Murray and Gerald Scarfe and based on Hogarth's prints of **The Rake's Progress.** The productions played to an average of 78.08% capacity.

1986

A second nationwide tour with the mobile theatre was mounted in the spring; between 7 April and 17 May **As You Like It** toured eleven venues from Carlisle to Crawley.

In July the Corporate Members Scheme – the first major initiative of the theatre's sponsorship and development programme – was officially launched with 20 founding firms. The Taittinger Bar off the foyer, a specially created private bar for the exclusive use of corporate members to entertain their guests, was opened on 9 December by Pierre Emmanuel Taittinger from the famous family-run French champagne company who sponsored the venture.

The theatre celebrated its Tenth Anniversary on 15 September with a private performance of the opening production of the season **Zack** and a birthday party for many former members of the company, staff, actors, directors, designers and other friends. Brian Matthew's *Round Midnight* programme on Radio 2 was broadcast live from the theatre that night. Other public events to mark the anniversary included an Open Day on 14 September attended by almost 6,000 people. An extended Craft Centre was re-opened by James Maxwell on 12 September.

1986 The newly extended Craft Centre
Photo: John Peters

Actor Ian McDiarmid was appointed an Associate Artistic Director at the beginning of the Tenth Anniversary Season and Fergus Early Associate Director (Movement). Jeff Noon and Iain Heggie became the theatre's first annual playwrights-in-residence. The publication of Noon's **Woundings** on 27 November marked the start of an association with the play publishers, Oberon Books. Richard Negri relinquished his position as an artistic director in October and became Honorary Artistic Director.

Behind Heaven, one of five new plays premiered that year, transferred to the Donmar Warehouse Theatre in London on 16 December for a limited run. The other premieres were Russell Hoban's **Riddley Walker,** the Mobil prize-winner **Mumbo Jumbo** in which Nigel Stock played his last role, **The Act** and **Woundings.** Sell-out productions included the British premiere of the farce **Court in the Act!** and **The Country Wife,** but overall the capacity was 78.68%.

1987

Court in the Act! was the first of four Royal Exchange productions to be seen outside Manchester that year when it opened a pre-London tour in Guildford on 21 January. It subsequently toured to seven other major theatres and transferred to the Phoenix Theatre in the West End on 21 April. **The Alchemist** was the third production to make a national tour in the mobile theatre. With sponsorship from the Prudential, the company visited 11 towns over an 8-week period from 31 March to 23 May.

The Mobil prize-winner **Mumbo Jumbo** was revived by Nicholas Hytner at the Lyric Hammersmith on 15 May for a six-week run and another Mobil play **A Wholly Healthy Glasgow** was presented at the Edinburgh International Festival in August, the company's first return there since the opening productions in 1968 of the 69 Theatre Company.

The second Mobil Playwriting Competition, by then established as the major contest for dramatists to be organised in Britain with prize money on offer of £33,000, was launched at Mobil Court in London on 25 March.

1987 Terence Stamp opening Willshaw's Theatre Bookshop
Photo John Peters

Willshaws Theatre Bookshop, a new retail outlet in the foyer, created by the Alto Design Partnership, was opened by Terence Stamp on 30 June. An ongoing series of literary events associated with the bookshop was initiated by visits from Simon Callow (11 September) and Arthur Miller (10 November).

Maggie Whitlum was succeeded as Administrator by Lynda Farran in May. The theatre's first education director was appointed in February and three other appointments were confirmed in September – those of Gregory Hersov as Artistic Director, Chris Monks as Associate Director (Music) and Nick Dear as Playwright-in-residence.

The repertoire included two premieres, Iain Heggie's comedy **A Wholly Healthy Glasgow** and the Woody Allen revue **The Bluebird of Unhappiness,** and two premieres of new translations, the company's 100th production – an **Oedipus** double-bill and James Maxwell's version of Schiller's **Don Carlos** directed by Nicholas Hytner. The average capacity of 80.05% was easily beaten by box office figures of 95% for **The Alchemist** and 92% for **Loot.**

1987 Arthur Miller reading from his autobiography with chairman, Casper Wrede
Photo Michael Arron

Entries for the second Mobil Playwriting Competition closed on 16 January. Judging of the 1600 scripts from 25 countries took three months and the Prize Ceremony was held at the theatre on 17 May. The first prize of £10,000 was won by Michael Wall for **Amongst Barbarians.**

A Wholly Healthy Glasgow transferred to the Royal Court Theatre from 28 January to 27 February and the play (filmed the previous March by BBC Scotland in the studio) was broadcast on BBC 1 on 16 February.

The Artistic Directors celebrated 20 years of continuous association on 12 February, the anniversary of the founding of the 69 Theatre Company in 1968.

The annual mobile theatre tour took to the road during May and June. Moliere's **Don Juan** was presented in ten venues and Marivaux's one-act comedy **Slave Island** as a late-night show in eight of them.

Box office figures for the 1987/88 financial year broke through the £1 million barrier for the first time.

In August the company returned to the Edinburgh International Festival with **A Midsummer Night's Dream** prior to the production opening the autumn season in Manchester.

Ian McDiarmid left the company in September, the same month in which Gabriel Gbadamosi, winner of the first Mobil Bursary, was appointed Playwright-in-residence.

Notable productions included the premiere of **American Bagpipes, All My Sons** in which John Thaw made his Royal Exchange debut to capacity audiences, and three Shakespeare plays **Twelfth Night, A Midsummer Night's Dream** and **Macbeth.** The repertoire achieved an average capacity of 81.05%.

On 16 and 23 October a Mobil prize-winner, **Assuming The Role** by Keith Wood, was staged as the first production in a new venture: the performance with limited decor of new full-length plays on Sunday evenings.

Other main productions scheduled in the 1988/89 Autumn/ Winter season are Shaw's **Arms and the Man** directed by Casper Wrede (22 December-4 February) and the premiere of **Amongst Barbarians** directed by James Maxwell (9-26 February). **Arms and the Man** will then tour major regional theatres throughout England for eight weeks under the banner of Mobil Touring Theatre.

1988 Albert Finney with Michael Wall, author of *Amongst Barbarians*
Photo John Peters

The Spring/Summer season plays include productions of Shelagh Delaney's **A Taste of Honey,** directed by Ian Hastings (2 March-1 April), the premiere of a Mobil-shortlisted play by Dolores Walshe **In The Talking Dark,** directed by Braham Murray (13 April-6 May), Greg Hersov's revival of **The Voysey Inheritance** by Harley Granville Barker (11 May-25 June) and Neil Simon's **The Odd Couple** (22 June-29 July). **A Taste of Honey** is the choice for the company's fifth tour in the mobile theatre and Patricia Routledge returns to the Royal Exchange in the first week of April with her show **Come for the Ride.**

Some quotes about
THE ROYAL EXCHANGE

The Building

"Theatrically the effect is stunning. The place seems poised for take-off. It is a masterstroke to have created Manchester's new theatre at the very heart of Mancunian tradition rather than to have set up yet another boarded-concrete cultural supermarket with no link to the past."
Irving Wardle, *The Times* (Sept 1976)

"Breath-taking . . . it is a symbol of what Manchester can become."
Louis Heren, *London Illustrated News* (Feb 1983)

"The best theatre in the regions and certainly the most original in its methods and setting . . . this peculiar auditorium (is) excitingly effective. Whatever the genre of show, it casts a spell we feel at no other theatre."
Eric Shorter, *Daily Telegraph* (June 1987)

"The result is breathtaking – a cream-coloured space module of metal and glass, half-hanging from the pillars of what must be the most impressive theatre foyer in the world. The conception of this new technology suspended within the old is riveting."
Paul Vallely, *Radio Times* (July 1980)

"That brilliant building within a building"
Colin Davies, *Architect's Journal* (Oct 1987)

". . . the Royal Exchange in Manchester, a fantastic and exciting example of the invasion of a non-theatrical space by a steep, galleried, tubular module that creates a sense equally of intimacy and occasion."
Michael Coveney, *Financial Times* (June 1986)

"A most ingenious and lively solution to a very familiar problem – what to do with an abandoned elephant of a Victorian commercial building of great grandeur for which no use could be found. The solution? Let a new theatre land in it like a helicopter, as a separate artefact with its own totally modern, glittering presence, which works like a dream and raises the spirits at first sight."
Sir Hugh Casson, *Vogue* (Sept 1980)

". . . an achievement which must be rated as one of the greatest advances in theatrical architecture of all time."
Sheridan Morley, *Punch* (Sept 1977)

"This architecurally exhilarating new theatre . . . The tubular steel arena, squatting like a giant crab between the marble pillars of the deep, heavily encrusted Victorian rock pool it lives in is the most exciting place I have been in for a long time – in its way the nearest thing in British arts to the technological bravura of the Paris Beaubourg."
Jeremy Treglown, *The Times* (Nov 1978)

"It is spectacular . . . one of the best theatres in England"
Jan Bielicki, *Suddeutsche Zeitung*, Germany (Jan 1988)

"The Royal Exchange is still my favourite theatre – after it all others seem old fashioned"
Tom Courtenay (Aug 1986)

"One of the most innovative and exciting pieces of theatre architecture in Britain of this century . . . and unlike so many of the new theatres of the post-War boom, the auditorium at the Exchange still manages to retain the extraordinary sense of occasion, intimacy and expectation that not only marks good theatre design but provides an ever-present springboard for theatrical adventure in the future."
George Rowell & Anthony Jackson, *The Repertory Movement* (Cambridge University Press 1984)

The Company

"What's important about this new venture is that it demolishes totally the notion that theatre outside London should ever be second best. Manchester is getting an international repertory, with as strong a team of actors and directors as you could wish for."
Michael Billington, *BBC Radio 4* (Sept 1976)

". . . the Mecca of all Northern theatre-goers."
Desmond Pratt, *Yorkshire Post* (Sept 1976)

"Under a four handed directorship the Royal Exchange has been flourishing artistically . . . not just a regional flagship but a national asset."
Jim Hiley, *The Listener* (July 1985)

"Manchester's famous Royal Exchange Theatre Company continues to beguile theatregoers with its adventurous repertoire . . . (it) amounts to an extremely catholic policy – one which compares favourably to the National's in the range of writers acted."
Eric Shorter, *Daily Telegraph* (May 1987)

"Britain's leading provincial repertory company."
Herb Greer, *Wall Street Journal* (Jan 1986)

"The current flagship of regional theatre is the Royal Exchange."
Paul Allen, *New Society* (July 1984)

"One of the most exciting theatres in Britain today and one which has achieved the unique distinction of challenging the London theatre's monopoly of excellence . . . there is more to its success, of course, than the amazing building itself. The loyalty of the audience, which consistently brings 90% houses, is based on an unflagging standard of productions . . . Classics, revivals, foreign plays and new plays; it all adds up to an exciting and adventurous policy."
Paul Vallely, *Radio Times* (July 1980)

"One of Britain's foremost theatres."
The Economist (Jan 1982)

"The success of the Royal Exchange's superb *All My Sons* shows that demand is undiminished for art which not only "takes you out of yourself", but also offers nourishment to the mind."
John Peter, *Sunday Times* (March 1988)

"If the success of a theatre can be measured in terms of audience support, then undoubtedly the Exchange has triumphed . . . the company has clearly amply justified the effort and money invested in the building by the strength and quality of the majority of its work .. there has certainly been an impressive number of finely wrought and often deeply satisfying productions."
George Rowell & Anthony Jackson *The Repertory Movement* (C.U.P. 1984)

"Manchester's Royal Exchange Theatre – perhaps Britain's other National Theatre."
The Independent (Aug 1988)

"The unofficial National Theatre of the North"
Martin Hoyle, *Financial Times* (May 1985)

"The Royal Exchange is a theatre company with great prestige on a par with the National Theatre in London."
Sydsvenska Dagbladet, Sweden (March 1985)

". . . an intimate theatre in the round, doing work of the highest standard . . . the major company based outside London."
The Guardian (June 1984)

THE ARTISTIC DIRECTORS

The artistic policy of the company has been the result of the collaboration between no less than five artistic directors and four associate directors. What is especially surprising is the length of time that the artistic directors have been working together, easily a record for any so-called group theatre. By the time the Royal Exchange Theatre Company celebrated its 10th birthday in 1986, three of them, James Maxwell, Richard Negri and Casper Wrede, had been formally associated for almost 28 years and the fourth, Braham Murray, joined them in 1968. The late Michael Elliott was also a founder and an inspirational member of the group until his death in 1984. Recently Richard Negri has ceased to play an active role in the artistic direction and is now an honorary artistic director.

Casper Wrede initiated this artistic association in 1959 when he founded the 59 Theatre Company at the Lyric Hammersmith. In that famous season Michael Elliott made his stage debut as a director, Richard Negri was one of the designers and James Maxwell was one of the leading actors. In 1962, Michael Elliott was invited to become the Artistic Director of the Old Vic and the team which joined him was the very same. In the interim the four worked together on many projects at other theatres, including the Royal Shakespeare Company and the National Theatre and over a long period on television, where, apart from their separate careers, Elliott and Wrede co-directed many productions.

Braham Murray was a schoolboy member of the audience at the Lyric Hammersmith in 1959, who from that date so admired the work of the group that in 1965 when he became the Artistic Director of the Century Theatre at the University Theatre in Manchester he persuaded James Maxwell and Michael Elliott to work with his company. This liaison led to the 69 Theatre Company founded in 1968 and has lasted through the formation of the Royal Exchange Theatre Company in 1976 to the present day.

During all this time the artistic directors have pursued individual careers in the theatre, television and films in this country and abroad, in design and teaching. This combination of diversity yet shared purpose is one of the major factors which gives the Royal Exchange Theatre Company its unique character. That diversity has been strengthened in recent seasons by the addition of several other directors. Gregory Hersov, who joined the company in 1979 as an assistant director with a particular interest in contemporary plays and later became an associate director, was appointed a full artistic director in 1987. Sophie Marshall, a founding staff member of the Royal Exchange and latterly casting director, has been an associate artistic director since 1983. Manchester-born Nicholas Hytner, with a background in opera, joined the group in 1985. Actor Ian McDiarmid was also an associate artistic director for the two seasons 1986-1988. Fergus Early (Movement) and Chris Monks (Music) are now additional associate directors.

CASPER WREDE was born in Finland and came to Britain to study at the Old Vic Drama School. When he left in 1952 he began directing, spending two years with the OUDS as professional producer. During this period he directed for BBC Television and with Michael Elliott directed *Uncle Vanya, Twelfth Night* and *The Lady from the Sea.*

He was the founder of the 59 Theatre Company and in their acclaimed season at the Lyric, Hammersmith, he directed *Danton's Death* (translated by James Maxwell), Strindberg's *Creditors* with Mai Zetterling, and the premiere of Alun Owen's *The Rough and Ready Lot.* Other notable productions included *Othello* at the Old Vic and *The Father* with Trevor Howard in the West End. At the 1968 Edinburgh Festival he directed the 69 Theatre Company's first production, *Hamlet* with Tom Courtenay, before the company's move to its Manchester home. His other 69 Theatre Company productions were Ronald Harwood's *Country Matters* and, at Manchester Cathedral, *A Man For All Seasons.*

His choice of productions for the Royal Exchange Theatre Company reflects major interests in European drama and new work. He has directed the British premieres of Heinrich von Kleist's *The Prince of Homburg,* Hofmannsthal's *The Deep Man* and Schnitzler's *The Round Dance (La Ronde)* as well as two Chekhov plays, *The Cherry Orchard* and the award-winning *Three Sisters,* two by Ibsen, *Rosmersholm* and *The Wild Duck,* Molière's *The Misanthrope* and a double bill of *Oedipus the King* and *Oedipus at Colonus,* the company's 100th production. New plays have included *A Family* with Paul Scofield, his own adaptation of Nadezhda Mandelstam's *Hope Against Hope, The Act* by Richard Langridge, and, most recently, Iain Heggie's *American Bagpipes.* He has also co-directed *Cymbeline,* a new adaptation of *Great Expectations, The Admirable Crichton* and Trevor Peacock's *Class K.* In 1988/89 he directs *Arms and the Man* in Manchester and on tour.

For television he directed Laurence Olivier in *John Gabriel Borkman,* Edith Evans in *Hay Fever,* Tom Courtenay in *Time and Time Again,* all the early television plays by Ronald Harwood, and five documentaries including *The Summer in Gossensass* (by Michael Meyer, about Ibsen in old age) and *Sibelius.* He has also directed extensively in theatre and television in Scandinavia. Among his feature films are *Private Potter, The Barber of Stamford Hill, One Day in the Life of Ivan Denisovich* and *Ransom* with Sean Connery.

BRAHAM MURRAY has directed more productions for the company than anyone else – 11 for 69 Theatre Company and 27 at the Royal Exchange. Although he is a Londoner, he has been working in Manchester

since he was appointed Artistic Director of Century Theatre at the end of 1965.

He made his first impact on British theatre, while still a student at Oxford University, as co-author and director of *Hang Down Your Head and Die,* an anti-capital punishment documentary musical which transferred to the West End in 1964 (winning the Variety Critics Award) and then to Broadway. He directed the revue *Chaganog,* which transferred from the Edinburgh Festival to the St Martin's Theatre, and other London productions before moving to the Century Theatre, then based at Manchester's University Theatre. During his two years in charge of Century, he directed 16 productions, including the first production of Joe Orton's revised version of *Loot, The Merchant of Venice, Uncle Vanya, The Ortolan,* the premiere of Gerard McLarnon's *The Saviour, Charley's Aunt* and *Romeo and Juliet,* the last two with Tom Courtenay.

He became an Artistic Director of the 69 Theatre Company at its inception in 1968 and directed many notable productions, six of which transferred to London – *She Stoops To Conquer* and *Charley's Aunt,* both with Tom Courtenay, the musicals *'Erb* by Trevor Peacock and Jack Good's *Catch My Soul,* J M Barrie's *Mary Rose* (which introduced Mia Farrow to the English stage) and Beckett's *Endgame.* For the West End his other musical productions have included Andre Previn's version of J B Priestley's *The Good Companions* with John Mills and Judi Dench and *The Black Mikado,* an updated version of the Gilbert and Sullivan operetta.

Since the opening production at the Royal Exchange of *The Rivals* he has directed most of the company's successful musicals – *Leaping Ginger, The Three Musketeers,* the award-winning *Andy Capp* by Alan Price and Trevor Peacock which transferred to the West End, *Class K* and *Who's A Lucky Boy?* – and a wide variety of plays including the rarely seen *The Dybbuk, The Winter's Tale* (which toured Europe), *Measure for Measure, The Beaux' Stratagem, Cymbeline* (co-directed with the other artistic directors), *Long Day's Journey Into Night,* the European premiere of *The Nerd* and the premiere of Russell Hoban's *Riddley Walker.* Four other productions have also been seen in London – *Waiting for Godot* with Max Wall and Trevor Peacock, Robert Lindsay's *Hamlet* which finished its English tour with a three-week run on the roof of the Barbican Centre and the farces *Have You Anything To Declare?* and *Court in the Act!,* both of which he adapted with Robert Cogo-Fawcett. His most recent productions have been *The Merchant of Venice,* the premiere of *The Bluebird of Unhappiness,* the Woody Allen revue adapted by John Lahr, Pinero's *The Cabinet Minister* and *Twelfth Night.* In the autumn of 1988 he directed David Threlfall and Frances Barber in *Macbeth.*

Braham has also directed at several other major English repertory companies and in America. He is married to the designer Johanna Bryant.

JAMES MAXWELL has combined the roles of actor and director throughout a very successful career. He was born in Worcester, Massachusetts and after studying at Yale came to England in 1950 to train at the Old Vic School. His first job was a tour of the musical *Kiss Me Kate*, after which he went to Bristol Old Vic and various other repertory companies, including a season for Frank Dunlop and Richard Negri for the Piccolo Theatre Company in Manchester. His first West End appearance was the lead in a musical version of *The Comedy of Errors*.

In 1959 he translated and adapted Büchner's *Danton's Death* for Casper Wrede's opening production at the Lyric Hammersmith and he also acted with the company. He was a member of Michael Elliott's Old Vic Company, playing Bassanio in *The Merchant of Venice* and the Duke in *Measure for Measure*. For a time he concentrated mainly on television work, starring in many drama series including *Frontier*, *The Hidden Truth*, *Blackmail* and as Henry VII in the BBC series *Shadow of the Tower*.

His work for the 69 Theatre Company included the adaptation of *Daniel Deronda* (which starred Vanessa Redgrave and was subsequently televised), appearances as Prospero in *The Tempest* and as Osborne in *Journey's End* (which transferred to the West End), directing Tom Courtenay and Jenny Agutter in *Arms and the Man*, the company's first production in the temporary tent theatre in the Royal Exchange, and playing Thomas More in *A Man For All Seasons* at Manchester Cathedral.

He became an artistic director of the company in 1973 and acted in the opening productions of *The Rivals* and *The Prince of Homburg* in 1976. For the Royal Exchange he has directed Albert Finney in *Present Laughter*, Patricia Routledge in *The Schoolmistress* and his wife Avril Elgar in *The Corn is Green*, his own adaptation of *Treasure Island*, *While the Sun Shines*, *Hay Fever* and the Tenth Anniversary production of *Zack*. Productions he has co-directed include *The Skin of Our Teeth*, *Cymbeline* (in which he also played the title role), *Great Expectations*, *The Admirable Crichton* and *Class K*. As an actor he has also taken leading roles in *The Winter's Tale*, *The Deep Man*, *The Cherry Orchard*, *The Lower Depths*, *Harvey*, *Doctor Faustus* opposite Ben Kingsley, *Philoctetes*, *Cat On A Hot Tin Roof*, *Long Day's Journey Into Night*, *Entertaining Mr Sloane* with Adam Ant and *Behind Heaven* (which transferred to London for a limited run). He played the Grand Inquisitor in Schiller's *Don Carlos*, which he also translated, and directs the premiere of Michael Wall's *Amongst Barbarians*, winner of the second Mobil Playwriting Competition, in February 1989.

Among his countless television appearances have been *Portrait of a Lady* with Richard Chamberlain, a series of Somerset Maugham plays, the BBC serialisation of *John MacNab*, the Play for Today *Under the Hammer* and *Bergerac*. Films include *Private Potter*, *Otley*, *Connecting Rooms*, *One Day In The Life Of Ivan Denisovich*, and the thriller *Ransom* with Sean Connery.

His interest in music led to the formation, under the directorship of pianist Anthony Goldstone, of the Musicians of the Royal Exchange in 1978. He has introduced many concerts, narrated many musical works and even directed one opera, Gordon Crosse's *Purgatory* for the Royal Northern College of Music. The RNCM honoured him by making him a Member in 1986.

GREGORY HERSOV was born in London. After Oxford he went on a Thames Television Regional Directors Scholarship to the Redgrave Theatre, Farnham for two years and directed over twenty plays there. In 1980 he formed the Stiletto Theatre Company in Bristol to produce

a season of five new plays and the same year he joined the Royal Exchange as an assistant director, working on *The Duchess of Malfi*, *Rosmersholm*, *Measure for Measure*, *Doctor Faustus* and *The Round Dance* amongst others. He directed two seasons of contemporary plays, *Philby – Going Home*, *Will* (which he also devised from the works

of Shakespeare), *Private Wars* and *The Soul of the White Ant*, *Painting a Wall*, and *The Unseen Hand*, following which he was made an associate director. *One Flew Over The Cuckoo's Nest* in September 1982 was his first major production and he directed *Cock Ups*, the first production in the Festival '83 season at the Corn Exchange for which he was also responsible. His other main house productions before his appointment as associate artistic director in the autumn of 1984 were *The Plough and the Stars* and *Cat On A Hot Tin Roof*. He joined the other directors on *Cymbeline*, *Great Expectations*, *The Admirable Crichton* and *Class K*, and directed Adam Ant in *Entertaining Mr Sloane*, Trevor Peacock in *Death of a Salesman* and the premiere of Jonathan Moore's *Behind Heaven* which transferred to London. His productions in the tenth anniversary season were *Woundings* by Jeff Noon and *The Alchemist* which toured the country in the mobile theatre. He was appointed an artistic director at the beginning of the 1987/88 season, during which he directed Brenda Blethyn in *A Doll's House* and Garson Kanin's comedy *Born Yesterday*, and John Thaw in an acclaimed production of *All My Sons*. He directed the Edinburgh Festival production of *A Midsummer Night's Dream* which then opened the 1988/89 season in Manchester.

SOPHIE MARSHALL became an associate artistic director at the end of 1983. Born and brought up in Altrincham she joined the 69 Theatre Company in 1973 as production and project secretary for the building of the new theatre. Over the years she progressed through various key

jobs from production assistant and assistant to the artistic directors to company manager and, finally, casting director and an associate artistic director.

NICHOLAS HYTNER was appointed an associate director of the Royal Exchange Theatre in August 1985, some eighteen months after he directed Julie Walters and Tom Courtenay in *Jumpers*, his first production for the company. He was born in Manchester and educated at Manchester

Grammar School and Cambridge University. His theatre work includes several productions at the Northcott Theatre, Exeter, including *The Recruiting Officer* and four at Leeds Playhouse including *Tom Jones*, *The Ruling Class* and *Chips with Everything*. He also directs opera — notably for Kent Opera (*The Turn of the Screw*, *The Marriage of Figaro* and Tippett's *King Priam*, recently broadcast on Channel 4), English National Opera (Wagner's *Rienzi*, nominated for the SWET Award, Handel's *Xerxes* which won both the Laurence Olivier Award and the Standard Award as Best Opera production in 1985, and *The Magic Flute*). The Royal Opera Covent Garden (the British premiere of Sallinen's *The King Goes Forth to France* and the first major revival of Tippett's *The Knot Garden*), and the Paris Opéra (Handel's *Julius Caesar*). Prior to his Royal Exchange appointment he directed Donald Sinden in *The Scarlet Pimpernel* at the Chichester Festival and in the West End and since then *As You Like It*, which also toured in the mobile theatre, the Mobil award-winning *Mumbo Jumbo*, which transferred to the Lyric Hammersmith, *Edward II* with Ian McDiarmid and *The Country Wife* with Cheryl Campbell and Gary Oldman. Following Schiller's *Don Carlos* which opened the 1987/88 season, he made his debut at the RSC with *Measure for Measure* for whom he has also directed *The Tempest*. He is soon to direct Joshua Sobol's *Ghetto* at the National Theatre.

RICHARD NEGRI was responsible for the concept of the Royal Exchange Theatre and he designed the building in collaboration with the architects Levitt Bernstein Associates. Of Italian extraction, he was born

in London and studied engineering and art before going to the Old Vic School. On leaving he spent a year as designer at Oldham Coliseum before founding the Piccolo Theatre Company with Frank Dunlop in 1954. In their two short seasons at Chorlton many of their fellow ex-Old Vic students who were later to become associated with the 69 Theatre Company and the Royal Exchange were in the company – James Maxwell, Avril Elgar, Dilys Hamlett, Rosalind Knight, Eric Thompson and George Hall.

He assisted Orson Welles in his productions of the ballet *Lady Into Ice* for Roland Petit and *The Merchant of Venice* for television, and designed the famous production of *Brand* for the 59 Theatre Company. Other productions he has designed include *Platonov* with Rex Harrison for the English Stage Company, *Richard II*, *Othello* and *Peer Gynt* (all at the Old Vic), Michael Elliott's *As You Like It* for the RSC, *Miss Julie* for the National Theatre and *The Story of Vasco* for English National Opera. For the 69 Theatre Company he designed *The Tempest* and *Peer Gynt* and co-directed and staged *The Cocktail Party* at Manchester Cathedral.

He was Director of the Theatre Department at the Wimbledon School of Art from 1963 but resigned ten years later to concentrate on designing the Royal Exchange Theatre. After its opening he returned to the Wimbledon School where he was Senior Lecturer until 1988. He has been involved in the design of several other theatre auditoria, the Piccolo Theatre, the Round House in London and the Royal Exchange's mobile theatre. For several years he was also involved in productions at the Royal Exchange where his work included co-directing *The Skin of Our Teeth* and directing the European premiere of Shusako Endo's *The Golden Country*, a double-bill of *The Chairs* and *The Emperor Jones*, designing Michael Elliott's production of *Twelfth Night* and *The Cherry Orchard*, co-adapting and designing the British premiere of *The Round Dance*, and directing Charlie Drake in *The Caretaker*. He relinquished his position as an artistic director of the Royal Exchange, which he had held since 1974, in 1986, becoming Honorary Artistic Director.

MICHAEL ELLIOTT 1931-1984

MICHAEL ELLIOTT was a founding Artistic Director of both the 69 and the Royal Exchange Theatre Companies. The son of a clergyman (Canon Elliott who was known for many years as "the Radio Parson") he was born in London and educated at Radley College and Keble College, Oxford. It was at Oxford that he first met Casper Wrede, then directing a new play by Michael Meyer with a drama student called Maggie Smith, and began an artistic association that lasted until his death in 1984.

He entered the theatre as a television director in 1956, co-directing several productions for the BBC with Casper Wrede; and he became Casper's assistant for the 59 Theatre Company season at the Lyric Hammersmith, making his own stage directing debut with the acclaimed production of Ibsen's *Brand* with Patrick McGoohan. In 1961/2 he directed Vanessa Redgrave in *As You Like It* for the Royal Shapespeare Company in Stratford and London before directing Trevor Howard in John Mortimer's *Two Stars for Comfort* in the West End. He was appointed Artistic Director of the Old Vic in 1962, for whom he directed *Peer Gynt* with Leo McKern, *The Merchant of Venice* and *Measure for Measure* in the last year before it became the National. Other notable productions were *Little Eyolf* at the 1963 Edinburgh Festival and *Miss Julie* for the National, with Maggie Smith and Albert Finney.

He first came to Manchester in 1967 to direct Tom Courtenay in *The Playboy of the Western World* for Braham Murray's Century Theatre and the following year directed Wendy Hiller in *When We Dead Awaken*, one of the 69 Theatre Company's opening productions. Subsequently he directed *Daniel Deronda*, *The Tempest*, *Peer Gynt* with Tom Courtenay, *The Family Reunion* and, in Manchester Cathedral, *The Cocktail Party*.

In the Royal Exchange's first season he directed Albert Finney and Leo McKern in *Uncle Vanya*. Three of his later productions – *The Ordeal of Gilbert Pinfold* with Michael Hordern, *The Lady from the Sea* with Vanessa Redgrave, and *The Family Reunion* with Edward Fox – transferred to London, another – *Crime and Punishment* – was seen in Germany, and *The Dresser* went on to New York after its West End success. His final productions were *Philoctetes*, Ronald Harwood's *After the Lions* and, at Christmas 1983, his own adaptation of *Moby Dick*.

Michael Elliott was a member of the Arts Council Drama Panel for eight years, a member of the Arts Council for three years, served on the Building Committee for the National Theatre, and was a member of the Board of Governors for the Central School of Speech and Drama. He produced two operas, both world premieres by Gordon Crosse – *The Story of Vasco* for ENO at the London Coliseum and *Potter Thompson* at the Aldeburgh Festival.

He was responsible for more than 50 major television productions in this country and several in Norway and Sweden, and directed the CBS Coast-to-Coast spectacular of *The Glass Menagerie* in New York. His memorable BBC plays included *Antigone* with Dorothy Tutin, *Time Remembered* with Edith Evans, *The Lower Depths*, *The Cherry Orchard* with John Gielgud and Peggy Ashcroft and *Ghosts* with Tom Courtenay, Celia Johnson and Donald Wolfit. His last television production was the award-winning *King Lear* with Laurence Olivier for Granada Television.

Awarded the OBE in the 1979 New Year's Honours List, he was married to the actress Rosalind Knight and had two daughters.

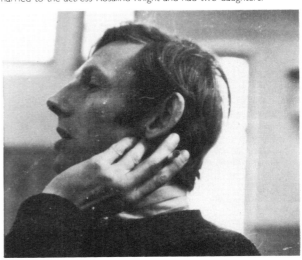

"To work with Michael Elliott was to embark on a voyage of discovery, a humbling and intensely exciting experience as that driving imagination gradually illuminated unexplored landscape. Michael combined technical mastery with a brilliant visual sense, the ability to penetrate to the heart of the most resistant text, and the gift of extracting the best from everyone he worked with.

Whether you were an actor, a writer or a stage hand, you knew he would get the best out of you and that neither of you would rest until he had done so. Yet all this was done with gentleness and courtesy: he made you feel a partner, not an inferior, and that in a small way you were helping to make theatrical history.

Michael's name is perhaps especially associated with his Ibsen productions, and he had much in common with that author; both possessed a rare combination of austerity, sensuality, poetry, strength of will and integrity. His productions of *Brand*, *Peer Gynt*, *Ghosts* (on television), *When We Dead Awaken* and *The Lady from the Sea* will hardly be equalled. Visual images from these productions, the memory of chained and tormented spirits seeking salvation, remain after 10 and even 25 years.

Yet one remembers equally his productions of the authors, Sophocles, Shakespeare, Strindberg, Chekhov, Synge, Gorki and T S Eliot, and of Dostoevsky, George Eliot and Melville in adaptation. His genius was for tragedy, yet his *As You Like It* in 1961 with the young Vanessa Redgrave was as unforgettable as his *Brand*.

If he had a fault as a director, it was that his intense truthfulness made him unwilling to paper the cracks in a flawed play, and this is perhaps why he directed comparatively little contemporary drama, though when a new play did take his fancy, such as *The Dresser*, he did it superbly. The theme of that play must have been close to his heart, for he too regarded himself as the servant of a series of demanding masters, the great dramatists.

For the last eight years of his life, Michael was on a kidney machine, which in his case meant that he only really slept every second night. Few of his friends were allowed to know this; self-pity was one of the things he despised most.

As a man, he had much in common with George Orwell. Both were more than usually tall, thin almost to the point of emaciation, plagued by persistent ill-health and cut off in their prime (Orwell at 46, Elliott at 52); both combined vision and a shining integrity with much warmth and humour lurking behind a veil of austerity."

MICHAEL MEYER

an appreciation reprinted from The Times 9 June 1984

An aerial view of the Royal Exchange
Photo: Airviews (M/c) Ltd

The theatre under construction 1975

Looking down on the theatre module;
the Craft Centre is in the background

View of the theatre from St Ann's Square entrance

Curtain call for Court in the Act! 1986

Entrance to the theatre, St Ann's Square

Staircase of module

The interior of the module during a curtain call for
Lord Arthur Savile's Crime 1982
Photo: Carlton Studios

Exhibition in foyer

Craft Centre

Café and Bar

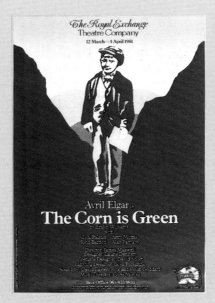

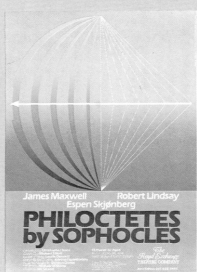

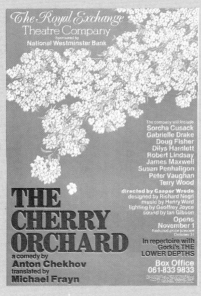

THE CORN IS GREEN 1981
THE DRAWING ROOM

TREASURE ISLAND 1981
THE DRAWING ROOM

THE PRINCE OF HOMBURG 1976
MEARNS

THE MISANTHROPE 1981
THE DRAWING ROOM

PHILOCTETES 1982
THE DRAWING ROOM

SEASON 1984/5
THE DRAWING ROOM

THE CHERRY ORCHARD 1979
HILLY BEVAN & ANTHONY LAWRENCE

TWELFTH NIGHT 1988
MICHAEL MAYHEW

ZACK 1986
ROGER SOUTHERN

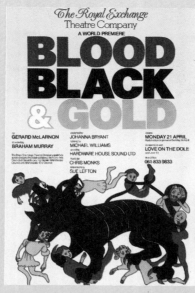

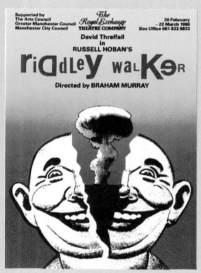

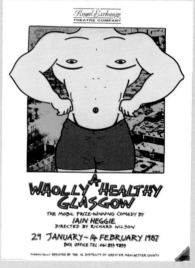

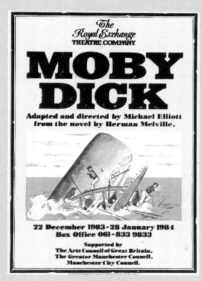

THE FAMILY REUNION 1979
PAUL BAILEY

RIDDLEY WALKER 1986
CENTRAL STATION DESIGN

MOBY DICK 1984
THE DRAWING ROOM

BLOOD, BLACK & GOLD 1980
HILLY BEVAN & ANTHONY LAWRENCE

A MIDSUMMER NIGHT'S DREAM 1988
THE DRAWING ROOM

HOPE AGAINST HOPE 1983
STEPHEN McCABE

THE PRIME OF MISS JEAN BRODIE 1984
THE DRAWING ROOM

A WHOLLY HEALTHY GLASGOW 1987
JOHN ANGUS

CYMBELINE 1984
THE DRAWING ROOM

We've mastered the arts

From our central position just off the M6, Holbrook provide a unique nationwide printing service exclusively devoted to the arts.

We understand that the demands of this specialised field are for print which requires the most ingenious versatility at the highest quality with the greatest economy – and that is what we know we give best – nobody does it better.

SPECIALIST PRINTERS TO THE ARTS

PRODUCTIONS
1976•1988

33

THE RIVALS Christopher Gable, Patricia Routledge & James Maxwell

Photo Brian Linney

15 September - 13 November 1976

THE RIVALS

by Richard Brinsley Sheridan

Mrs Malaprop	PATRICIA ROUTLEDGE
Jack Absolute	CHRISTOPHER GABLE
Faulkland	TOM COURTENAY
Sir Anthony Absolute	JAMES MAXWELL
Lydia Languish	SUSAN TRACY
Julia	JUDI BOWKER
Acres	TREVOR PEACOCK
Fagg	JOHN BARDON
Mrs M's servant	JOHN BOSWALL
Acres' servant	CHRISTOPHER BRAMWELL
Thomas, the Coachman	FRANK CROMPTON
Sir Lucius O'Trigger	JOHN CUNNINGHAM
Lucy	LINDSAY DUNCAN
David	ENN REITEL
The Boy	RICHARD SPEIGHT
Julia's servant	MARJORIE SUDELL
Director	BRAHAM MURRAY
Designer	JOHANNA BRYANT
Lighting	MICK HUGHES
Sound	IAN GIBSON

The Rivals played in repertoire with The Prince of Homburg

"an uncommonly clear blueprint of the play ... For sheer fun Miss Routledge's Malaprop is the main delight of the evening, not an old dragon but a giggling would-be merry widow ... Altogether a great send-off for a fine new house"
Irving Wardle *The Times*

BRITISH PREMIERE

16 September - 13 November 1976

The Prince of Homburg

by Heinrich von Kleist
translated by Jonathan Griffin

Prince Friedrich Arthur of Homburg	TOM COURTENAY
Count Hohenzollern	CHRISTOPHER GABLE
The Electress	OLIVE McFARLAND
Princess Natalie of Orange	JUDI BOWKER
Friedrich Wilhelm	JAMES MAXWELL
Baron von der Golz	IAN HASTINGS
Bork	SUSAN TRACY
Winterfield	LINDSAY DUNCAN
The Chamberlain	JOHN BOSWALL
Prittwitz	RICHARD SPEIGHT
Field-Marshall Dorfling	WILLOUGHBY GRAY
Count Truchss	FRANK COMPTON
Hennings	DON TROEDSEN
Colonel Kottwitz	TREVOR PEACOCK
Siegfried von Morner	JOHN BARDON
Count Reuss	CHRISTOPHER BRAMWELL
A young officer	LEO DOVE
A peasant woman	MARJORIE SUDELL
A peasant	ENN REITEL
Count Georg von Sparren	JOHN CUNNINGHAM
Franz	JOHN BARDON
Stranz	ENN REITEL
Director	CASPER WREDE
Designer	STEPHEN McCABE
Lighting	MICK HUGHES
Sound	IAN GIBSON
Music	JEAN-YVES BOSSEUR

The Prince of Homburg played in repertoire with The Rivals

"Casper Wrede brings the theatre to thrilling life ... he uses the new auditorium for unforeseen spectacular and aural effects ... a masterpiece, it functions on every level: as an Anthony Hope thriller, as a study in moral integrity, and as a drama of strong personalities in serious dispute"
John Barber *Daily Telegraph*

THE PRINCE OF HOMBURG Trevor Peacock, Tom Courtenay & Christopher Gable

Photo Brian Linney

THE PRINCE OF HOMBURG James Maxwell & Judi Bowker

Photo Brian Linney

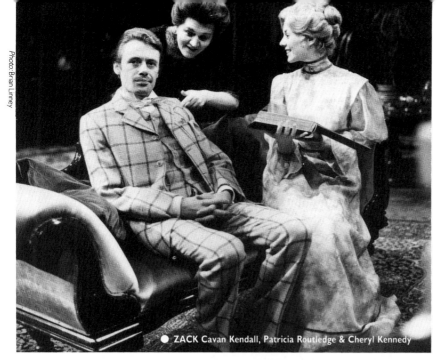

Photo: Brian Linney

● ZACK Cavan Kendall, Patricia Routledge & Cheryl Kennedy

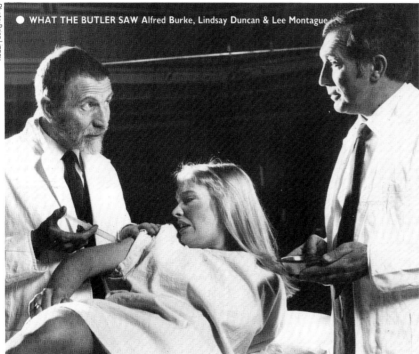

Photo: Brian Linney

● WHAT THE BUTLER SAW Alfred Burke, Lindsay Duncan & Lee Montague

Photo: Brian Linney

● DICK WHITTINGTON Enn Reitel, Ian Hastings & Derek Griffiths

17 November - 18 December 1976

ZACK

by Harold Brighouse

Mrs Munning	PATRICIA ROUTLEDGE
Sally Teale	LINDSAY DUNCAN
Paul Munning	CAVAN KENDALL
Virginia Cavander	CHERYL KENNEDY
Zachariah Munning	TREVOR PEACOCK
Martha Wrigley	SUSAN TRACY
James Abbott	ENN REITEL
Joe Wrigley	JOHN BARDON
Thomas Mowatt	FRANK CROMPTON
Harry Shoebridge	IAN HASTINGS
Director	ERIC THOMPSON
Designer	LAURIE DENNETT
Lighting	MICHAEL WILLIAMS

"This superb production is a highly polished gem ... warm, human, bursting with life, funny, moving and vastly entertaining"
Alan Hulme *Manchester Evening News*

---

23 December 1976 - 29 January 1977

WHAT THE BUTLER SAW

by Joe Orton

Dr Prentice	LEE MONTAGUE
Geraldine Barclay	LINDSAY DUNCAN
Mrs Prentice	ROSALIND KNIGHT
Nicholas Beckett	MICHAEL FEAST
Dr Rance	ALFRED BURKE
Sergeant Match	TREVOR PEACOCK
Director	BRAHAM MURRAY
Designer	PETER BENNION
Lighting	MICHAEL OUTHWAITE

"Against all expectation Braham Murray's revival of *What The Butler Saw* sails blithely round the problems of arena staging to establish itself as the best constructed modern farce we have."
Eric Shorter *Daily Telegraph*

PREMIERE
27 December 1976 - 22 January 1977
(Daytime performances)

DICK WHITTINGTON

devised and composed by Derek Griffiths

The Cast
DEREK GRIFFITHS
JENNY McGUSTIE
IAN HASTINGS
PENELOPE POTTER
JULIAN EVANS
ENN REITEL
JOHN ROGAN

Staged by	JUDY GRIDLEY and DEREK GRIFFITHS
Designer	DAVID SHORT
Lighting	GEOFFREY JOYCE
Sound	GEORGE GLOSSOP

"...bursting with originality. Derek Griffiths has come up with a mixture of fun, song and mime which also takes a new irreverent look at the mummified panto tradition"
Alan Hulme *Manchester Evening News*

13 January - 12 February 1977

THE SKIN OF OUR TEETH
by Thornton Wilder

Mr Fitzpatrick, stage manager	IAN HASTINGS
Sabina	MARSHA HUNT
Mrs Antrobus	OLIVE McFARLAND
Frederick, the dinosaur	KEVIN MOORE
Dolly, the mammoth	JENNIE McGUSTIE
Telegraph boy	ENN REITEL
Henry	MICHAEL FEAST
Gladys	LINDSAY DUNCAN
Mr Antrobus	LEE MONTAGUE
Doctor	TAYLOR McAULEY
Professor	DAVID HUSCROFT
Judge Moses	JOHN BOSWALL
Homer	JULIAN EVANS
Miss E Muse, crippled girl	PENELOPE POTTER
Miss T Muse, supermarket girl	JENNIE McGUSTIE
Miss M Muse, nun	LUCITA LIJERTWOOD
Road labourer	JOHN ROGAN
Man on stretcher	KEVIN MOORE
Mourner	ENN REITEL
TV Interviewer	JOHN ROGAN
TV Cameraman	TAYLOR McAULEY
TV Floor Manager	PENELOPE POTTER
TV Assistant Floor Manager	KEVIN MOORE
Chair Attendant	DAVID HUSCROFT
Lifeguard	ENN REITEL
Esmerelda	LUCITA LIJERTWOOD
Defeated Candidate	JOHN BOSWALL
Defeated Candidate's Bodyguard	JULIAN EVANS
Masseuse	JENNIE McGUSTIE
BBC Broadcast Official	KEVIN MOORE
Mr Tremayne	JOHN BOSWALL
Hester	PENELOPE POTTER
Ivy	JENNIE McGUSTIE
Fred Bailey	DAVID HUSCROFT
Directors	RICHARD NEGRI and JAMES MAXWELL
Costumes	CHARLOTTE HOLDICH
Properties	GERTRUDE PFAFFINGER
Lighting	MICHAEL WILLIAMS
Sound	IAN GIBSON
Songs arranged by	JULIAN EVANS

"a most engaging and cleverly staged evening of home-spun American thoughtfulness"
Eric Shorter *Daily Telegraph*

"the direction capitalises on all the opportunities for spectacle. The theatre continues to excite, and the company to charm"
Robert Cushman *The Observer*

17 February - 26 March 1977

Uncle Vanya
by Anton Chekhov
translated by Ariadne Nicolaeff

Aleksandr Vladimirovich Serebryakov	ALFRED BURKE
Elena Andreyevna	ELEANOR BRON
Sofia Aleksandrovna (Sonia)	JOANNA DAVID
Maria Vassilyevna Voinitskaya	PEGGY THORPE-BATES
Ivan Petrovich Voinitsky (Vanya)	LEO McKERN
Mikhail Lvovich Astrov	ALBERT FINNEY
Ilya Ilyich Telegin	MICHAEL FEAST
Marina	SUSAN RICHARDS
Workman	CHRISTOPHER MILES
Director	MICHAEL ELLIOTT
Designer	CLARE JEFFERY
Lighting	MICHAEL WILLIAMS
Sound	IAN GIBSON
Music arranged by	GEORGE HALL

"A hauntingly memorable *Uncle Vanya*"
Robin Thornber *The Guardian*

Leo McKern's Vanya is an unqualified triumph ... his performance is real, rich and rewarding"
Bernard Levin *Sunday Times*

"(Finney's) is a wonderfully chilly performance matched perfectly by the icy aristocratic grandeur of Eleanor Bron"
Sheridan Morley *Punch*

● THE SKIN OF OUR TEETH Kevin Moore, Jennie McGustie, Lee Montague & Olive McFarland

Photo: Brian Linney

● UNCLE VANYA Leo McKern & Albert Finney

Photo: Brian Linney

Photo: Brian Linney

● PRESENT LAUGHTER Lindsay Duncan, Polly James, Eleanor Bron, Albert Finney, Peggy Thorpe-Bates, Diana Quick & Rosalind Knight

31 March - 14 May 1977

PRESENT LAUGHTER
by Noel Coward

Daphne Stillington	LINDSAY DUNCAN
Miss Erikson	ROSALIND KNIGHT
Fred	JOHN BARDON
Monica Reed	ELEANOR BRON
Garry Essendine	ALBERT FINNEY
Liz Essendine	POLLY JAMES
Roland Maule	MICHAEL FEAST/ IAN HASTINGS
Henry Lyppiatt	JOHN BOSWALL
Morris Dixon	GARY WALDHORN
Joanna Lyppiatt	DIANA QUICK
Lady Saltburn	PEGGY THORPE-BATES
Director	JAMES MAXWELL
Designer	STEPHEN DONCASTER
Lighting	MICHAEL SWEETLAND

"as funny a Coward revival as I have seen"
Irving Wardle *The Times*

"James Maxwell's production treats *Present Laughter*, with exhilerating success, as physical farce as well as verbal comedy"
Michael Billington *The Guardian*

"Finney is masterly. He makes the role of the slightly ageing matinee idol entirely his own, successfully transforming Coward's foppish conception into a much more red-blooded animal"
Alan Hulme *Manchester Evening News*

"a marvellously-evocative vision of the Old South ... Huck himself is played with a gritty integrity by Enn Reitel ... the overall impression is irresistible"
Gerard Dempsey *Daily Express*

"The special effects are superb. Through light and sound, the Mississippi becomes real, the wrecking paddle boat steams terrifyingly by and the lantern lights of the towns and villages blink silently through the mist"
Patrick O'Neill *Daily Mail*

Photo: Brian Linney

● THE ADVENTURES OF HUCKLEBERRY FINN

19 May - 18 June 1977

THE ADVENTURES OF
HUCKLEBERRY FINN

a play by David Terence from the novel by Mark Twain

Huck	ENN REITEL	Miss Watson, Widow Bartlett	DEDDIE DAVIES
Jim	WILLIE JONAH	Charlotte Grangerford,	
"The King"	FREDDIE JONES	Joanna Wilks	DÉBORAH MACLAREN
"The Duke"	MALCOLM RENNIE	Mrs Judith Loftus,	
Pap Finn, First Preacher,		Mary Jane Wilks	JIGGY BHORE
Auctioneer	RONALD FORFAR	Sophia Grangerford	DIANE MERCER
Buck Grangerford, Young Man	JEFFREY PERRY	Townspeople	STUART HOBDAY
Colonel Grangerford,			DAVE BARTLETT
Mr Phelps	WILLOUGHBY GRAY		CHRIS MONKS
Harney Shepherdson,			
Revivalist Preacher	JOHN CURLESS	Director	DAVID TERENCE
Tom Grangerford,		Costumes	CLARE JEFFERY
Rev Hobart	IAN HASTINGS	Sets	PETER BENNION
Bob Grangerford	TIM MYERS	Lighting	DAVID MARCHMENT
Dr Robinson, Shepherdson	MICHAEL GUNN	Sound	ALAN STRETCH
Widow, Mrs Grangerford	IRENE RICHMOND	Songs	GEORGE HALL

● LEAPING GINGER Christopher Neil

Photo: Brian Linney

38

● LEAPING GINGER Alibe Parsons & Christopher Neil

Photo: Roger Geldard

PREMIERE
28 June - 23 July 1977

a musical by Trevor Peacock

King's Head Barmaid, Duchess, Gracie, Punter	BEATRICE ASTON
Screw, Moses, Poofter, Edie, Sporty Businessman, Sergeant Roger Bone, Punter	JOHN BARDON
Prison Governor, Sheik's Man, Gertie, Jock McKay, Ollie	IAN BURFORD
Prisoner, Lenny, Norman, Dora, Punter	RON EMSLIE
Prisoner, American Tourist, Ethel, Chauffeur, Cameraman, Punter	JULIAN EVANS
Debutante, Lil, Choo-Choo, Marylin, Punter	BELINDA LANG
Lulu, Debutante, Queenie, Brit, Punter	ANNA MACLEOD
Prisoner, Poofter, Elsie, Jones, Punter, Policeman	MICHAEL MAYNARD
Ginger Carmody	CHRISTOPHER NEIL
Rosie Prince	ALIBE PARSONS
Jack Palace	MALCOLM RENNIE
American Tourist, May, Big Blonde Pam, Greyhound Track Barmaid	BARBARA ROSENBLAT
Arthur, Auctioneer, Flo, Frozen Foods Importer, Punter	WALLY THOMAS
Duchess, Miss Solkit, Masseuse from Cheadle Hulme, Punter	TILLY TREMAYNE
Prisoner, Pudding, Doris, Sergeant Paul Hollis, Punter	TERRY WOOD

Director	BRAHAM MURRAY
Designer	JOHANNA BRYANT
Lighting	MICHAEL WILLIAMS
Sound	TIM FOSTER
Musical supervision and orchestration	ANTHONY BOWLES
Musical director	NIGEL HESS
Choreography	MICHELE HARDY

"In one breathtaking bound *Leaping Ginger* soars into the smash-hit category ... the best British musical for years ... it takes off like a rocket and bursts into spine-tingling life"
Alan Hulme *Manchester Evening News*

"It all hangs together exceptionally well, certainly uplifts and entertains, and at times reaches high points of comedy"
Philip Radcliffe *Sunday Times*

THE ORDEAL OF GILBERT PINFOLD Michael Hordern

Photo: Brian Linney

"(Hordern's) performance is surely the crown of an immensely distinguished career"
Bernard Levin *Sunday Times*

PREMIERE
15 September - 15 October 1977

THE ORDEAL OF Gilbert Pinfold

a play by Ronald Harwood
from the novel by Evelyn Waugh

Gilbert Pinfold	MICHAEL HORDERN
Mrs Pinfold	MARGARET INGLIS
Reggie Graves-Upton/ 1st General	LOCKWOOD WEST
Dr Drake/2nd General	WILLOUGHBY GRAY
Angel	GEOFFREY BATEMAN
Margaret	LINDSAY DUNCAN
Fosdyke/Fosker/Spanish Official	IAN HASTINGS
Murlock/Murdoch	KEN RANDLE
Indian Steward	DERRICK BRANCHE
English Steward	RON EMSLIE
Captain Steerforth	MYLES HOYLE
Glover	GARETH FORWOOD
Mr Scarfield	FRANK CROMPTON
Mrs Scarfield/Mother	GWEN CHERRELL
Norwegian Lady/ Voice of Goneril	DILYS HAMLETT
Young Gentleman	JEFFREY PERRY
Young Girl	TILLY TREMAYNE
Director	MICHAEL ELLIOTT
Designer	STEPHEN DONCASTER
Lighting	MICHAEL WILLIAMS
Sound	TIM FOSTER and GEORGE GLOSSOP
Song by	GEORGE HALL

"Ronald Harwood's stage version, from the crotchety hero's ominous radio interview in his secluded country residence to his nightmare health cruise, succeeds beyond all my expectations"
Irving Wardle *The Times*

The Ordeal of Gilbert Pinfold transferred to The Round House, London, 14 February - 17 March 1979 with the following changes:

Fosdyke/Fosker/Clergyman/ Officer	GEOFFREY McGIVERN
Captain Steerforth	JOHN RINGHAM
Mrs Scarfield/Mother	PAULINE JAMESON
Norwegian Lady/Goneril	CAROL GILLIES
Lighting	MARK HENDERSON

THE ORDEAL OF GILBERT PINFOLD Geoffrey Bateman, Michael Hordern & Lindsay Duncan

Photo: Brian Linney

39

19 October - 14 December 1977

SEE HOW THEY RUN

a farce by Philip King

Ida	SALLY WATTS
Miss Skillon	OLWEN GRIFFITHS
The Reverend Lionel Toop	NORMAN BIRD
Penelope Toop	PRISCILLA MORGAN
Lance-Corporal Clive Winton	PHILIP LOWRIE
The Intruder	GEOFFREY BATEMAN
The Bishop of Lax	JAMES BERWICK
The Reverend Arthur Humphrey	IAN HASTINGS
Sergeant Towers	RON EMSLIE
Director	MIKE OCKRENT
Designer	PETER RICE
Lighting	MICHAEL SWEETLAND
Sound	DAVID EASTERBROOK

See How They Run played in repertoire with *The Golden Country*

"played to perfection ... an evening of joint triumph for author, actors and director"
Eric Shorter *Daily Telegraph*

"a frantically funny evening"
Ned Chaillet *The Times*

SEE HOW THEY RUN Philip Lowrie & Priscilla Morgan

Photo: Brian Linney

Photo:Brian Linney

● THE GOLDEN COUNTRY Ian Hastings & Jenny Twigge

16 November - 17 December 1977

The Golden Country

by Shusaku Endo
translated by Francis Mathy

Inoue Chikugo-No-Kami	WOLFE MORRIS
Hirata Shuzen	GEOFFREY BATEMAN
Kano Gennosuke	IAN HASTINGS
Father Christopher Ferreira	JOHN CHURCH
Tomonaga Sakuemon	JOHN SHARP
Yuki	JENNY TWIGGE
Hatsu	FINOLA KEOGH
Kasuke	DAVID HUSCROFT
Mokichi	TAYLOR McAULEY
Hisaichi	JULIAN EVANS
Norosaku	MICHAEL COLYER
Tome	EDITH HART

Directed and staged by	RICHARD NEGRI
Costumes	CHARLOTTE HOLDICH
Lighting	GEOFFREY JOYCE
Sound	DAVID BURROWS
Music composed by	JULIAN EVANS

The Golden Country played in repertoire with
See How They Run

"Written ten years ago by Shusaku Endo, a Japanese
Roman Catholic, it is a play about the apostasy of
a Portuguese missionary, Christopher Ferreira,
during the 17th century persecution of Christians in
Japan ... as a thoughtful political thriller, it succeeds
superbly, thanks to some very fine acting from Wolfe
Morris, Geoffrey Bateman and John Church ... a
stimulating theatrical experience"
Robin Thornber *The Guardian*

● TWELFTH NIGHT Tom Courtenay

Photo:Brian Linney

22 December 1977 - 28 January 1978

Twelfth Night

by William Shakespeare

Orsino	CLIVE ARRINDELL
Curio	MICHAEL COLYER
Valentine	JULIAN EVANS
Viola	LINDSAY DUNCAN
A Sea Captain	GERARD McLARNON
Sir Toby Belch	WOLFE MORRIS
Maria	SALLY WATTS
Sir Andrew Aguecheek	GARETH FORWOOD
Feste	JOHN CHURCH
Olivia	ELIZABETH ROMILLY
Malvolio	TOM COURTENAY
Sebastian	JEFFREY PERRY
Antonio	HARRY WALKER
Fabian	ENN REITEL

Director	MICHAEL ELLIOTT
Designer	RICHARD NEGRI
Music	GEORGE HALL
Lighting	MICHAEL WILLIAMS

"This is the first shot at Shakespeare by the most
exciting of Britain's post-war theatres . . . Michael
Elliott's production is intelligently spoken and
deliberately low-keyed . . . Tom Courtenay's
Malvolio is a carefully conceived and finely executed
booby, complete with rolled umbrella and shabby
morning suit to echo both Chaplin and Samuel
Beckett."
Eric Shorter *Daily Telegraph*

"Tom Courtenay is the undisputed star of the
company. Every line he speaks is audible, intelligible,
and irresistibly funny"
Irene McManus *New Manchester Review*

● THE DYBBUK John Bennett

"All credit to the Royal Exchange Company who gave us a rarity last seen in the 1965 World Theatre Season in London"
Rosemary Say *Sunday Telegraph*

"You don't have to be Jewish ... to have one of the most amazing evenings of your life at *The Dybbuk*, a play based on an ancient Jewish legend of a dead soul that enters into a living body and is ultimately exorcised with tragic results ... Braham Murray makes no concessions whatever and simply defies us, with total success, even to think about incredulity while it is going on"
Bernard Levin *Sunday Times*

● THE GENTLE PEOPLE Harry Landis

2 February - 4 March 1978

The DYBBUK

by S Anski, translated by Henry G Alsberg and Winifred Katzin

First Batlon	JOHN CHURCH
Second Batlon	TERRY WOOD
Third Batlon	GEORGE LITTLE
The Messenger	JOHN WATTS
Meyer	WOLFE MORRIS
Hannah Esther	DIANA FLACKS
Channon	IAN HASTINGS
Chennoch	JEFFREY PERRY
Leah	ELIZABETH ROMILLY
Frade	SUSAN RICHARDS
Gittel	CARYN HURWITZ
Asher	PAUL BENTLEY
Sender	MICHAEL POOLE
A Wedding Guest	JOHN CHURCH
A Beggar Woman with Child	DIANA FLACKS
A Lame Beggar	RITA LESTER
A Hunchback	PAUL BENTLEY
Bassia	ALISON LEE ROSE
Nachmon	TERRY WOOD
Rabbi Mendel	GEORGE LITTLE
Menashe	JEFFREY PERRY
A Beggar Man on Crutches	GERARD McLARNON
A Blind Beggar	MAUREEN MORRIS
A Tall Pale Beggar	ELAINE IVES-CAMERON
First Chassid	JEFFREY PERRY
Second Chassid	TERRY WOOD
Third Chassid	PAUL BENTLEY
Fourth Chassid	GEORGE LITTLE
Rabbi Azrael	JOHN BENNETT
Michoel	GERARD McLARNON
First Judge	JOHN CHURCH
Second Judge	GEORGE LITTLE
Rabbi Samson	WOLFE MORRIS
Minyen	DAVE BARTLETT, GILES FAVELL, CRISPIN WEDELL, RICK FREEMAN, DUNCAN MOORE, MARK WHELEHAN, CHARLES BATEMAN
Children	SOPHIA, NATASHA & VICTORIA WILLIAMS
Director	BRAHAM MURRAY
Designer	PETER BENNION
Music	ANTHONY BOWLES
Choreography	MICHELE HARDY
Lighting	MICHAEL WILLIAMS
Sound	TIM FOSTER and GEORGE GLOSSOP

41

9 March - 1 April 1978

THE GENTLE PEOPLE

by Irwin Shaw

Jonah Goodman	JOHN BENNETT
Philip Anagnos	HARRY LANDIS
Harold Goff	GEOFFREY BATEMAN
Magruder	TERRY WOOD
Stella Goodman	CYD HAYMAN
Eli Lieber	ROBERT WHELAN
Florence Goodman	ROSE HILL
Angelina Esposito	ELEANOR McCREADY
The Judge	WILLOUGHBY GRAY
Lammanawitz	ALFRED HOFFMAN
Polack	DEREK ETCHELLS
Flaherty	GEOFFREY McGIVERN
Director	ERIC THOMPSON
Costumes and Set	JOHANNA BRYANT
Lighting	MICK HUGHES
Sound	DAVID EASTERBROOK

"It is a rare sight to see a first-rate company take a run-of-the-mill play, and turn it into superb theatre ... Excellent acting, especially from John Bennett and Harry Landis as the fisherman and Geoffrey Bateman as the hoodlum ... absorbing entertainment"
G.A. Oldham *Evening Chronicle*

● CRIME AND PUNISHMENT Leo McKern & Tom Courtenay

PREMIERE OF A NEW ADAPTATION

6 April - 6 May 1978

CRIME AND PUNISHMENT

by Fyodor Dostoevsky adapted by Paul Bailey additional material by Gerard McLarnon

Rodion Raskolnikov	TOM COURTENAY	Pyotry Luzhin	MICHAEL POOLE
Alyona Ivanovna	LILA KAYE	Workman	TOM HARRISON
Lisaveta	JUDITH BARKER	1st Coachman	GEOFFREY McGIVERN
Nastasya	MAUREEN MORRIS	2nd Coachman	MICHAEL COLYER
Inn Keeper	MICHAEL COLYER	Witness	TERRY WOOD
Marmeladov	ESMOND KNIGHT	Nicolay	MICHAEL COLYER
Sonia Marmeladov	ELIZABETH ROMILLY	Townsfolk and Prisoners	MICHAEL COLYER,
Pulcheria	OLIVE McFARLAND	TOM HARRISON, GEOFFREY McGIVERN,	
Dounia	JANE HOW		TERRY WOOD
Officer	GEOFFREY McGIVERN		
Student	TERRY WOOD	Director	MICHAEL ELLIOTT
Razumihin	ROY SAMPSON	Designer	LAURIE DENNETT
Zametov	IAN HASTINGS	Lighting	GEOFFREY JOYCE
Porfiry Petrovitch	LEO McKERN	Sound	DAVID EASTERBROOK,
Messenger	TOM HARRISON	TIM FOSTER and GEORGE GLOSSOP	

Toured to Münster, West Germany for the International Festival of Arena Theatre 23-24 May 1978

"Once again the Royal Exchange Theatre turns out to be the real star of one of its own shows ... it is the Exchange's arena staging which allows them to unroll the episodic narrative so fluidly and evocatively ... That and the company's loving attention for the detailed texture of the production, the rags, the limps, the cobwebs, the timber, the echoing voices, the background chatter in a bar and a spectacular Siberian snowfall"
Robin Thornber *The Guardian*

"The joy of the production ... is Leo McKern's wheezing, avuncular Porfiry ... perfectly balancing the remorseless policeman against the benevolent confessor" Irving Wardle *The Times*

"Mr Courtenay's Raskolnikov is a telling blend of coldness and emotion – a mind conscious of its superiority put to intolerable strain by the forces of poverty, hunger and sickness"
B A Young *Financial Times*

● A FAMILY Paul Scofield, Celia Gregory & Trevor Peacock

"An admirable play, honest, well conceived, properly worked out, freshly and fittingly written"
Bernard Levin *Sunday Times*

"A stunning cast ... Paul Scofield is beautiful to watch"
Irving Wardle *The Times*

PREMIERE

11 May - 3 June 1978

A Family

a new play by Ronald Harwood

Freddie Kilner	PAUL SCOFIELD
Paula Barrett	CELIA GREGORY
Margaret Barrett	ELEANOR BRON
Emma Kilner	IRENE HANDL
Tom Price	TREVOR PEACOCK
Millicent Price	SALLY BAZELY
Marc Barrett	GARY WALDHORN
Ivan Kilner	HARRY ANDREWS
Director	CASPER WREDE
Designer	PETER BENNION
Lighting	MICHAEL WILLIAMS
Sound	TIM FOSTER and GEORGE GLOSSOP
Music arranged by	GEORGE HALL
Sung by	EIRA HEATH

Following visits to the Alexandra Theatre, Birmingham (12-17 June), The Grand Theatre, Leeds (19-24 June) and The Theatre Royal, Brighton (26 June - 1 July), *A Family* transferred to the Theatre Royal, Haymarket, London 6 July - 30 September 1978 with the following change:
Lighting   JOE DAVIS

"In a splendid performance Paul Scofield switched moods with masterly assurance ... Under Casper Wrede's direction and with the help of this theatre's admirable sound effects, Ronald Harwood's play provided an absorbing evening and surely deserves a wider showing"
Ian Stewart *Country Life*

Photo: Brian Linney

● **LEAPING GINGER** Robert Lindsay

"Robert Lindsay shines as Ginger ... in Braham Murray's sparkling production"
Ned Chaillet *The Times*

Photo: Brian Linney

● **LEAPING GINGER** John Bennett & Robert Lindsay

Photo: Brian Linney

● **SISTERS** Paul Copley, Malcolm Terris, Anita Carey, Paul Kelly, & Pauline Moran

---

8 June - 15 July 1978

LEAPING GINGER
(Revised Version)

The musical by Trevor Peacock

Screw, Moses, Poofter, Edie, Sporty Businessman, Sergeant Roger Bone, Punter	JOHN BARDON
Jack Palace	JOHN BENNETT
Prison Governor, Mr Todd, Sheik's Man, Gertie, Jock McKay, Ollie	IAN BURFORD
Duchess, Miss Davis, Gracie, Masseuse from Cheadle Hulme, Punter	SANDRA CARRIER
American Tourist, Ethel, Cameraman, Punter	JULIAN EVANS
Rosie Prince	COLETTE GLEESON
Ginger Carmody	ROBERT LINDSAY
Prisoner, Lenny, Norman, Dora, Punter	GEOFFREY McGIVERN
Debutante, Lil, Choo-Choo, Marylin, Punter	ALISON ROSE
American Tourist, May, Big Blonde Pam, Greyhound Track Barmaid	BARBARA ROSENBLAT
Arthur, Auctioneer, Flo, Frozen Food Importer, Punter	WALLY THOMAS
Duchess, Mrs Solkit, Punter	TILLY TREMAYNE
Prisoner, Poofter, Elsie, Jones, Colin, Punter	JOHN WATTS
Prisoner, Mr Nuttard, Doris, Sergeant Paul Hollis, Punter	TERRY WOOD
Debutante, Queenie, Brit, Punter	WENDY YOUNG
Director	BRAHAM MURRAY
Designer	JOHANNA BRYANT
Lighting	MICHAEL WILLIAMS
Sound	TIM FOSTER and GEORGE GLOSSOP
Musical supervision and orchestration	ANTHONY BOWLES
Musical director	NIGEL HESS
Choreography	MICHELE HARDY

"That enormously talented little man – actor, writer and composer – Trevor Peacock has turned it into that rare theatrical phenomenon, a smash hit British musical ... Robert Lindsay and Colette Gleeson are superb ... the magnificent John Bennett gives the part of Jack Palace depth, strength and a razor sharp edge ... the best of the old has been preserved, including the two scenes with the old ladies and the show-stopper – 'Roger and I are naughty' – with John Bardon and Terry Wood as the two bent coppers, one of the funniest satirical numbers written ... Ginger is not only leaping – it is all set to take off"
R W Shakespeare *New Manchester Review*

PREMIERE
12 September - 30 September 1978

SISTERS

by David Storey

Mrs Donaldson	NOËL DYSON
Adrienne	JENNIFER HILARY
Carol	NATASHA PYNE
Tom	PAUL KELLY
Beryl	PAULINE MORAN
Joanna	ANITA CAREY
Terry	PAUL COPLEY
Crawford	MALCOLM TERRIS
Director	ERIC THOMPSON
Designer	TIM GOODCHILD
Sound	COLIN GODDARD
Lighting	GEOFFREY JOYCE

"A remarkable, stimulating and unsettling gem of a play ... Jennifer Hilary gives a luminous performance as the older sister, Pauline Moran is a splendidly sluttish harlot, and Noel Dyson is so exactly right as the neighbour in a pinafore that you feel she can't possibly be acting"
Gerard Dempsey *Daily Express*

"A rich, untidy, fascinating piece of theatre"
Ron Lawson *Bolton Evening News*

1978 1979

5 October - 4 November 1978

The Lady from the Sea

by Henrik Ibsen
translated by Michael Meyer

Dr Wangel	GRAHAM CROWDEN
Ellida	VANESSA REDGRAVE
Bolette	SHERRIE HEWSON
Hilde	LYNSEY BAXTER
Arnholm	JOHN FRANKLYN-ROBBINS
Lynstrand	CHRISTOPHER GOOD
Ballested	RONALD HERDMAN
A Stranger	MICHAEL BYRNE
Tourists	JULIA COTTON, ALISON DARKE
	SIABHRA WOODS, PAUL BRADLEY
	PETER FIELDSON, YANNIS LAZARIDES

Director	MICHAEL ELLIOTT
Set designer	LAURIE DENNETT
Costume designer	CLARE JEFFREY
Lighting	MARK HENDERSON
Sound	TIM FOSTER and GEORGE GLOSSOP

The Lady from the Sea transferred to The Round House Theatre, London 16 May - 7 July 1979 with the following changes:

A Stranger	TERENCE STAMP
Tourists	JANE BUTLER, VICTORIA CONSTAN
	CAMILE DAVIS, ANDREW CUTHBERT
	CHRIS MORTON, IAN SWANN

"It is, like all this company's work, a beautifully tactile experience, with the action taking place on a rocky outcrop and wooden landing stages designed by Laurie Dennett with the stage flooded with 1,000 gallons of water reflecting the limpid Scandinavian clarity of Mark Henderson's lighting ... It is, most of all, a production which makes you realise what an assured masterpiece of Ibsen's maturity this play is ... a production which casts a magic spell that is all its own." Robin Thornber, *The Guardian*

"Miss Redgrave can make you share her belief in any number of impossible things; happiness, bewilderment, loneliness, loss and happiness again suffuse her every inch. She gives an amazingly unstrained performance ... Seventeen years ago Miss Redgrave and Mr Elliott gave us the 'As You Like It' of a generation; their joint return to form could hardly be happier"
Robert Cushman *The Observer*

"this exceptionally complete and powerful performance" Bernard Levin *The Sunday Times*

● WINTER'S TALE Helen Ryan & John Turner

"Just returned from an acclaimed European tour in proscenium arched theatres ... the power of Braham Murray's (production) holds the audiences' attention in an unevadeable grip. The rather ridiculous story of Leontes' jealousy and reformation becomes credible and involving."
Charles Petry *Bolton Evening News*

● CINDERELLA Wendy Morgan & Gabrielle Drake

9 November - 16 December 1978

The Winter's Tale

by William Shakespeare

Leontes	JAMES MAXWELL
Hermione	HELEN RYAN
Mamillius	SARAH WEBB
Perdita	JACQUELINE TONG
Camillo	JEFFRY WICKHAM
Antigonus	MORRIS PERRY
Cleomenes	PETER GUINNESS
Dion	PAUL CLAYTON
Paulina	DILYS HAMLETT
Emilia	ANGELA ROOKS
Polixenes	JOHN TURNER
Florizel	RICHARD DURDEN
Archidamus	PETER GUINNESS
Autolycus	HARRY LANDIS
Old Shepherd	HAROLD GOODWIN
Clown	IAN HASTINGS
Mopsa	PHILIPPA HOWELL
Dorcas	SARAH WEBB
A Gaoler/A Mariner	KEITH TAYLOR
A Gentleman Poet	KNIGHT MANTELL
An Officer	KEITH TAYLOR
Servants	PETER GUINNESS, NICHOLAS GECKS
Lords, Ladies, Gentlemen	
& Peasants	KNIGHT MANTELL
	JON GLENTORAN, PHILIPPA HOWELL
	LESLEY NICOL, PAUL CLAYTON
	MORRIS PERRY, KEITH TAYLOR
	& ANGELA ROOKS
Time	KNIGHT MANTELL

Director	BRAHAM MURRAY
Designer	PETER BENNION
Lighting	MICHAEL WILLIAMS
Music composed and	
supervised by	ANTHONY BOWLES
Choreography	MICHELE HARDY
Sound	TIM FOSTER and GEORGE GLOSSOP

Prior to the run at the Royal Exchange, *The Winter's Tale* made a European tour. Following visits to the New Theatre, Oxford (12-16 September) and the New Theatre, Cardiff (18-23 September), the Company toured Germany, Holland, Belgium, Luxembourg, Switzerland, Hungary and Romania 24 September - 26 October 1978.
During the tour the parts of Dorcas and A Lady were played by Chloe Salaman, and Sarah Webb also played A Peasant.

PREMIERE
22 December 1978 - 3 February 1979

CINDERELLA
by Trevor Peacock
additional music by Nigel Hess

Cinderella	WENDY MORGAN
Fairy Godmother	EILEEN PAGE
Stepmother	ROSALIND KNIGHT
Ugly Sister	TERRY WOOD
Ugly Sister	JOHN BARDON
Baron Hardup	CLIVE SWIFT
Prince Charming	GABRIELLE DRAKE
Hen, Soldier, Guest	TRICIA DEIGHTON
Hen, Duchess, Martin's Wife	JOANNA HORLOCK
Soldier, "Low, lonely and blue"	
solo, Maid	LESLEY NICOL
Hen, Soldier, Guest	TINA PARRY
Mole, Prime Minister, Messenger	ROBERT HOWIE
Mole, General	NEIL REID
Mole, Admiral	TREVOR T SMITH
The Voice, Messenger, Master	
of Ceremonies, Martin	RICHARD WALSH

Directors	ANTHONY BOWLES
	and MICHELE HARDY
Musical director	NIGEL HESS
Designer	BOB RINGWOOD
Lighting	MICK HUGHES
Sound	TIM FOSTER and GEORGE GLOSSOP

"The whole thing sparkles like silver"
Frank Bruckshaw *The Stage*

45

8 February - 17 March 1979

THE SCHOOLMISTRESS
by Arthur Wing Pinero

Tyler	CLIVE DUNCAN
Jane Chipman	JOYCE GRUNDY
Gwendoline Hawkins	SOPHIE THOMPSON
Ermyntrude Johnson	FIONA GRAY
Peggy Hesslerigge	ANN HASSON
Dinal	FELICITY DEAN
Miss Dyott	PATRICIA ROUTLEDGE
Mr Otto Bernstein	TERRY WOOD
The Hon Vere Queckett	CLIVE FRANCIS
Mrs Rankling	ROSALIND KNIGHT
Rear Admiral Archibald Rankling	MICHAEL ROBBINS
Mr Reginald Paulover	IAN HASTINGS
Lieutenant John Mallory	PETER SETTELEN
Mr Saunders	MARK ROGERS
Goff	MALCOLM HEBDEN
Jaffray	PAUL CLAYTON
Director	JAMES MAXWELL
Set designer	LAURIE DENNETT
Costume designer	MICHAEL STENNETT
Lighting	GEOFFREY JOYCE
Sound	DAVID EASTERBROOK and COLIN GODDARD
Music	NIGEL HESS
Dances by	JOHN HAYNES

"The Exchange's production effectively proves the durability and sheer enjoyment to be found in unregarded Victorian plays and shows this company at its very best – a good enjoyable play, strongly cast, inventively and lovingly directed by James Maxwell, and handsomely mounted by Laurie Dennett"
David Mayer *Plays & Players*

22 March - 14 April 1979

The Family Reunion
by T S Eliot

Amy, Dowager Lady Monchensey	BEATRIX LEHMANN/ PAULINE JAMESON
Violet	DAPHNE OXENFORD
Ivy	CONSTANCE CHAPMAN
Agatha	AVRIL ELGAR
Charles	JEFFRY WICKHAM
Gerald	WILLIAM FOX
Mary	JOANNA DAVID
Harry, Lord Monchensey	EDWARD FOX
Downing	HARRY WALKER
Dr Warburton	ESMOND KNIGHT
Sergeant Winchell	HARRY WALKER
Denman	HILDA SCHRODER
Director	MICHAEL ELLIOTT
Set designer	LAURIE DENNETT
Costume designer	CLARE JEFFERY
Lighting	MICHAEL WILLIAMS
Sound	IAN GIBSON

The Family Reunion transferred to The Round House, London 18 April - 12 May 1979 and then to The Vaudeville Theatre 19 June - 17 November 1979 with the following changes:

Amy, Dowager Lady Monchensey	PAULINE JAMESON
Lighting	MICHAEL WILLIAMS and MARK HENDERSON

"I am glad to have seen Michael Elliott's superb production of this elusive poetic drama ... The in-the-round staging undeniably gives the entries of the Eumenides a shock impact. And the acting is extremely good"
Michael Billington *The Guardian*

"Michael Elliott's beautiful production now emerges from theatre-in-the-round into the proscenium with its virtues intact. This is nothing less than a directorial triumph which gives the play a sense of ominous excitement and tension I would not have thought possible" Nicholas de Jongh *The Guardian*

● THE SCHOOLMISTRESS Patricia Routledge

"The jewel of James Maxwell's production is Miss Routledge, who crowns a beautiful performance of anxious determination with a rousing display of her musical talents" Michael Coveney *Financial Times*

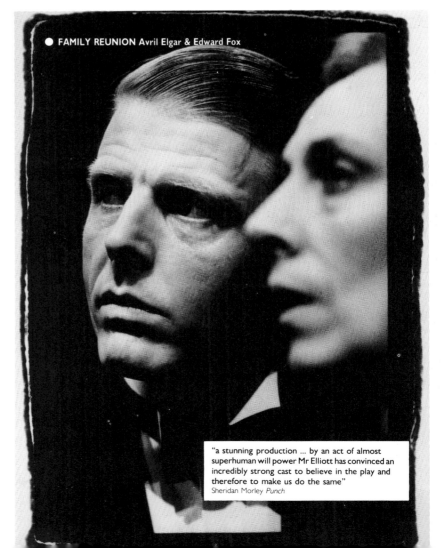

● FAMILY REUNION Avril Elgar & Edward Fox

"a stunning production ... by an act of almost superhuman will power Mr Elliott has convinced an incredibly strong cast to believe in the play and therefore to make us do the same"
Sheridan Morley *Punch*

● LAST OF THE RED HOT LOVERS Georgina Hale & Lee Montague

BRITISH PREMIERE
19 April - 19 May 1979

Last of the Red Hot Lovers

by Neil Simon

Barney Cashman	LEE MONTAGUE
Elaine Navazio	FRANCES TOMELTY
Bobbi Michele	GEORGINA HALE
Jeannette Fisher	BRIDGET TURNER
Director	ERIC THOMPSON
Designer	JOHN BLOOMFIELD
Lighting	DEBORAH GOODKIN
Sound	DAVID EASTERBROOK
	and COLIN GODDARD

Last of the Red Hot Lovers transferred to the Criterion Theatre, London 13 November 1979 - 31 May 1980 with the following change:
Elaine Navazio   SUSAN ENGEL

"A delectable trio of attempted seductions. Lee Montague, quiet and sedate but hopeful, fails in turn with Frances Tomelty who shocks him, Georgina Hale (superbly weird) who ignores him, and Bridget Turner who depresses the hell out of him. American comedy has rarely been so well served by British actors." Robert Cushman *The Observer*

"Lee Montague can have never acted better ... and none of the actresses miss a trick in their unconsummated triumph ... the only mystery is how such a comedy of reassuring (if impotent) sexual ritual and sophisticated, cosy fun could have fallen into the hands of the Royal Exchange before the West End. Not for the first time this enterprising theatre has stolen a march on London" Eric Shorter *Daily Telegraph*

● THE DEEP MAN Dilys Hamlett

"The best comedies are at once funny, elegant, courteous and profound. 'The Deep Man', which is all of these things, belongs to the tradition of Shakespeare, Molière and Chekhov. (It) is an affectionate elegy for the aristocratic Vienna of 1921: wealthy, refined, affronted by the new materialism and, without knowing it, dying on its feet. Director, translator and designer succeed surprisingly well in staging a slap-up *soirée* where smooth gentlemen and elaborately coiffed ladies plot to exchange an old lover or arrange a new match ... the whole experience, admirable in its boldness, gives great pleasure" John Barber *Daily Telegraph*

BRITISH PREMIERE
24 May - 16 June 1979

The Deep Man

by Hugo von Hofmannsthal
translated by Jonathan Griffin

Vinzenz	ROBERT DUNCAN
Lukas	GERARD McLARNON
Hans Karl, Count Buhl	JAMES MAXWELL
Crescence, Countess Freudenberg	DILYS HAMLETT
Neugebauer	CHRISTOPHER BRAMWELL
Agathe	OLIVE McFARLAND
Stani, Count Freudenberg	DANIEL GERROLL
Baron Theophil Neuhoff	JOHN SOMMERVILLE
Wenzel	DON TROEDSON
A Young Servant	PAUL BRADLEY
Count Altenwyl (Poldo)	WILLOUGHBY GRAY
Helene Altenwyl	TESSA DAHL
Edine, Countess Meerenberg	ANNE MAXWELL
A Famous Man (Professor Brucke)	MICHAEL POOLE
Antoinette, Countess Hechingen	CLARE HIGGINS
Huberta	ROSEMARY KINGSTON
Nanni	MOIRA BROOKER
Adolf, Count Hechingen	GARY WALDHORN
Director	CASPER WREDE
Set designer	NORMAN JAMES
Costume designer	MICHAEL STENNETT
Lighting	GEOFFREY JOYCE
Sound	DAVID EASTERBROOK
	and COLIN GODDARD

"A comedy of elegance, grace and wit to which James Maxwell — who carries easily the weight of the evening — responds in a quietly fastidious performance" J C Trewin *Birmingham Post*

THE THREE MUSKETEERS Trevor Peacock, Derek Griffiths & Terry Wood

21 June - 21 July 1979

The Three Musketeers!

by Braham Murray and Derek Griffiths
adapted from the novel
by Alexandre Dumas
music and lyrics by Derek Griffiths

A Blind Accordion Player	NIGEL HESS
D'Artagnan	ROBERT LINDSAY
Athos	DEREK GRIFFITHS
Porthos	TERRY WOOD
Aramis	TREVOR PEACOCK
King Louis	JEFFREY PERRY
Queen Ann, D'Artagnan's Mother	TILLY TREMAYNE
Constance Bonacieux	CAROLYN COURAGE
Cardinal Richelieu	GARY WALDHORN
De Rochefort	ANDREW McCULLOCH
Milady De Winter	DIANA WESTON
Duke of Buckingham	KEITH VARNIER
Planchet	DOUG FISHER
M. De Treville, Old D'Artagnan, Sea Captain, Others	BARRY MARTIN
Cyrano De Bergerac, Dupont, Chef, Others	ALAN McMAHON
First Englishman, Flunkey, Others	ROBERT HOWIE
Second Englishman, Landlord of Jolly Miller, Others	JOHN FOLEY
Patrick, Jussac, Peasant, Others	DAVID TYSALL
Director	BRAHAM MURRAY
Designer	JOHANNA BRYANT
Music directed and arranged by	NIGEL HESS
Choreographer	MICHELE HARDY
Fight arranger	MALCOLM RANSON
Lighting	MICHAEL WILLIAMS
Sound	TIM FOSTER and GEORGE GLOSSOP

"This Dumas-land extravaganza amounts to an outrageously enjoyable evening of pure entertainment ... it is a complete take-off of romantic swashbuckling" Desmond Pratt *Yorkshire Post*

"As light and delectable as a meringue glacé ... the company showed an incredible strength throughout, and sustained for two and a half hours a show of non-stop visual and verbal gags ... Robert Lindsay's D'Artagnan will have the ladies swooning as he swings from the chandeliers, and takes on five of Cardinal Richelieu's guards single-handed. His back-up trio (Derek Griffiths, Terry Wood and Trevor Peacock) hilariously bungle their way to victory over Gary Waldhorn's megalomaniac Richelieu in a series of triumphant ruses and disguises."
Diana Harker *Daily Telegraph*

13 September - 13 October 1979

PEOPLE ARE LIVING THERE

by Athol Fugard

Milly, a landlady	MARGARET TYZACK
Don, one of her lodgers	RALPH LAWFORD
Shorty, another of her lodgers	PAUL HERZBERG
Sissy, Shorty's wife	KAY ADSHEAD
Director	ANDY JORDAN
Designer	LAURIE DENNETT
Lighting	DEBORAH GOODKIN
Sound	DAVID EASTERBROOK and COLIN GODDARD

PEOPLE ARE LIVING THERE Margaret Tyzack

"*People are Living There* is a marvellous play — kitchen sink realism with an exotic Afrikaans accent. Andy Jordan's production festers and soars, with wonderful performances from the whole cast"
Robin Thornber *The Guardian*

"Margaret Tyzack as Milly dominates the action like a grotesque prima donna, swooping from the highest notes of aggressive hysteria to the lowest register of humiliation and despair"
Jane King *Morning Star*

·1979·

1980

● SEPERATE DEVELOPMENT Robert Kirby

16 October - 27 October 1979

SEPARATE DEVELOPMENT

an evening of South African Gothic

written and directed by Robert Kirby

with
ROBERT KIRBY	BRUCE MILLAR
HAL ORLANDINI	MICHELLE FINE

"A revue from South Africa, it is written by Robert Kirby, whose satirical attacks on the society, and particularly the authorities, of his country have earned him a considerable reputation"
Stella Flint *Daily Telegraph*

"a moving testimony to the pain of being sensitive, intelligent and sceptical in a country which is built on brute, crass conformity"
Robin Thornber *The Guardian*

"*Separate Development* is a rarity; a revue which mixes stark tragedy with outrageous ribaldry"
Jane King *Morning Star*

1 November 1979 - 12 January 1980

THE CHERRY ORCHARD

by Anton Chekhov
translated by Michael Frayn
Sponsored by
♻ National Westminster Bank

Dunyasha	SUSAN PENHALIGON
Lopakhin (Yermolay)	PETER VAUGHAN
Yepikhodov	DOUG FISHER/
	JONATHAN BARLOW
Firs	GERARD McLARNON
Anya	MOIRA BROOKER
Mme Ranyevskaya (Lyuba)	DILYS HAMLETT
Varya	SORCHA CUSACK
Gayev (Lenya)	JAMES MAXWELL
Charlotta Ivanovna	GABRIELLE DRAKE
Simeonov-Pischik	TERRY WOOD
Yasha	WILLIAM HOPE
Trofimov (Pyetya)	ROBERT LINDSAY
A Passer-by	MICHAEL POOLE
The Station Master	PETER CHILDS
The Postmaster	JONATHAN BARLOW
A Guest	EDWARD BRYANT
Guest, Servants	JONATHAN BARLOW
	EDWARD BRYANT
	ISABEL CROSSLEY
	DONA DI STEFANO
Director	CASPER WREDE
Designer	RICHARD NEGRI
Lighting	GEOFFREY JOYCE
Sound	IAN GIBSON
Music	HENRY WARD
Choreography	BARBARA CAISTOR

The Cherry Orchard played in repertoire with
The Lower Depths

"The production lays the action out with clarity and has good performances ... Mr Wrede also makes good use of the vast space around the auditorium to present us with chuffing trains, howling dogs, rushing winds and the famous breaking string that betokens historical transition"
Michael Billington *The Guardian*

"Dilys Hamlett as Ranyevskaya gives a performance to equal the best that I have seen in this theatre ... (she) offers a woman painfully open to feeling and responsive to others, miserably acknowledging the destruction wrought on her family by her compulsion to love a worthless man. Hers is a performance ruthless in its honesty"
David Mayer *Plays & Players*

"Robert Lindsay was superb as the fumbling student"
John Thompson *Lancashire Evening Telegraph*

● THE CHERRY ORCHARD Robert Lindsay

● THE LOWER DEPTHS Peter Vaughan

15 November 1979 - 8 January 1980

THE LOWER DEPTHS

by Maxim Gorky
translated by David Magarshack
Sponsored by
♻ National Westminster Bank

The Baron	JOHN WATTS
Kvashnya	JUDITH BARKER
Andrey Kleshch	PETER CHILDS
Anna	MOIRA BROOKER
Bubnov	MICHAEL POOLE
Nastya	SUSAN PENHALIGON
Satin	JAMES MAXWELL
The Actor	DOUG FISHER/BRAHAM MURRAY
Mikhail Kostylyov	GERARD McLARNON
Vassilly Pepel	ROBERT LINDSAY
Luka	PETER VAUGHAN
Natasha	GABRIELLE DRAKE
Alyoshka	EDWARD BRYANT
Vassillissa	SORCHA CUSACK
Medvedev	TERRY WOOD
The Tartar	JONATHAN BARLOW
Zob	WILLIAM HOPE
Director	BRAHAM MURRAY
Designer	LAURIE DENNETT
Lighting	MICHAEL WILLIAMS
Sound	DAVID EASTERBROOK
	and COLIN GODDARD
Music	CHRIS MONKS
Fight arranger	MALCOLM RANSON

The Lower Depths was played in repertoire with
The Cherry Orchard

"*The Lower Depths* encompasses death, murder,
laughter and defiance in the face of oppression. Its
effect in the Russia of 1902 was explosive. Braham
Murray's moving production gives fresh relevance to
this powerful and compassionate play"
Stella Flint *Daily Telegraph*

50

PREMIERE
22 December 1979 - 5 January 1980
(Daytime performances)

CHRISTMAS FUN & A FAIRYTALE

devised by Dilys Hamlett, Doug Fisher,
Colin Goddard and Chris Monks
music and lyrics by Colin Goddard and
Chris Monks

Christmas Fun

Rose	JUDITH BARKER
Alice	MOIRA BROOKER
Kevin	EDWARD BRYANT
TV Repairman	PETER CHILDS
Mavis	SORCHA CUSACK
Sandra	GABRIELLE DRAKE
Albert	JOHN WATTS
Melvin	WILLIAM HOPE
Ralph	MICHAEL POOLE
Arthur	TERRY WOOD

A Fairytale

Rosa	JUDITH BARKER
Alicia	MOIRA BROOKER
Vasha	EDWARD BRYANT
TV Repairman	PETER CHILDS
Baba Yaga	SORCHA CUSACK
Tabitha	GABRIELLE DRAKE
Felix	JOHN WATTS
Boski	WILLIAM HOPE
Ralphsky	MICHAEL POOLE
Stephan	DONA DI STEFANO
Ninny	TERRY WOOD
Directors	DILYS HAMLETT and DOUG FISHER
Designer	STEPHEN DONCASTER
Choreography	ISABEL CROSSLEY
	and DIANA FAVELL
Lighting	GEOFFREY JOYCE
Sound	DAVID EASTERBROOK

● CHRISTMAS FUN AND A FAIRYTALE John Watts

● ROLLO Jack Hedley

"Freddie Jones recreated that kind of beknighted theatrical dinosaur with melodramatic relish ... He ranted. He raved, wept and roared, scowled and shook, boasted, bullied, bleated and bellowed. It was a magnificent, a gigantic and at the same time a pitiful performance" Patrick O'Neill *Daily Mail*

● THE DRESSER Freddie Jones

● THE DRESSER Freddie Jones & Tom Courtenay

---

17 January - 1 March 1980

ROLLO

by Marcel Achard
adapted by Felicity Douglas

Leon Rollo	LEO McKERN
Edith Rollo	BARBARA SHELLEY
Eugène	ANTHONY WINGATE
Véronique Carradine	ANNE ROGERS
Noel Carradine	JACK HEDLEY/
	GARY WALDHORN
Alexa Rollo	CLARE HIGGINS
Director	DAVID THOMPSON
Designer	ANN BEVERLEY
Lighting	GLYN PEREGRINE and GEOFFREY JOYCE

"At the centre we have Mr McKern stamping and gurgling his way through an incomparable performance. At one point he brings down the house by flopping on to a chair that collapses before resuming his needling inquisitions ... It is an irresistible display of inspired and varied ingenuity ... Jack Hedley is supremely skilful as the stoical adulterer ..." Michael Coveney *Financial Times*

PREMIERE
6 March - 12 April 1980

THE DRESSER

by Ronald Harwood

Norman	TOM COURTENAY
Her Ladyship	ISABEL DEAN
Irene	JACQUELINE TONG
Madge	CAROL GILLIES
Sir	FREDDIE JONES
Geoffrey Thornton	LOCKWOOD WEST
Mr Oxenby	GEOFFREY McGIVERN
Players in King Lear	
Gloucester	REX ARUNDEL
Knight, Albany	ANTHONY BENSON
Knight, Gentleman	JOE HOLMES
Kent	GUY NICHOLLS
Director	MICHAEL ELLIOTT
Set designer	LAURIE DENNETT
Costume designer	STEPHEN DONCASTER
Lighting	MARK HENDERSON
Sound	IAN GIBSON
Deputy director	MICHAEL CAMERON

The Dresser transferred to the Queen's Theatre, London 30 April - 17 January 1981 with the following cast changes:

Her Ladyship	JANE WENHAM
Madge	JANET HENFREY
Knight, Albany	KENNETH OXTOBY
Knight, Gentleman	PETER O'DWYER
Kent	DAVID BROWNING
Electrician	TREVOR GRIFFITHS

The Dresser later opened on Broadway in New York at the Brooks Atkinson Theatre, 9 November 1981 - 1 May 1982 with TOM COURTENAY playing Norman, PAUL ROGERS as Sir, RACHEL GURNEY as Her Ladyship and MICHAEL ELLIOTT directing

"A theatrical play in the best sense of the word, Ronald Harwood is not afraid to draw characters in affectionate caricature, and to give them situations of the kind known to inspire instant laughter, instant tears ... a masterly production"
B A Young *Financial Times*

"Much the best new piece yet unveiled by the Royal Exchange Company ... Tom Courtenay, too, has discovered sources of rage and wild comedy beyond its original reach, but his portrait of Norman, sulking, cajoling, and keeping himself going with a half bottle of Scotch in the back of his baggy wartime trousers, was definitive from the start: once seen, never forgotten" Irving Wardle *The Times*

● BLOOD, BLACK AND GOLD Dilys Hamlett

21 April - 13 June 1980

BLOOD BLACK & GOLD

by Gerard McLarnon

Mat	ALAN PARNABY
Chingo	ALAN McMAHON
Vinty	RON EMSLIE
Dinny	JOSEPH PETERS
King	NICK STRINGER
Madam	CARMEL McSHARRY/
	ROSALIND KNIGHT
Judith	CLARE HIGGINS
Deidre	SHIRLEY CASSEDY
Delia	VIVIENNE RITCHIE
Dymphna	LINDSAY BLACKWELL
Silver	JOHN WATTS
Mrs Clay	DILYS HAMLETT
Atty	ISHIA BENNISON
Pet	LISA TRAMONTIN
Cepta	LESLEY NICOL
Director	BRAHAM MURRAY
Designer	JOHANNA BRYANT
Lighting	MICHAEL WILLIAMS
Sound	TIM FOSTER and MARTIN NOAR
Music	CHRIS MONKS
Movement	SUE LEFTON
Assistant director	DION McHUGH

Blood Black and Gold played in repertoire with
Love on the Dole

"A fantastic confection of Irish religion and folklore ... Braham Murray's production shows off the resources of the theatre, including a slaughter house version of a Chinese dragon"
James Fenton *Sunday Times*

"Gerard McLarnon has a weird, wild, wonderful way with words. His new play is set in a strange Celtic twilight world of Irish tinker fairground folk and it has the hypnotic effect of a Gypsy's curse ... Visually exciting and technically slick, it has rich and powerful performances from John Watts, as the godly man, and Dilys Hamlett as the devilish hag"
Robin Thornber *The Guardian*

22 April - 14 June 1980

LOVE ON THE DOLE

by Ronald Gow
from Walter Greenwood's novel

Sally Hardcastle	JOHANNA KIRBY
Mrs Hardcastle	CARMEL McSHARRY/
	JUDITH BARKER
Larry Meath	JOSEPH PETERS
Harry Hardcastle	ALAN PARNABY
Mr Hardcastle	JOHN BARDON
Mrs Jike	ROSALIND KNIGHT
Mrs Dorbell	JUDITH BARKER/
	SALLY GIBSON
Mrs Bull	RITA LESTER
Helen Hawkins	LINDSAY BLACKWELL
Policeman	ALAN McMAHON
Charlie	RON EMSLIE
Sam Grundy	NICK STRINGER
O'Leary	ALAN McMAHON
Director	ERIC THOMPSON
Designer	PETER BENNION
Lighting	MICHAEL WILLIAMS
Sound	TIM FOSTER and MARTIN NOAR

Love on the Dole played in repertoire with
Blood Black and Gold

"Coming fresh to the piece in a buoyant new revival I am impressed by both its staying power and dramatic vivacity ... truthfully observed and truthfully played" Michael Coveney *Financial Times*

"*Love on the Dole* seldom gets the kind of lavish treatment of Eric Thompson's revival. It proves well worth the trouble"
Eric Shorter *Daily Telegraph*

● LOVE ON THE DOLE Johanna Kirby & Alan Parnaby

BRITISH PREMIERE
19 June - 26 July 1980

HAVE YOU ANYTHING TO DECLARE?

a farce by Maurice Hennequin and Pierre
Veber, adapted and translated by Robert
Cogo-Fawcett and Braham Murray

Sponsored by **DINERS CLUB INTERNATIONAL**

Lise Dupont	SUSANNA BISHOP
Gontran des Barbettes	JEFFREY PERRY
Ernestine	SALLY WATTS
La Baule	ENN REITEL
Adelaide Dupont	DILYS HAMLETT
Benjamin Dupont	JOHN PHILLIPS
Philippe Couzan	NOEL HOWLETT
Frontignac	MALCOLM RENNIE
Paulette de Trivelin	MICHELLE NEWELL
Vicomte Robert de Trivelin	BRIAN COX
Zézé	MADELINE SMITH
Mariette	CASSIE McFARLANE
The Prize Winner	PADDY WARD
Police Commissioner	BARRY JARVIS
Policeman	PAUL DORAN
Director	BRAHAM MURRAY
Designer	JOHANNA BRYANT
Lighting	GEOFFREY JOYCE
Song composed by	CHRIS MONKS

Have You Anything to Declare? transferred to
The Round House, London 13 May - 6 June 1981
with the following cast changes:

Zézé	SUSAN LITTLER
Frontignac	DEREK GRIFFITHS
Lise Dupont	TRACY BOOTH
Ernestine/Mariette	GLORIA CONNELL
La Baule	DOUG FISHER
Police Commissioner	DAVID BLUESTONE
Policeman	SCOTT THOMSON

Braham Murray subsequently directed *Have You
Anything to Declare?* for Milwaukee Repertory
Theater (23 October - 29 November 1981)
with Dilys Hamlett reprising the role of Adelaide
Dupont

"A plush, beautifully dressed show; crackling with
energetic desperation, guilty panic, and lust ... not
to be missed" Irving Wardle *The Times*

"The company is splendidly led by Brian Cox, bullish,
driven and very fast as the count. It is the sort of
performance you could have expected from Albert
Finney ten years ago, only, I suspect, a lot better. The
last act is graced by an impeccable display by John
Phillips as the judicial father"
Michael Coveney *Financial Times*

"The company could hardly have chosen a better
production with which to visit London. Any theatre
that can manage this and *The Duchess of Malfi* in the
same season has to be of national status"
Sheridan Morley *Punch*

● THE DUCHESS OF MALFI Helen Mirren

16 September - 18 October 1980

The Duchess of Malfi

by John Webster

THE HOUSE OF ARAGON
The Cardinal	JULIAN CURRY
Ferdinand	MIKE GWILYM
The Duchess of Malfi	HELEN MIRREN

THE COURT
Count Malateste	ALAN McMAHON
The Marquis of Pescara	RAYMOND LLEWELLYN
Lord Silvio	RICHARD CUBISON
Lord Roderigo	ROBERT REYNOLDS
Castruchio	AUBREY MORRIS
Delio	ROBERT SWANN
Julia	SORCHA CUSACK
Cariola	DIANA HARDCASTLE

THE PROFESSIONAL CLASSES
Daniel de Bosola	BOB HOSKINS
Antonio Bologna	PETER POSTLETHWAITE
Old Lady – a midwife	BARBARA KEOGH
The Doctor	AUBREY MORRIS
Officer	ALBIE WOODINGTON
Officer	ROBERT DEMEGER

Attendants, madmen, soldiers, executioners
RICHARD CUBISON, ROBERT DEMEGER,
RAYMOND LLEWELLYN, ALAN McMAHON,
ROBERT REYNOLDS, ALBIE WOODINGTON
Children (played at various performances by)
JEANNE-LOUISE BRINCAT, JOSEPH MURRAY,
MARIE LOWNDES, NICOLA-LOUISE
RICHARDSON, DUNCAN FLEMING,
PHILIP GLANCY

Director	ADRIAN NOBLE
Designer	BOB CROWLEY
Lighting	GEOFFREY JOYCE
Music	GEORGE FENTON
Sound	DAVID EASTERBROOK
	and COLIN GODDARD
Fight arranger	MALCOLM RANSON

The Duchess of Malfi transferred to The Round
House, London 1 April - 9 May 1981
with the following cast changes:
Castruchio/The Doctor	GEORGE RAISTRICK
Delio	BOSCO HOGAN
Officer	NIGEL COOKE

Children (played at various performances by)
RUPERT BADERMAN, SIOBHAN HAYES,
CHARLES RENDALL, SARAH CHATWYN,
LUKE HOPE, NAOMI RUSSELL

"It's grisly, it's gripping, it's spell-binding magic – John
Webster himself couldn't have hoped for a more
compelling enactment of his awesomely cynical
vision of human nastiness and nobility"
Robin Thornber *The Guardian*

"If it is anybody's evening it is Miss Mirren's ...
a performance of tragic stature. At her strangling we
all hold our breath. And at her famous assertions,
'I have youth and a little beauty' or 'I am not mad',
the actress achieves a rare degree of pathos"
Eric Shorter *Daily Telegraph*

"a really distinguished production. The lines are
spoken very quietly, but justice is done to the
unbearable richness of the poetry ... One is
continually surprised and convinced by Bob Hoskins'
performance" James Fenton *Sunday Times*

"This is Mr Noble's first production at the Royal
Exchange, but he has mastered its resources. Not
only in his use of the outer perimeter to carry the
sounds from the outer world (beautifully employed
in the echo scene), but in projecting the open and
secret elements of the play through frozen tableaux,
decisive alternations of full light and spotlit gloom,
and the substitution for the white carpet of a long
blood-stained rag bleeding to a prison chair"
Irving Wardle *The Times*

"In a word, it's brilliant"
Alan Hulme *Manchester Evening News*

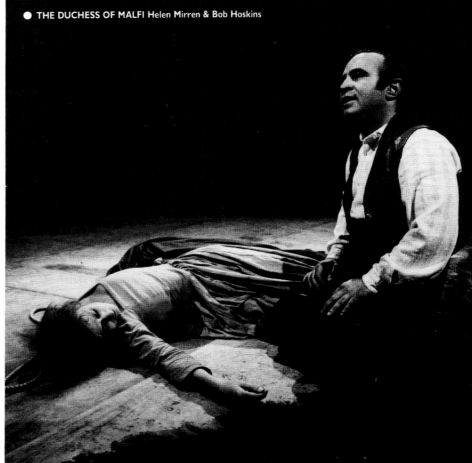

● THE DUCHESS OF MALFI Helen Mirren & Bob Hoskins

● THE CHAIRS Gwen Nelson & Frank Thornton

23 October - 8 November 1980
A double bill of

The Chairs

by Eugene Ionesco
translated by Donald Watson

GWEN NELSON
FRANK THORNTON

Director	RICHARD NEGRI
Designer	STEPHEN DONCASTER
Lighting	GEOFFREY JOYCE
Sound	IAN GIBSON

and

The Emperor Jones

by Eugene O'Neill

Brutus Jones	PETER POSTLETHWAITE
Smithers	ALBIE WOODINGTON
Lem/Witchdoctor	CARL CAMPBELL
Native Woman	LUCITA LIJERTWOOD
The Auctioneer	ALBIE WOODINGTON
Native soldiers, slaves	AKINTAYO AKINBODE
	CHRIS ROUDETTE
Director	RICHARD NEGRI
Designer	PETER BENNION
Lighting	GEOFFREY JOYCE
Sound	IAN GIBSON
The Dance of the Witchdoctor choreographed by	CARL CAMPBELL

Assistant to Richard Negri   GREGORY HERSOV

"An imaginative double bill ... Mr Negri, as architect of this exciting space, displays an admirable grasp of its potential. The realism of O'Neill's stage directions – with the walls of the forest closing in on the Emperor, white traders and crocodile gods looming out of the darkness – is transposed in a sustained exercise of technical wizardry. Best of all is the sacraficial climax, with the witch doctor drawing Mr Postlethwaite into a pulsating dance of death that clarifies his fate.
(In *The Chairs*) the Old Man and the Old Woman who fantasise an assembly arriving to hear the Old Man's message for posterity are quite beautifully played by Frank Thornton and Gwen Nelson ... Again, sound effects and lighting are deployed with thrilling ingenuity ... Sheer delight from start to finish" Michael Coveney *Financial Times*

55

● THE EMPEROR JONES Peter Postlethwaite

13 November - 20 December 1980

Waiting for Godot

by Samuel Beckett

Vladimir	MAX WALL
Estragon	TREVOR PEACOCK
Pozzo	WOLFE MORRIS
Lucky	GARY WALDHORN
Boy	JACOB MURRAY
	or CLIVE MYERS
Director	BRAHAM MURRAY
Designer	JOHANNA BRYANT
Lighting	GLYN PEREGRINE

Waiting for Godot transferred to The Round House, London 9-27 June 1981
The Boy was played by   JOSHUA WALDHORN
or JOSEPH GITTINGS

"It was a monumental performance as Max Wall's bloodhound features, etched by half a century of comedy, softened into the sadness of Beckett's tramp. With Trevor Peacock, Max created a double act which combined the best of vaudeville with the demanding virtuosity of modern theatre. I don't know where Godot was last night, but he missed the performance of a life-time"
Patrick O'Neill *Daily Mail*

"Max Wall has joined the Royal Exchange to score another triumph ... the great Wall inhabits Beckett's world with effortless grace. As always, his discomfort is the cause of our joy ... Braham Murray's outstanding production ..."
Michael Coveney *Financial Times*

56

● HARVEY Trevor Peacock

"Well directed by Eric Thompson, with good designs by Stephen Doncaster"
James Fenton *Sunday Times*

"As the drunk who is accompanied wherever he goes by a 6ft invisible white rabbit, Trevor Peacock loiters engagingly through the attempts of his sister, played with outraged perplexity by Patricia Routledge, to get him shut up in a sinister sanitarium ... hilariously funny" Charles Petry *Bolton Evening News*

24 December 1980 - 31 January 1981

HARVEY

by Mary Chase

Myrtle Mae Simmons	TILLY TREMAYNE
Veta Louise Simmons	PATRICIA ROUTLEDGE
Elwood P Dowd	TREVOR PEACOCK
Mrs Ethel Chauvenet	BERYL COOKE
Ruth Kelly RN	GLORIA CONNELL
Duane Wilson	GEOFFREY BATEMAN
Lyman Sanderson MD	ALAN PARNABY
William R Chumley MD	JAMES MAXWELL
Betty Chumley	JUDITH BARKER
Judge Omar Gaffney	FRANK CROMPTON
E J Lofgren	MALCOLM HEBDEN
Director	ERIC THOMPSON
Designer	STEPHEN DONCASTER
Lighting	MICK HUGHES

5 February - 7 March 1981

Rosmersholm

by Henrik Ibsen
translated by Michael Meyer

John Rosmer	CHRISTOPHER GABLE
Rebecca West	CELIA GREGORY
Dr Kroll	JEFFRY WICKHAM
Ulrik Brendel	ESPEN SKJØNBERG
Peter Mortensgaard	MILES ANDERSON
Mrs Helseth	RACHEL THOMAS
Director	CASPER WREDE
Designer	KIT SURREY
Lighting	MICHAEL WILLIAMS
Sound	DAVID EASTERBROOK
	and COLIN GODDARD
Assistant director	GREGORY HERSOV

"The Exchange Theatre was designed by a group who first made their names with Ibsen, and it is a perfect instrument for this play; capable at once of projecting grand-scale symbolic effects in the outer perimeter, and examining the naturalistic action almost in laboratory conditions ... The performance exerts a continuous spell such as I have never before experienced from this play. It is truly nuanced ..."
Irving Wardle *The Times*

"Espen Skjønberg possesses all the (Ralph) Richardson qualities, with an irresistible ability to destroy the distinction between comic and tragic, so that one is both vastly amused and rendered incapable of laughter, fearing to miss a moment's tragic nuance"
James Fenton *Sunday Times*

● ROSMERHOLM Christopher Gable & Celia Gregory

● THE CORN IS GREEN Avril Elgar

● MEASURE FOR MEASURE Alfred Burke

12 March - 4 April 1981

The Corn is Green
by Emlyn Williams

John Goronwy Jones	ARTRO MORRIS
Miss Ronberry	JANETTE LEGGE
Idwal Morris	MARTIN MURPHY
Sarah Pugh	IONA BANKS
A Groom	PHILIP GOODHEW
The Squire	JOHN BARDON
Bessie Watty	TINA MARIAN
Mrs Watty	TONI PALMER
Miss Moffatt	AVRIL ELGAR
Robbart Robbatch	ROBBIN JOHN
Will Hughes	PHILIP GOODHEW
John Owen	JEFFREY THOMAS
Morgan Evans	ALAN PARNABY
Old Tom	MICHAEL CUNNINGHAM
Grandparents	BARBARA DOWLING
	ROGER BOURNE
Children	VICTORIA WILLIAMS
	SOPHIA WILLIAMS
	NATASHA WILLIAMS
	BENEDICK WILLIAMS
Director	JAMES MAXWELL
Designer	LAURIE DENNETT
Costume designer	DAVID SHORT
Lighting	GLYN PEREGRINE
Sound	COLIN GODDARD
	and DAVID EASTERBROOK
Music arranged by	CHRIS MONKS
Welsh adviser	GLYN PEREGRINE

"Alan Parnaby is the model pupil. Avril Elgar's Miss Moffat counters his gentle compliance with a single-minded matter-of-fact sense of purpose. Her performance is a joy." Stella Flint *Daily Telegraph*

"With such a cast and direction, this is a production to cherish" Philip Key *Liverpool Daily Post*

9 April - 16 May 1981

Measure for Measure
by William Shakespeare
Sponsored by
IBM United Kingdom Limited **IBM**

Vincentio	ALFRED BURKE
Angelo	CHRISTOPHER NEAME
Escalus	PAUL CURRAN
Claudio	RICHARD REES
Lucio	ZIA MOHYEDDIN
Provost	MICHAEL POOLE
Friar Peter/Froth	COLIN PROCKTER
Elbow	ROY SAMPSON
Pompey	JOHN ABINERI
Abhorson/2nd Gentleman	ALAN PARTINGTON
Barnadine/1st Gentleman	CONRAD ASQUITH
Isabella	CLARE HIGGINS
Mariana/Whore	DIANA KATIS
Juliet	VIVIENNE RITCHIE
Francisca/Whore	DAPHNE ROGERS
Mistress Overdone	FANNY CARBY
Clerk to the Court/Transvestite	ALAN POLONSKY
Director	BRAHAM MURRAY
Designer	JOHANNA BRYANT
Lighting	MICHAEL WILLIAMS
Sound	TIM FOSTER and GEORGE GLOSSOP
Music	CHRIS MONKS
Assistant director	GREGORY HERSOV

"*Measure for Measure* is a director's dream. Its themes are so universal – illusion and reality, corruption, lust and heartless virtue – that its setting translates happily to almost any time and place ... Duke Vincentio is played by Alfred Burke with a parchment-voiced mystic ascetisism which is a joy to hear and watch."
Robin Thornber *The Guardian*

"An exceedingly stylish and powerful production. It has the exceptional virtues of utter clarity and complete conviction."
Alan Hulme *Manchester Evening News*

● THE MISANTHROPE Tom Courtenay & Amanda Boxer

21 May - 27 June 1981

The Misanthrope

by Molière
translated by Richard Wilbur
Sponsored by **(I) DINERS CLUB INTERNATIONAL**

Alceste	TOM COURTENAY
Philinte	CHRISTOPHER GABLE
Oronte	GEOFFREY BATEMAN
Célimène	CECILIA RICHARDS
Basque	NICHOLAS AMER
Eliante	JANET ELLIS
Clitandre	TIM McINNERNY
Acaste	IAN HASTINGS
Guard	PHILIP GOODHEW
Arsinoé	AMANDA BOXER
Dubois	IVAN STEWARD
Director	CASPER WREDE
Designer	MALCOLM PRIDE
Lighting	JOE DAVIS
Sound	DAVID EASTERBROOK
	and COLIN GODDARD
Assistant to the Director	DAVID SUGARMAN

The Misanthrope transferred to The Round House, London 1 July - 1 August 1981

"Richard Wilbur's translation is excellent and the rhymes earn a great proportion of the laughs ... What a wonderful play it is, and how sorry one feels when it's over so soon ... don't miss them in London" James Fenton *Sunday Times*

"The costumes are stunning with the men visually outpointing the women in their magnificent display of velvet, satin, bows, ruffles and wigs ... Mr Courtenay's performance is beautifully judged and balanced" Alan Hulme *Manchester Evening News*

"Tom Courtenay expresses both the self-deluding absurdity and self-lacerating pathos of this 17th-century Timon superbly well; and there are excellent performances from Christopher Gable as his philosophical confidant and from Amanda Boxer as that lubricious prude, Arsinoé" *Sunday Telegraph*

PREMIERE
2 July - 1 August 1981

devised by Anthony Bowles

SIMON CLARK	JONATHAN OWEN
BARRY JAMES	NEIL REID
ANNABEL LEVENTON	CHRISTINA THORNTON
LESLEY NICOL	JOHN WATTS
Director	ANTHONY BOWLES
Designer	TIM GOODCHILD
Lighting	GEOFFREY JOYCE
Sound	TIM FOSTER
Musical director	GARETH VALENTINE

"*Take Eight* derives its title from the company of eight singer-actors. It is a string of songs – more than two dozen of them – which are widely different in style. They range from Morley through Gershwin to Richard Rodgers and Leonard Bernstein. All of them have been re-arranged by Anthony Bowles with results that are often surprising, and his treatment is sometimes amusingly irreverent ... Tim Goodchild has devised a novel setting consisting of a triple circular rostrum which uses the hovercraft principle to move it about the stage ... a pleasant, light-hearted summer entertainment." Frank Bruckshaw *The Stage*

● TAKE EIGHT

59

17 September - 24 October 1981

DR FAUSTUS

by Christopher Marlowe

Wagner/Sloth/Frederick/ A Friar	DAVID BANNERMAN
The Bad Angel/Horse-Courser/ Bruno	KEN BONES
Cornelius/A Friar	JOHN BOSWALL
Belzebub/Pope Adrian/ Duke of Saxony	ROWLAND DAVIES
2nd Scholar/Gluttony/ Cardinal 2/Martino	DAVID FOXXE
A Devil/Wrath/Benvolio/ Cardinal 3	JAMES GADDAS
Chorus/1st Scholar/ Cardinal 1/Darius	JAMES GRIFFITHS
A Devil/A Friar/Alexander/ 3rd Scholar	NIGEL HARRISON
Doctor Faustus	BEN KINGSLEY
Lucifer/Emperor Charles/ Cardinal 4	JEFFERY KISSOON
Helen of Troy/Lechery/ Paramour/A Devil	JENIFER LANDOR
The Good Angel/Dick/ Archbishop of Rheims	IAN MACKENZIE
Mephistophilis	JAMES MAXWELL
Robin/Envy/A Friar	ALAN PARNABY
Valdes/Vintner/Pride/Raymond	WILLIAM SLEIGH
Devils/Choirboys	MAXTON BEESLEY
	PAUL BIBBY, or SIMON DANSON
	NIGEL PHIPPS

Director	ADRIAN NOBLE
Designer	BOB CROWLEY
Music	GEORGE FENTON
Lighting	BRIAN HARRIS
Sound	DAVID EASTERBROOK
Fight arranger	IAN McKAY
Assistant director	GREGORY HERSOV

"Last night Ben Kingsley moved from the company of very good actors to the elite of the truly great ... with a frightening range of noise, an exhausting virtuosity of emotion, and a fearsome nervous energy, Kingsley turned Faustus into a man who took all his pleasures seriously and a necromancer with enough black magic in his art to bewitch audiences. It was a performance which was shamelessly perfect ... if you'll pardon a shameless pun, it was a damned good show.
Patrick O'Neill *Daily Mail*

"The Royal Exchange, which show-for-show has a recent track record as impressive as that of the National or the RSC, now has another winner in Adrian Noble's masterly production ... in all the essentials a spare and tense triumph ... There is a clarity and a confidence here, as well as the arrival of Kingsley at major straight-stage stardom."
Sheridan Morley *Punch*

29 October - 28 November 1981

HEARTBREAK HOUSE

by George Bernard Shaw

Ellie Dunn	LYNSEY BAXTER
Nurse Guinness	PEGGY AITCHISON
Captain Shotover	ALFRED BURKE
Lady Utterword	DIANE FLETCHER
Hesione Hushabye	ELEANOR BRON
Mazzini Dunn	PETER HOWELL
Hector Hushabye	NORMAN ESHLEY
Alfred (Boss) Mangan	NIGEL STOCK
Randall Utterword	CHRISTOPHER GOOD
The Burglar	RICHARD BEALE

Director	JONATHAN HALES
Set designer	ROGER BUTLIN
Costume designer	DEIRDRE CLANCY
Lighting	NICK CHELTON
Sound	COLIN DUNCAN

"In a word, this Shaw classic is dazzling"
Gerard Dempsey *Daily Express*

"Here Miss Bron has the opportunity – indeed the duty – to dazzle us in her full Edwardian splendour. And oh boy does she dazzle ... a fine production"
James Fenton *Sunday Times*

"A newcomer to the Exchange, Mr Hales is not afraid to hold static groupings in powerful eye-to-eye contact: and the movement he does use is beautifully calculated to build climaxes and surprises."
Irving Wardle *The Times*

"In adapting Robert Louis Stevenson's story James Maxwell has aschewed all whimsey. Authenticity is the hallmark. The detailed care shown in everything, from Laurie Dennett's set design and David Short's costumes to the least of the props, provides a fascinating background to enough spine-chilling menace, clashing swords and gun shots to curdle the blood of any self-respecting schoolboy."
Stella Flint *Daily Telegraph*

● **TREASURE ISLAND** Ian Hastings & Clive Duncan

PREMIERE
3 December - 26 December 1981

TREASURE ISLAND

by Robert Louis Stevenson
adapted by James Maxwell

Jim Hawkins	CLIVE DUNCAN
Billy Bones/Redruth	ALEC LINSTEAD
Taylor/Job Anderson	WILLIAM ILKLEY
Mrs Hawkins	SALLY GIBSON
Dr Livesey	MATTHEW GUINNESS
Black Dog/Merry	KEN BONES
Blind Pew/Joyce	DAVID FOXXE
Johnny/Benn Gunn	IAN HASTINGS
Tom Morgan	ANTHONY WINGATE
Mr Dance/O'Brien	PHIL BANYARD
Dogger/Israel Hands	ANTHONY HEATON
Mr Trelawney	ROWLAND DAVIES
Alan/Young John	PETER NICHOLLS
Dick	OKON JONES
Abraham Gray	JAMES GADDAS
Tom/Pirate	NIGEL HARRISON
Long John Silver	RONALD FORFAR
Captain Smollett	OLIVER SMITH
Director	JAMES MAXWELL
Set designer	LAURIE DENNETT
Costume designer	DAVID SHORT
Music	CHRIS MONKS
Lighting	GLYN PEREGRINE
Sound	TIM FOSTER
Fight arranger	IAN McKAY
Assistant director	GREGORY HERSOV

BRITISH PREMIERE
1 January - 30 January 1982

The ROUND DANCE

by Arthur Schnitzler
translated by Charles Osborne
adapted by Richard Negri and Casper Wrede

The Prostitute	MELANIE KILBURN
The Soldier	DANIEL PEACOCK
The Nursemaid	CINDY O'CALLAGHAN
The Young Man	WILLIAM HOPE
The Young Married Woman	GABRIELLE DRAKE
The Husband	GARY WALDHORN
The Sweet Girl	CHERYL PRIME
The Poet	GEOFFREY BATEMAN
The Actress	BERNICE STEGERS
The Earl	NORMAN ESHLEY
Dancers	LORRAINE LOCKETT
	SEAN CURRAN
Director	CASPER WREDE
Designer	RICHARD NEGRI
Lighting	MICHAEL WILLIAMS
Sound	COLIN DUNCAN
Assistant Director	GREGORY HERSOV

Systime sponsored the week beginning 10 January

"Wrede has set an Austrian play, redolent of the Vienna of Freud, Hofmannsthal and Rilke, in modern London ... This is a remarkable production, faithful to Schnitzler's acerbity without ever losing his malicious sense of fun." John Barber *Daily Telegraph*

"... a beautifully, elegantly written comedy. It is an ingenious tarantella of temptations, but by no means today erotic enough to raise an eyebrow ...
Mr Wrede directs with a fleet hand in an amusing, often hilarious production with a keen sardonic eye"
Desmond Pratt *Yorkshire Post*

Photo: Catherine Ashmore

● **THE ROUND DANCE** Geoffrey Bateman & Cheryl Prime

4 February - 13 March 1982

The Beaux' Stratagem

by George Farquhar

Cherry	SALLY WATTS
Boniface	ARTRO MORRIS
Archer	ROBERT LINDSAY
Aimwell	CHRISTOPHER NEAME
Tapster	NIVEN BOYD
Mrs Sullen	SARAH BADEL
Dorinda	JOANNE PEARCE
Sullen	CHRISTOPHER GOOD
Scrub	IAN HASTINGS
Gibbet	JOHN CORDING
Foigard	COLIN PROCKTER
Gipsy	TRACY BOOTH
Count Bellair	CHRISTOPHER BRAMWELL
Countrywoman	SALLY GIBSON
Lady Bountiful	DOROTHY ALISON
Sir Charles Freeman	PETER GALE
Hounslow	NIGEL HARRISON
Bagshot	NIVEN BOYD
Director	BRAHAM MURRAY
Designer	JOHANNA BRYANT
Lighting	MICHAEL WILLIAMS
Music	CHRIS MONKS
Choreography	SUE LEFTON
Fight arranger	WILLIAM HOBBS
Sound	CHRIS COXHEAD

"Manchester's Royal Exchange have discovered in
The Beaux Stratagem a neglected costume classic,
and they have brought it back to vibrant life with wit
and flair. Written in 1707, the play is a comedy of
manners in the tradition of Restoration comedy —
all fops and frills, romantic intrigue and colourful
serving folk ... The casting of Robert Lindsay and
Christopher Neame as the fortunate hunting young
gents sets the tone – it's vital, romantic, and never
misses an opportunity of a nudging aside."
Robin Thornber *The Guardian*

"Particularly excellent is the leading performance by
Robert Lindsay ... irresistible"
James Fenton *Sunday Times*

● THE BEAUX' STRATAGEM Robert Lindsay & Sarah Badel

PREMIERE OF NEW TRANSLATION

18 March - 10 April 1982

PHILOCTETES

by Sophocles
translated by Christopher Stace

Odysseus	ESPEN SKJØNBERG
Neoptolemus	ROBERT LINDSAY
Philoctetes	JAMES MAXWELL
Heracles	CHRISTOPHER GOOD
Leader of the Chorus	JOHN CORDING
Chorus of Sailors	CLIVE DUNCAN

CHRISTOPHER GOOD, NIGEL HARRISON
IAN RUSKIN, ROBERT VAHEY, BENNY YOUNG

Director	MICHAEL ELLIOTT
Set designer	LAURIE DENNETT
Costume designer	IOANNA PAPANTONÌOU
Music composed by	GORDON CROSSE
Lighting	MICHAEL WILLIAMS
Sound	IAN GIBSON

"This was a Greek drama expressed with rare
realism, superbly staged with memorable and chilling
sound effects"
Gerard Dempsey *Daily Express*

"Eliott has waited 18 years to direct Greek Tragedy;
the result shows the advantage of a long, loving
engagement with the genre. Brisk, yet relaxed, the
production gives full value to the moral issues raised
while sustaining the excitement of the story."
Timothy Ramsden *Times Educational Supplement*

"... a gripping and entertaining production ...
As usual, the setting, lighting and effects draw praise,
from the first and last eerie swathes of mist on the
rocky shore to the thunder-and-lightning Heracles
spectacle."
Oldham Evening Chronicle

● PHILOCTETES Robert Lindsay & James Maxwell

● THE NERD Derek Griffiths

EUROPEAN PREMIERE
15 April - 15 May 1982

The Nerd
by Larry Shue

Willum	DAVID HOROVITCH
Axel	GARY WALDHORN
Tansy	SHELLEY BORKUM
Waldgrave	DON HENDERSON
Clelia	SALLY GIBSON
Thor	MATTHEW BARKER/OLIVER FINDLAY
Rick	DEREK GRIFFITHS
Kemp	LLOYD COOPER
Director	BRAHAM MURRAY
Designer	JOHANNA BRYANT
Lighting	CLIVE ODOM
Sound	TIM FOSTER and GEORGE GLOSSOP

"Derek Griffiths is a nerd of epic awfulness –
a monster of ineptitude and tactlessness. It is a
performance to treasure .. never less than hilarious."
Gerard Dempsey *Daily Express*

20 May - 19 June 1982

DETECTIVE STORY
by Sidney Kingsley

Detective Dakis	ANDY PANTELIDOU
Shoplifter	SANDY RATCLIFF
Detective Gallagher	ERIC MASON
Patrolman Keogh/Mr Feeney	PHILIP BARNES
Mrs Farragut/Mrs Feeney/	
The Lady	THOMASINE HEINER/SYBIL ALLEN
Joe Feinson	IAN HASTINGS
Detective Callaghan	GEOFFREY BATEMAN
Detective O'Brien/Crumb-bum/	
Mr Bagatelle	ANDY RASHLEIGH
Detective Brody	PAUL IMBUSCH
Endicott Sims	JOHN STERLAND
Detective McLeod	DANIEL MOONEY
Arthur Kindred	ALAN PARNABY
Patrolman Barnes	RICK JAMES
1st Burglar (Charlie)	TIM McINNERNY
2nd Burglar (Lewis)	ROY SAMPSON
Mrs Bagatelle	RITA HOWARD
Willy	ALLISTER BAIN
Dr Schneider/Gentleman	MICHAEL ROBERTS
Lt Monoghan	JAMES BERWICK
Susan Carmichael	JOANNE PEARCE
Miss Hatch/Indignant Citizen	MAUREEN BEATTIE
Mr Gallantz/Photographer	ROBERT DEMEGER
Mr Pritchett	MICHAEL POOLE
Mary McLeod	SORCHA CUSACK
Tami Giacoppetti	JACK KLAFF
Director	JOHN DILLON
Designer	LAURIE DENNETT
Lighting	GLYN PEREGRINE
Sound	CHRIS COXHEAD
Fight arranger	MALCOLM RANSON
Assistant director	GREGORY HERSOV

● DETECTIVE STORY Daniel Mooney

"Watching *Detective Story* is a pleasure ... in its
exciting and amusing atmosphere and in its range of
attitudes and expressive character, this is probably
the best play of its kind ... the whole company
deserves praise for its snap and sensibility and above
all for its teamwork." Eric Shorter *Daily Telegraph*

● ANDY CAPP Tom Courtenay & Val McLane

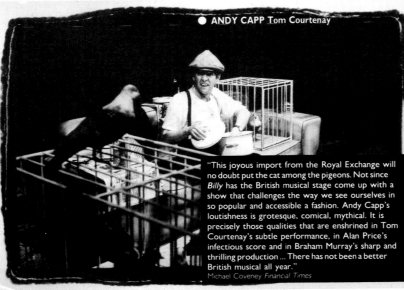

● ANDY CAPP Tom Courtenay

"This joyous import from the Royal Exchange will no doubt put the cat among the pigeons. Not since *Billy* has the British musical stage come up with a show that challenges the way we see ourselves in so popular and accessible a fashion. Andy Capp's loutishness is grotesque, comical, mythical. It is precisely those qualities that are enshrined in Tom Courtenay's subtle performance, in Alan Price's infectious score and in Braham Murray's sharp and thrilling production ... There has not been a better British musical all year."
Michael Coveney *Financial Times*

● ONE FLEW OVER THE CUCKOO'S NEST Jonathan Hackett

"Gregory Hersov's stunning production ... the performances are, totally compelling – from Jonathan Hackett's McMurphy, so powered it's exhausting just to watch, Linda Marlowe's chillingly smug Nurse Ratched, Nick Brimble's smouldering Chief Bromden, and Eric Richard's sensitive-to-a-fingertip patient's president to the coolly twitching black orderlies." Robin Thornber *The Guardian*

PREMIERE
29 June - 21 August 1982

ANDY CAPP

a musical by Alan Price and Trevor Peacock
Supported by the
makro Sponsors' Scheme

Geordie	ALAN PRICE
Vicar	JEFFREY PERRY
Linda	NICKY CROYDON
Jack	TREVOR COOPER
Andy Capp	TOM COURTENAY
Percy	RON EMSLIE
Olga	ANGELA MORAN
Chalkie	JOHN BARDON
Pauline	EVE MATHESON
Elvis Horsepole	MICHAEL MUELLER
Shern	JEFFREY PERRY
Ron	ROBERT VAHEY
Passerby	TREVOR COOPER
Ruby	JUDITH BARKER
Florence Capp	VAL McLANE
Raquel Scrimmett	NICKY CROYDON
Mrs Scrimmett	VIVIENNE ROSS
Mr Scrimmett	ROBERT VAHEY
Director	BRAHAM MURRAY
Designer	JOHANNA BRYANT
Musical arranger	DEREK WADSWORTH
Musical supervisor and vocal arrangements by	DAVID FIRMAN
Choreography	SUE LEFTON
Fight arranger	WILLIAM HOBBS
Lighting	MICHAEL WILLIAMS
Sound	TIM FOSTER and GEORGE GLOSSOP

From 9 August the following cast changes were made prior to transferring to the Aldwych Theatre, London where *Andy Capp* ran from 28 September 1982 - 22 January 1983

Vicar/Percy	COLIN PROCKTER
Pauline	FIONA MATHIESON
Big Mad Ron/Usher	DAVID BLUESTONE

"... one of the least sentimental musicals around. It's funny, tuneful and often ingenious."
James Fenton *Sunday Times*

---

16 September - 9 October 1982

One flew over the cuckoo's nest

by Dale Wasserman
based on the novel by Ken Kesey

Chief Bromden	NICK BRIMBLE
Aide Warren	ALAN IGBON
Aide Williams	STANLEY FINNI
Nurse Ratched	LINDA MARLOWE
Nurse Flinn	JUDY HOLT
Dale Harding	ERIC RICHARD
Ellis	SIMON TREVES
Billy Bibbitt	TIM McINNERNY
Scanlon	BILL LEADBITTER
Cheswick	IAN HASTINGS
Martini	JOHN SESSIONS
Ruckly	STUART RICHMAN
Randle McMurphy	JONATHAN HACKETT
Dr Spivey	KENNETH WALLER
Aide Turkle	LLOYD ANDERSON
Candy Starr	HAZEL O'CONNOR
Sandra	EVE FERRET
Technician	PAUL WALKER
Director	GREGORY HERSOV
Designer	DAVID SHORT
Lighting	PAUL W JONES
Sound	CHRIS COXHEAD
Music	COLIN GODDARD
Fight arranger	MALCOLM RANSON
Movement	JANE GIBSON
Assistant director	CHRISTINA BURNETT

"Gregory Hersov's direction is so intimate and telling, it compels and engrosses."
Stella Flint *Daily Telegraph*

1982·1983

14 October - 13 November 1982

LORD ARTHUR SAVILE'S CRIME

by Oscar Wilde
adapted by Constance Cox

Sponsored by

National Westminster Bank

Baines	BARRY FOSTER
Lord Arthur Savile	ALAN PARNABY
Sybil Merton	KIKA MIRYLEES/
	ELIZABETH WATTS
The Dean of Paddington	TREVOR BAXTER
Lady Windermere	ROSALIND KNIGHT
Lady Clementina	GWEN NELSON
Lady Julia Merton	PATSY BYRNE
Mr Podgers	JOHN TORDOFF
Nellie	ELIZABETH WATTS/SONIA KENSON
Herr Winkelkopf	HARRY LANDIS
Director	ERIC THOMPSON
Set designer	LAURIE DENNETT
Costume designer	STEPHEN DONCASTER
Lighting	MARK HENDERSON
Sound	JOHN DEL'NERO

"Theatrically, *Lord Arthur Savile's Crime* is
extremely well contrived. It contains a great many
characteristic Wildeisms and brings to the stage in
Lord Arthur and Baines a master and butler
relationship which predates Wodehouse by a good
many years. Above all it is extremely funny so that
throughout its two hours there is an almost
continuous ripple of laughter from the audience.
Casting, as always at the Exchange, is first-rate. Barry
Foster is a bland and urbane Baines, almost
completely unruffled, slickly whisking away the
poisoned sweet when it is in danger of getting in the
wrong mouth and removing the about-to-explode
bomb with almost equal aplomb. Alan Parnaby, slimly
handsome and wearing some superb suits,
personifies the rich man."
Frank Buckshaw *The Stage*

● LORD ARTHUR SAVILE'S CRIME Barry Foster

65

18 November - 18 December 1982

AFTER THE LIONS

a new play by Ronald Harwood

Major Denucé	JOHN CORDING
Sarah	DOROTHY TUTIN
Pitou	RUSSELL HUNTER
Madame de Gournay	SHEILA REID
Old Carpenter/	
Wounded Soldier	TOM HARRISON
Young Carpenter/	
Military Orderly	RICHARD GALLAGHER
The Woman	WENDY GERRARD
Director	MICHAEL ELLIOTT
Set designer	LAURIE DENNETT
Costume designer	MALCOLM PRIDE
Lighting	MICHAEL WILLIAMS
Sound	IAN GIBSON
Assistant director	CHRISTINA BURNETT

"The triumph of the human spirit over suffering and
hardship is one of the fundamental recurring themes
at the Royal Exchange Theatre. And you could hardly
ask for a clearer exposition of his faith than Ronald
Harwood's new show. It's a simple, sometimes
subtle, morality play. After his success with *The
Dresser*, the setting is again theatrical, being based
with sympathetic imagination on Sarah Bernhardt's
later years. It is a part, decked out with purple
passages of high-flown acting in a single spot, for
which most actresses would give their all. And
Dorothy Tutin – often spell-binding in a lower key
– rises to it as if it was written for her...
Harwood has also created a complex, winsome
character for her shadowy secretary, Pitou, played
with droll, abrasive wit by Russell Hunter...
For the theatrical, the combination of sentiment and
luscious settings – big cat skins and an elephant's foot
– designed by Laurie Dennett will be a treat."
Robin Thornber *The Guardian*

● AFTER THE LIONS Dorothy Tutin

23 December 1982 - 29 January 1983

RING ROUND THE MOON

by Jean Anouilh
adapted by Christopher Fry

Joshua	BRIAN OULTON
Hugo/Frederic	RUPERT FRAZER
Diana Messerschmann	EMMA WATSON
Lady India	ROSALIND KNIGHT
Patrice Bombelles	CHRISTOPHER GOOD
Madame Desmermortes	SHEILA BALLANTINE
Capulat	ANN WAY
Messerschmann	HARRY LANDIS
Romainville	HUGH SULLIVAN
Isabelle	NATALIE SLATER
Her Mother	MARGERY MASON
The General	JOHN KEYWORTH
Footman	RICHARD TALBOT
Other appearances by	ROBIN BURCH
Director	STEVEN PIMLOTT
Set designer	DAVID FIELDING
Costume designer	MICHAEL STENNETT
Lighting	MARK HENDERSON
Music composed by	JEREMY SAMS
Choreography	TERRY JOHN BATES
Sound	JOHN DEL'NERO

PREMIERE

3 February - 26 February 1983

HOPE AGAINST HOPE

adapted by Casper Wrede, from the writing of Nadezhda Mandelstam, the prose, poetry and letters of Osip Mandelstam and the poetry and reminiscences of Anna Akhmatova

Nadezhda Mandelstam	AVRIL ELGAR
Osip Mandelstam	DAVID HOROVITCH
Anna Akhmatova	DILYS HAMLETT
Elena Bulgakova/Nurse/Zinaida Pasternak/	
Secretary to Literary Fund	SYBIL ALLEN
1st Agent/Abel Yenukidze/1st Soldier/	
Voice of Stalin/Victor Scklovski/	
Kazarnowski	DICKEN ASHWORTH
2nd Agent/Demian Bedny/Hospital	
Attendant/Militia Officer/	
1st Officer	DAVID BAUCKHAM
Janitor's Wife/Nadezhda's Mother/	
Housekeeper/Sec in the Writers'	
Union	HELEN BLATCH
Man/Evgeni/Hospital Attendant/	
2nd Agent/2nd Officer	PAUL BUTTERWORTH
Doctor/British Literary	
Historian	PATRICIA HENEGHAN
Brodski/The Interrogator/Kornei	
Chukovski	PAUL IMBUSCH
Conductor/Nurse/Telegraph Girl/	
Housing Committee Secretary/	
Vassilissa Scklovski	MELANIE KILBURN
3rd Agent/Lev Gumilev/Shura Mandelstam/	
Commandant/American University	
Professor	BILL LEADBITTER
Lidia Seifullina	BRIGID MACKAY
Alexei Tolstoi/Boris Pasternak/Man with	
the Axe/The Physicist	ROY SAMPSON
2nd Soldier/1st Informer/Printer's	
Apprentice/Militia Clerk	FERGUS McLARNON
3rd Soldier	ROBIN BURCH
Director	CASPER WREDE
Set designer	STEPHEN McCABE
Costume designer	DAVID SHORT
Lighting	MICHAEL WILLIAMS
Sound	JOHN DEL'NERO
Music	GEORGE HALL
Assistant director	CHRISTINA BURNETT

● RING ROUND THE MOON Sheila Ballantine

"... romantic, spectacular and sparkling with aristocratic wit; frivolous and light-hearted, yet still sound and sharp enough not to insult your intelligence ... Rupert Frazer's command was masterly as he distinguished the twins Hugo and Frederic ... the texture was as rich as ever – beautifully evocative settings by David Fielding and costumes by Michael Stennett suggesting an awesomely opulent world of good taste and breeding." Robin Thornber The Guardian

● HOPE AGAINST HOPE Avril Elgar & Dilys Hamlett

"*Hope Against Hope* is the great exception among books by literary widows. It certainly has the purpose of restoring the name of a forgotten man. But its real theme is the prison house of Russia under Stalin. Osip Mandelstam was a great poet, full stop. If such torments can befall a totally non-political victim, consider the lives of his fellow citizens. Casper Wrede, adaptor and director of the production, is absolutely faithful to the scope of the book." Irving Wardle The Times

"David Horovitch and Avril Elgar, as the poet and his wife, provide tour de force performances which register alternating hope and despair with telling effect." Walter Huntley Liverpool Echo

● WHILE THE SUN SHINES Caroline Goodall & Paul Barber

3 March - 2 April 1983

While the SUN SHINES

by Terence Rattigan

Horton	CHRISTOPHER HANCOCK
Bobby, Earl of Harpenden	MICK FORD
Lieutenant Mulvaney	PAUL BARBER
Colbert	PAUL HERZBERG
Lady Elisabeth	CAROLINE GOODALL
Mabel Crum	JULIE PEASGOOD
The Duke of Ayr and Stirling	KEN WYNNE
Director	JAMES MAXWELL
Designer	STEPHEN DONCASTER
Lighting	GLYN PEREGRINE
Fight arranger	MALCOLM RANSON

"Terence Rattigan's light-hearted look at love in the Second World War makes a good nostalgic night out, with plenty of fun. The audience rocks with laughter at a production that is sheer entertainment from beginning to end. Despite its 40-year-old setting, it is not at all dated – the wit and slapstick remain fresh and funny."
C.W. *Oldham Evening Chronicle*

"*While the Sun Shines* captures the full power of that 1940s nostalgia, fuelled by dance halls, patriotic music and the arrival in Britain of hundreds of thousands of Allied soldiers preparing for the invasion of Europe. James Maxwell's production explores to the full the comic potential of the labyrinthine relationships."
David Harrison *Liverpool Echo*

7 April - 14 May 1983

THE WILD DUCK

by Henrik Ibsen
translated by Michael Meyer

Haakon Werle	JOHN PHILLIPS
Gregers Werle	IAN McDIARMID
Old Ekdal	ESPEN SKJØNBERG
Hjalmar Ekdal	JONATHAN HACKETT
Gina Ekdal	STEPHANIE COLE
Hedvig	SALLY COOKSON
Mrs Soerby	ANGELA BROWNE
Relling	GEOFFREY BATEMAN
Molvik	STUART RICHMAN
Petterson	DAVID BAUCKHAM
Jensen	PAUL BUTTERWORTH
Dinner Guests:	
Flabby Gentleman	GEOFFREY ANDREWS
Balding Gentleman	FRANK CROMPTON
Short-Sighted Gentleman	STUART RICHMAN
Other Guests	JOHN KEYWORTH
	PETER PENDLEBURY
	DON POOLE
Director	CASPER WREDE
Set designer	STEPHEN McCABE
Costume designer	STEPHEN DONCASTER
Lighting	GLYN PEREGRINE
Sound	JOHN DEL'NERO
Assistant director	CHRISTINA BURNETT

"This production makes one regret all the more that with the Roundhouse's future uncertain, there is no London theatre ready to take even a small selection of Manchester's best work that intermittently came to Chalk Farm ... Casper Wrede's staging has a clarity and a tenderness that do the play exceptional justice. Hard to know how far to attribute that clarity to the production alone, because Ian McDiarmid's performance as Gregers is so remarkable ... Espen Skjønberg, an Ibsen veteran, makes an Old Ekdal of extraordinary ripeness and presence. His shame-faced entry into the act one party is masterly ..."
Anthony Masters *The Times*

● THE WILD DUCK Ian McDiarmid & Sally Cookson

● THE CARETAKER Charlie Drake

19 May - 18 June 1983

THE CARETAKER

by Harold Pinter

Davies	CHARLIE DRAKE
Aston	JONATHAN HACKETT
Mick	TIM McINNERNY
Director	RICHARD NEGRI
Designer	NADYA COHEN
Lighting	GEOFFREY JOYCE
Sound	CHRIS COXHEAD

"The star was fluent enough delivering his lines with painstaking detachment, but it was the stillness, the watchful silence scrupulously maintained, that made his performance so impressive. As Pinter's barely articulate tramp, Charlie Drake erased the memory of that desperately lovable and, to many, utterly resistable little funny man. A minor blessing; a major triumph." Gerard Dempsey Daily Express

"Charlie Drake brought a rare dignity and poise to Pinter's pathetic tramp, with a lived-in performance" Patrick O'Neill Daily Mail

"Gogol's savage jibe can rarely have been delivered with such relish ... this is comedy with its inhibitions down and its pecker up – raw, rude, raucous and rakish. It's a hit."
Patrick O'Neill Daily Mail

"... there are some lovely actors in this company – Philip Madoc as the toy town mayor, Val McLane putting on airs as his wife and Tina Marian lacking the graces as his daughter; Christopher Hancock, Colin Prockter and Ian Hastings running the school, hospital and post office and relishing the cameos. It's a play that's a gift to strong character actors"
Robin Thornber The Guardian

PREMIERE OF NEW ADAPTATION   23 June - 6 August 1983

The Government Inspector

by Nikolai Gogol
adapted by Gerard McLarnon

Supported by the
makro Sponsors' Scheme

The Mayor	PHILIP MADOC
The Judge	MICHAEL POOLE
Schools Superintendent	CHRISTOPHER HANCOCK
Charity Warden	COLIN PROCKTER
Postmaster	IAN HASTINGS
Dobsky	HARRY LANDIS
Bobsky	BARRY MARTIN
Constable	THOMAS HENTY
Police Superintendant/ A Shopkeeper	GEOFFREY ANDREWS
The Mayor's Wife, Anna Andreyevna	VAL McLANE
The Mayor's Daughter, Marya Antonovna	TINA MARIAN
Avdotya/Sergeant's Wife/School Superintendent's Wife	MELANIE KILBURN
Osip	SAM KELLY
Khlestakov	DEREK GRIFFITHS
Korobkin/Waiter	JAMES WOOLLEY
Mishka	MARTIN ALLAN
A Special/A Shopkeeper	DAVID BAUCKHAM
A Special/Battered Man	ANDREW KAZAMIA
Gendarme/A Shopkeeper	JOHN KEYWORTH
Locksmith's Wife/Korobkin's Wife	HELEN BLATCH
Director	BRAHAM MURRAY
Designer	JOHANNA BRYANT
Lighting	CLIVE ODOM
Sound	JOHN DEL'NERO
Assistant director	CHRISTINA BURNETT

● THE GOVERNMENT INSPECTOR
Derek Griffiths

THE GOVERNMENT INSPECTOR
Philip Madoc

15 September - 22 October 1983

The Dance of Death

by August Strindberg
translated by Michael Meyer

Captain	EDWARD FOX
Alice	JILL BENNETT
Kurt	PETER BALDWIN
Jenny/Old Woman	SUE BURTON

Director	KENNETH MACMILLAN
Costume designer	BARRY KAY
Set designer	LAURIE DENNETT
Lighting	JOHN B READ
Sound	COLIN DUNCAN

27 October - 17 December 1983

HAMLET

by William Shakespeare

Hamlet	ROBERT LINDSAY
Claudius/Ghost	PHILIP MADOC
Gertrude	ALISON FISKE
Horatio	IAN HASTINGS
Polonius/Osric	DEREK SMITH
Laertes/Player Queen	MICHAEL CROMPTON
Player King/Priest/Sailor	JOHN WATTS
Musical Player	AKINTAYO AKINBODE
Guildenstern/Barnardo/Clerk	TREVOR COOPER
Player King/Gravedigger	NICK STRINGER
Marcellus/Player Poisoner	ANDREW KAZAMIA
Prologue Player/Priest/Sailor	BARRY EWART
Musical Player	CHRIS WALTON

Director	BRAHAM MURRAY
Designer	JOHANNA BRYANT
Lighting	MICHAEL WILLIAMS
Fights	MALCOLM RANSON
Sound	COLIN DUNCAN
Mime	DEREK GRIFFITHS
Music	CHRIS MONKS

Hamlet was the first touring production to go out in the mobile touring theatre in 1984:
Lowton High School (9-14 April), Huddersfield Sports Centre (16-19 April), Whitehaven Sports Centre (20-24 April), Macclesfield Leisure Centre (26-28 April), Kirkby Sports Centre (30 April - 1 May), Dolphin Centre Darlington (3-5 May), Newbiggin Sports and Community Centre (8-10 May), Stour Centre Ashford (11-12 May), Bletchley Leisure Centre (15-17 May), Crawley Leisure Centre (18-19 May), Barbican Centre London (22 May - 9 June)
The following cast changes were made for the tour:

Laertes/Player Queen	MICHAEL CROMPTON
Player King/Priest/Sailor	JOHN WATTS
Musical Player	AKINTAYO AKINBODE

"This *Hamlet's* freshness – and it does achieve a new vitality – comes from startling directorial strokes. Visually (Murray) has abandoned the trappings of theatrical illusion. The auditorium is flooded with a harsh shadowless light – that of an operating theatre ... The stage is bare, a boarded floor. And the company is dressed by the designer in costumes that look as if they could be their own street clothes. It looks like a rehearsal. But it is an honest approach, dispensing with the distractions of doublet and hose. And it does serve to emphasise the acting and the words. And the acting here is something to be seen. Robert Lindsay roars and twitches spectacularly like one whose great moment has come."
Robin Thornber *The Guardian*

"Lindsay has become an actor of major stature with his extraordinary intense reading of the ultimate actor's role – cracked voice, eyes starting from sockets, floor-rolling and bitter tears attending speech after exhausting speech ... All in all, a shrewd, literate and fierce production."
Irene McManus *Yorkshire Post*

"Sir Kenneth MacMillan's play-directing debut in a major theatre ... Strongly cast, it has a quietness and straightness and dry humour ... Mr Fox extends his usual line in well-bred gentleman for this complete, convincing, carefully studied old buffer. The voice's brittle, aged hardness and firm turn-down at the end of most sentences are most pleasurable. He keeps an unnerving balance between intolerable boredom and vicious alertness as he and Miss Bennett resume oft-repeated nagging rituals or virtually come to blows." Anthony Masters *The Times*

● THE DANCE OF DEATH Peter Baldwin & Jill Bennett

69

● HAMLET Robert Lindsay

22 December 1983 - 28 January 1984

MOBY DICK

adapted by Michael Elliott
from the novel by Herman Melville

Captain Ahab	BRIAN COX
Ishmael	NIGEL TERRY
Mr Starbuck	JOHN CORDING
Mr Stubb	TIM HEALY
Mr Flask	ANDREW BYATT
Queequeg	TERENCE WILTON
Tashtego	MARK LEWIS
Daggoo	LEO WRINGER
The Carpenter	ESMOND KNIGHT
The Blacksmith	HARRY WALKER
The Irishman	P G STEPHENS
Pip	GARY BEADLE
The Cook	ALFRED FAGON
John Corey (Leader of the forecastle)	PETER GUINNESS
Alberto Sholez (Shantyman)	TAYLOR McAULEY
Ivan Brodsky	RICHARD GRAHAM
Anatol Shevalov	ROY MITCHELL
Wilhelm Graben	RON DONACHIE
Benjamin Hatch	CLIVE DUNCAN
Lars Ohlson	ROBERT HOPKINS
Ezva T Howland	EWART JAMES WALTERS
Father Mapple	PHILIP MADOC
Captain Peleg	ESMOND KNIGHT
Captain Bildad	JOHN BOSWALL
The Stranger	P G STEPHENS
The Landlord	HARRY WALKER
Director	MICHAEL ELLIOTT
Settings	LAURIE DENNETT
Costumes	DAVID SHORT
Lighting	MICHAEL WILLIAMS
Sound	IAN GIBSON
Music	GORDON CROSSE
Movement	LITZ PISK and SUE LEFTON
Movement assistant	ROBERT HOPKINS
Shanties arranged by	TAYLOR McAULEY

"Very like a whale, this show is enormous, intelligent and difficult to get hold of ... it is a leviathan of a success which makes superlatives seem as diminutive as a man alone in the ocean ... a triumph of technical teamwork. The Royal Exchange's arena stage, intricately decked with rigging by designer Laurie Dennett, becomes a Nantucket whaler so realistically that when you notice the theatre's lights you wonder what they're doing there. The company, coached in movement by Litz Pisk, mimes the capsize of a longboat so convincingly that you duck to avoid the splash. With superb sound and lighting effects by Ian Gibson and Michael Williams, it is the ultimate in theatrical illusion, brilliantly conceived and immaculately executed. Michael Elliott wrote, directed, and master-minded this masterpiece. I for one was spell-bound. Sharing an illusion like that is one of the things that theatre – and this theatre in particular – is about."
Robin Thornber *The Guardian*

"Michael Elliott's courageous, fierce adaptation of *Moby Dick* could hardly be bettered. I doubt whether this theatre has ever seen more impassioned, committed acting. Brian Cox's furious, foaming Ahab is exactly right – utterly convincing as the tragically heroic Nantucket whaling captain with murder and blasphemy on his mind. Almost everything about this production – the ingenious sets, the costumes, sound, lighting, brilliant movement – contributes to an evening of terror and extreme beauty. The varying states of the ocean are wonderfully evoked – now stormy, lightning-struck; now enchanted, luscious calm. There are moments of real magic; the blacksmith tempering Ahab's evil harpoon over a cindery forge fire; or the selfsame harpoon – apparently untouched – bursting in lurid flame at the height of an electric storm."
Irene McManus *Yorkshire Post*

"Reports so far have been discreetly quiet about how Michael Elliott conjures the white whale in the final moments of his own adaptation. Suffice it to say that the effect is one of the most satisfying and remarkable I have witnessed in a theatre."
Michael Coveney *Financial Times*

70

● MOBY DICK

● MOBY DICK

2 February - 25 February 1984

THE PLOUGH AND THE STARS

by Sean O'Casey

Jack Clitheroe	LIAM NEESON
Nora Clitheroe	DEIRDRA MORRIS
Peter Flynn	FRED PEARSON
The Young Covey	CHRISTOPHER FULFORD
Bessie Burgess	VAL McLANE
Mrs Gogan	EILEEN O'BRIEN
Mollser	CATHERINE CLARKE
Fluther Good	BERNARD HILL
Lieutenant Langon	TAYLOR McAULEY
Captain Brennan	COLIN TARRANT
Corporal Stoddart	JONATHAN STRATT
Sergeant Tinley	TAYLOR McAULEY
Rosie Redmond	FRANCES LOW
A Bar Tender	GEOFFREY WILKINSON
A Woman	PAULINE JEFFERSON
The Voice	COLIN TARRANT
Director	GREGORY HERSOV
Designer	DAVID SHORT
Sound	TIM FOSTER
Lighting	PAUL W JONES
Singing supervised by	TAYLOR McAULEY

1 March - 7 April 1984

JUMPERS

by Tom Stoppard

George	TOM COURTENAY
Dotty	JULIE WALTERS
Archie	JOHN BENNETT
Bones	BARRY JACKSON
Crouch	JOHN GAY
Secretary	AMANDA ORTON
Clegthorpe	ROBERT KINGSWELL
Jumpers	BEN BENSON, STEPHEN BRIDGEN
	NORMAN COOLEY, STEVE DIXON
	INGRAM HOOD, PAUL JAYNES
	SUMAR KHAN, ROBERT KINGSWELL
Musicians	JEREMY SAMS
	JOHN ABENDSTERN
	JONATHAN DOVE
Director	NICHOLAS HYTNER
Designer	MARK THOMPSON
Lighting	MARK HENDERSON
Sound	PHIL CLIFFORD
Movement	BARRY JACKSON
	and ISABEL CROSSLEY
Music composed and arranged by	JEREMY SAMS

"The first major revival of Tom Stoppard's lunatic farce was a delight. Tom Courtenay plays George Moore, the professor of moral philosophy, with superb comic urgency and he benefits from this theatre's intimacy in the long, wonderfully entertaining speeches which comprise his tortured preparation of his lecture ... Julie Walters as his wife Dotty is absolutely first-rate, matching eccentricity and desperation in much juster proportions than did Diana Rigg at the National. Nicholas Hytner's vigorous and intelligent production lays out the play with exemplary clarity and allows you to enjoy the myriad felicities of Stoppard's invention ... Stoppard's complex sight-gags prove the greatest challenge to the in-the-round treatment, but Mr Hytner gets away with most of them and drives the evening on to a splendidly Expressionist finale."
Michael Coveney *Financial Times*

"In the original production Michael Hordern gave a memorable display of moral confusion. But Mr Courtenay, though giving us an equally funny assembly of academic tics such as knee-bends and circular hand movements, adds something crucial to the part: spiritual passion. You feel he genuinely cares about moral absolutes ... It is fine acting."
Michael Billington *The Guardian*

"... the Royal Exchange has not only done honour to a 20th century classic but also done it successfully in-the-round ... Gregory Hersov's staging is admirably smooth and finally stirring."
Eric Shorter *Daily Telegraph*

"Bernard Hill's highly comic and courageous performance as Fluther contrasted beautifully with Val McLane's magnificently angry Dublin doxy"
Patrick O'Neill *Daily Mail*

● THE PLOUGH AND THE STARS Bernard Hill

● JUMPERS Julie Walters

12 April - 12 May 1984

Cat on a Hot Tin Roof

by Tennessee Williams

Maggie	CONNIE BOOTH
Brick	JONATHAN HACKETT
Big Mamma	LIBBY MORRIS
Big Daddy	JAMES MAXWELL
Mae	PAM FERRIS
Gooper	SEAN ARNOLD
Doctor Baugh	RICHARD MAYES
Rev Tooker	ARTHUR NIGHTINGALE
Lacey	JIM LAKESON
Children:	
Dixie	KIMBERLEY WALKER/ ROSALYN EDWARDS
Trixie	ZOE CORDINGLEY/ LESLEY BELLIS
Polly	JANE REYNOLDS/ EMMA GREENHALGH
Buster	PAUL WILKINSON/ MATTHEW BARKER
Sonny	ADAM SUNDERLAND/ JOSEPH MURRAY
Director	GREGORY HERSOV
Designer	JOHANNA BRYANT
Lighting	GEOFFREY JOYCE
Sound	ERIC PRESSLEY

17 May - 23 June 1984

The Prime of Miss Jean Brodie

by Jay Presson Allen
adapted from the novel by Muriel Spark

Sponsored by
♻ National Westminster Bank

Sister Helena	MADELEINE CHRISTIE
Mr Perry	KENNETH PRICE
Photographer	BARRY STEAD
Jean Brodie	ELEANOR BRON
Sandy	VALERIE WHITTINGTON
Jenny	LUCY DURHAM MATTHEWS
Monica	AMANDA WARING
Mary	CAROLINE MILMOE
Susan	LISA EAST
Louise	RACHEL RUTTER
Schoolgirl	PIPPA LAY
Schoolgirl	KIM BENSON
Miss MacKay	MARY WIMBUSH
Gordon Lowther	HUGH ROSS
Teddy Lloyd	JAMES AUBREY
McReady	BARRY STEAD
Other Schoolgirls and Girl Guides	DEBRA GILLETT ANN RHEUBOTTOM
Director	JOHN DOVE
Designer	STEPHEN DONCASTER
Lighting	BRIAN HARRIS
Sound	PHIL CLIFFORD

"The issues raised by the book's fascinating but dangerous heroine are presented with impressive clarity in John Dove's beautiful Royal Exchange production. Eleanor Bron as the elegant Edinburgh school mistress is an unceasing delight, a treat for eye and ear ... Bron lends the part a warm humanity, an appealing delicacy, and, at the end, a surprising pathos ... every part has been perfectly cast. The six creme de la creme girls are marvels. Indeed, everything about this production is first rate."
Irene McManus *Yorkshire Post*

"Gregory Hersov's powerful production reveals (the play) for what it is: an expertly crafted, bitter melodrama ... Connie Booth plays poor Maggie with tense and brittle dignity ..."
John Peter *Sunday Times*

"Under director Gregory Hersov's restrained direction, the production grew in stature, developing into a challenging, uncompromising, weirdly entertaining, strangely charming theatrical triumph ..." Patrick O'Neill *Daily Mail*

● CAT ON A HOT TIN ROOF Jonathan Hackett

● THE PRIME OF MISS JEAN BRODIE Eleanor Bron

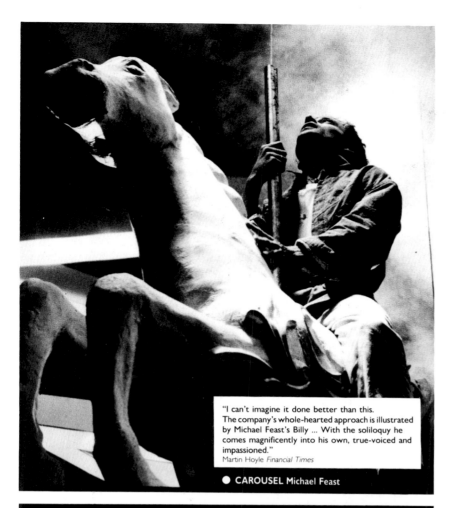

"I can't imagine it done better than this. The company's whole-hearted approach is illustrated by Michael Feast's Billy ... With the soliloquy he comes magnificently into his own, true-voiced and impassioned."
Martin Hoyle *Financial Times*

● CAROUSEL Michael Feast

3 July - 18 August 1984

Music by Richard Rodgers
Book and lyrics by Oscar Hammerstein II

Billy Bigelow	MICHAEL FEAST
Julie Jordan	JANET DIBLEY
Carrie Pipperidge	TRACIE BENNETT
Enoch Snow	RICHARD FREEMAN
Nettie Fowler	LUDMILLA ANDREW
Jigger Craigin	JONATHAN HACKETT
Mrs Mullin	DARLENE JOHNSON
David Bascombe	JAMES TOMLINSON
Arminy	BEVERLEY KLEIN
Hannah	GAYNOR SINCLAIR
Virginia	SUSAN HOLLAND
Jonathan	CHRISTOPHER BLADES
Captain	BRIAN HICKEY
Heavenly Friend	GRAHAM CALLAN
Starkeeper	BRIAN SMITH
Louise	SUE BURROWS
Carnival Boy	MICHAEL HAIGHTON
Acrobat	CHLOE LAGNADO
Enoch Snow Jnr	OLIVER BEAMISH
High School Principal	STEVE KLIGERMAN
Director	STEVEN PIMLOTT
Designer	SUE BLANE
Musical director/arranger	JEREMY SAMS
Choreographer	TERRY JOHN BATES
Lighting	GERRY JENKINSON
Sound	IAN GIBSON
Fights	PETER MacQUEEN
Circus tricks	JIM CARTER

"... great delight at the Royal Exchange, where Steven Pimlott (director) and Jeremy Sams (musical arranger) have been bold, original and affectionate with Rodgers and Hammerstein's neglected second masterpiece, in the process transforming it from a slightly luxurious operetta into the intimate, tough and tender 'musical play' Hammerstein had in mind ... The result is a triumph of intelligence and resourcefulness, simplicity and sophistication."
Michael Ratcliffe *The Observer*

● CYMBELINE Maurice Colbourne & Hugh Quarshie

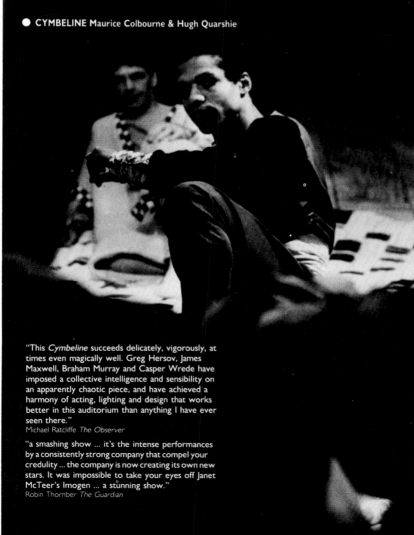

"This *Cymbeline* succeeds delicately, vigorously, at times even magically well. Greg Hersov, James Maxwell, Braham Murray and Casper Wrede have imposed a collective intelligence and sensibility on an apparently chaotic piece, and have achieved a harmony of acting, lighting and design that works better in this auditorium than anything I have ever seen there."
Michael Ratcliffe *The Observer*

"a smashing show ... it's the intense performances by a consistently strong company that compel your credulity ... the company is now creating its own new stars. It was impossible to take your eyes off Janet McTeer's Imogen ... a stunning show."
Robin Thornber *The Guardian*

13 September - 20 October 1984

CYMBELINE

by William Shakespeare

Cymbeline/Jupiter	JAMES MAXWELL
Posthumus/Cloten	HUGH QUARSHIE
Belarius/Philario/Sicilianus	MAURICE COLBOURNE
Guiderius/2nd Lord/Leonatus	RORY EDWARDS
Arviragus/1st Lord/Leonatus	MICHAEL MUELLER
Iachimo/Gaoler	ART MALIK
Caius Lucius	MICHAEL ELWYN
Pisanio	TREVOR COOPER
Cornelius	JOHN SOUTHWORTH
Queen/Mater/Soothsayer	AVRIL ELGAR
Imogen/Fidele	JANET McTEER
Helen	AMANDA DONOHOE
A Lady in Waiting	JENNI GEORGE
Roman Patrician	KEVIN DOYLE
Roman Patrician/2nd Gaoler/ Frenchman	CYRIL NRI
British Lords	ADEN GILLETT/RENNY KRUPINSKI
Directors	BRAHAM MURRAY
	GREGORY HERSOV, JAMES MAXWELL
	CASPER WREDE
Designer	STEPHEN McCABE
Lighting	MICHAEL WILLIAMS
Sound	PHIL CLIFFORD
Music composed by	CHRIS MONKS
Fight arranger	MALCOLM RANSON
Harpist	ELEANOR HUDSON
Assistant director	ELISABETH LAWLESS

1984•1985

GREAT EXPECTATIONS Art Malik & Michael Mueller

"You can expect anything of a play in which 18 performers appear as 70 different characters, don and doff 100 costumes and 30 masks, and help out with the incidental music and sound effects ... this bold new adaptation works astonishingly well."
Gerard Dempsey *Daily Express*

74

74

30 October - 8 December 1984

GREAT EXPECTATIONS
adapted from the novel by
Charles Dickens

Pip	MICHAEL MUELLER
Magwitch	NICK STRINGER
Mrs Joe/Molly	JANET McTEER
Joe	TREVOR COOPER
Compeyson	SEAN ARNOLD
Biddy	JENNI GEORGE
Estella	AMANDA DONOHOE
Miss Havisham	AVRIL ELGAR
Jaggers	WOLFE MORRIS
Sarah Pocket	AMANDA JESSIMAN
Herbert Pocket	ART MALIK
Orlick	RORY EDWARDS
Trabb	JOHN SOUTHWORTH
Trabb's boy	CYRIL NRI
Wemmick	RENNY KRUPINSKI
Startop	KEVIN DOYLE
Drummle	ADEN GILLETT
Figure	CHARLOTTE PLOWRIGHT
Other parts played by the company	
Directors	GREGORY HERSOV
	JAMES MAXWELL, BRAHAM MURRAY
	CASPER WREDE
Designer	DI SEYMOUR
Lighting	GEOFFREY JOYCE
Sound	JULIAN BEECH
Music	CHRIS MONKS
Movement and	CHRISTOPHER GABLE
choreography	and MOLLIE GUILFOYLE
Fights	MALCOLM RANSON
Percussionist	JOHN O'HARA
Assistant director	ELISABETH LAWLESS

"... the evening is continuously exciting ... there is some colourful playing – Avril Elgar's Miss Havisham, as mouldy as her wedding-cake, Wolfe Morris's Jaggers; Amanda Donohoe is properly cold and beautiful as Estella."
B A Young *Financial Times*

"... an elegant, unsentimental and brilliantly designed production. Casting a black actor as Crichton makes Barrie's imaginary Edwardian revolution both more unreal and infinitely more dangerous, and Hugh Quarshie plays the part with tense and wary dignity."
John Peter *Sunday Times*

"... it was a brilliant idea to cast a black actor, Hugh Quarshie, in the title role. The play remains a delight; and though there is no star in this inventive production the ensemble playing reaches the highest standard." Francis King *Sunday Telegraph*

THE ADMIRABLE CRICHTON Janet McTeer, Aden Gillett & Jenni George

13 December 1984 - 19 January 1985

The Admirable Crichton

by J M Barrie

Crichton	HUGH QUARSHIE
The Hon Ernest Woolley	ADEN GILLETT
Lady Agatha Lasenby	CHARLOTTE PLOWRIGHT
Lady Catherine Lasenby	AMANDA DONOHOE
Lady Mary Lasenby	JANET McTEER
The Rev John Treherne	KEVIN DOYLE
The Earl of Loam	MICHAEL CRAIG
Lord Brocklehurst	CHRISTOPHER BRAMWELL
Mrs Perkins/Countess of	
Brocklehurst	AVRIL ELGAR
Eliza ('Tweeny')	JENNI GEORGE
Monsieur Fleury	PETER BARTON
Mr Rolleston/A Naval Officer	ROBERT GARRETT
Mr Tompsett	TREVOR NELSON
Miss Fisher	CAROL NOAKES-GORMAN
Miss Simmons	SUSAN PENDLEBURY
Mademoiselle Jeanne	SUSANNA SHELLING
John	BOB WELLS
Stable Boy	DOM BOYDELL
Kitchen Wench	SHARON ROSE HILL
Directors	JAMES MAXWELL
	GREGORY HERSOV, BRAHAM MURRAY
	CASPER WREDE
Designer	JOHANNA BRYANT
Lighting	ROBERT BRYAN
Sound	ERIC PRESSLEY
Song	AKINTAYO AKINBODE
Entr'acte songs sung by	JENNI GEORGE
Assistant director	ELISABETH LAWLESS

29 January - 9 March 1985

Book and lyrics by Trevor Peacock
Music by Chris Monks and
Trevor Peacock

Mrs MacKenzie	JUDY LOE
Mr Smith/Mrs Pavitt's boyfriend	BRIAN SOUTHWOOD
Mr Barrett	COLIN PROCKTER
Mrs Thorn	ROSALIND KNIGHT
Bernard	CRISPIN LETTS
Clint	STEPHEN McGANN
Joanne	SARA SUGARMAN
Josh	IAN ROBERTS
Richmond	CYRIL NRI
Rose	JEANNE DOWNS
Tina	ELAINE LORDAN
Mr Fern	RORY EDWARDS
Mr Proudfoot/Dr Brian	STUART RICHMAN
Lennox/Ambulanceman	TIM DONNELLY/ MARTIN SADOFSKI
Sgt Hall/Mr Eastwood	ROY HEATHER
Mrs Pavitt/Ward Sister	ROBERTA KERR
Directors	GREGORY HERSOV BRAHAM MURRAY, JAMES MAXWELL CASPER WREDE
Designer	DAVID SHORT
Musical director	STEPHEN WARBECK
Choreography	FERGUS EARLY
Lighting	PAUL W JONES
Sound	PHIL CLIFFORD
Fights	MALCOLM RANSON
Assistant director	ELISABETH LAWLESS

"Trevor Peacock's *Class K* astonishingly mines an affecting musical from the depths of comprehensive education ... With neatly integrated songs it is concerned, compassionate, funny, touching."
Kenneth Hurren *The Mail on Sunday*

● CLASS K Sara Sugarman

"... the show as an entity is superb at constructing out of classroom cross chat a succession of human sculptures set to pulsating music ... there can be no real quarrel with a show that has such blissful explosions as the countryside outing, the kids climbing all over the circular theatre's structure, or the slickly fantastic hairdressing salon song. Judy Loe avoids do-gooding winsomeness, while her young mates are, without exception, brilliantly played."
Michael Coveney *Financial Times*

14 March - 6 April 1985

Long Day's Journey into Night

by Eugene O'Neill

James Tyrone	JAMES MAXWELL
Mary Cavan Tyrone	DILYS HAMLETT
James Tyrone Jnr	JONATHAN HACKETT
Edmund Tyrone	MICHAEL MUELLER
Cathleen	VICTORIA HASTED
Director	BRAHAM MURRAY
Designer	JOHANNA BRYANT
Lighting	MICHAEL WILLIAMS
Sound	PHIL CLIFFORD

"this play has provoked Miss Hamlett to a hitherto unsuspected range of desperate ferocity. The performance is beautifully graded, beginning with the nervous twitching of her swollen fingers when she feels the presence of suspicious eyes. When her suppressed feelings do burst out, as if torn up from her bowels, the effect is shocking enough to make you look away. She is superbly in command of the lines." Irving Wardle *The Times*

"The overall effect is a dramatic triumph for the Exchange." Jim Williams *Oldham Evening Chronicle*

● LONG DAY'S JOURNEY INTO NIGHT Dilys Hamlett

75

THREE SISTERS Niamh Cusack

PREMIERE OF A NEW TRANSLATION
11 April - 11 May 1985

THREE SISTERS

by Anton Chekhov
translated by Michael Frayn

Andrey Prozorov	NICHOLAS BLANE
Natasha	CHERYL PRIME
Olga	EMMA PIPER
Masha	JANET McTEER
Irina	NIAMH CUSACK
Kulygin (Fyodor)	DAVID ASHTON
Lieutenant-Colonel Vershinin	SVEN-BERTIL TAUBE
Lieutenant The Baron Tusenbach	CHRISTOPHER BRAMWELL
Junior Captain Solyony	RORY EDWARDS
Dr Chebutykin	ESPEN SKJØNBERG
Second-Lieutenant Fedotik	ADRIAN PALMER
Second-Lieutenant Rode	MARK ADDY
Ferapont	ROY HEATHER
Anfisa	HELENA McCARTHY
The Maid	JACKIE MORGAN
Beggar Boy	DAVID SMITH
Beggar Girl	CATRIN MARTIN
Officers	DAN MAXWELL
	DEREK BURRELL
Director	CASPER WREDE
Designer	DI SEYMOUR
Lighting	JEFFREY BEECROFT
Sound	IAN GIBSON
Music composed and researched by	MICK WILSON
Dances arranged by	SALLY ISERN
Assistant director	ELISABETH LAWLESS

"The new *Three Sisters* at the Royal Exchange really is the glory of the garden ... Such acting is a pleasure to watch because it's so natural and authentic ... Such performances as this fully justify the claim that this company is the National Theatre of the North."
John Peter *Sunday Times*

"If the Royal Exchange had to justify its entire existence, it could do so on the basis of this inspired and beautiful production ... Ian Gibson's stunning sound effects, including a flock of geese flying over the dome of the theatre and when combined with Jeffrey Beecroft's lighting, from spring sunshine to icy moonlight, these create moments which send shivers down one's spine. Di Seymour's superb set emphasises the sense of exile and hopeless optimism – the dining table of the Prozorov's provincial house has settings for 18. And, when the french windows are finally opened in Act 4, the panorama they reveal is of an endless grey mist."
Charlotte Keatley *Yorkshire Post*

"Wrede's marvellous production illuminates the play's every aspect ... all the cast are excellent. London could do with seeing them – it hasn't had a Chekhov production as good as this for years."
Kenneth Hurren *The Mail on Sunday*

THREE SISTERS Mark Addy, Janet McTeer & Adrian Palmer

16 May - 29 June 1985

● ENTERTAINING MR SLOAN Sylvia Syms & Adam Ant

by Joe Orton

Sloane	ADAM ANT
Kath	SYLVIA SYMS
Ed	JAMES MAXWELL
Kemp	JOHN SOUTHWORTH
Director	GREGORY HERSOV
Designer	DAVID SHORT
Lighting	PAUL W JONES
Sound	ROSALIND ELLIMAN
Fight arranger	MALCOLM RANSON

"Like its hero, *Entertaining Mr Sloane* is just over 20 years old. Unlike many scandals, both the play and its protagonist reach their majority with impact undiminished. Greg Hersov's new production for Manchester's Royal Exchange proves Sloane a child as much of the 1980s, as he was of the 1960s ... Adam Ant excells at Sloane's naive self-satisfaction."
Martin Hoyle *Financial Times*

"... a sadistic comedy of low life, directed with relish and expertise by Gregory Hersov, and designed by David Short in a style of superbly repellent working-class baroque ... The star of the show is Sylvia Syms, who gives a bravura performance as poor besotted Kath: blowsy gentility combined with middle-aged lust, teetering at the edge of sadness."
John Peter *Sunday Times*

"Adam Ant, in his first venture outside the world of pop, turned in a deft and alluring performance. But this was Sylvia Syms's night – a rare tour de force by an actress in her prime."
Patrick O'Neill *Daily Mail*

Adam Ant's performance is both believable and threatening – the sort of credibility essential to make farce funny, a grotesque acceleration of reality."
Charlotte Keatley *Yorkshire Post*

● ENTERTAINING MR SLOANE Adam Ant & James Maxwell

PREMIERE
9 July - 10 August 1985

a musical by Alan Price
based on an idea by Braham Murray,
Alan Price and Gerald Scarfe

Tom Rakewell	MICHAEL MUELLER
Sarah	ALISON THOMAS
The Fixer	ADRIAN DUNBAR
Announcer/No-Parent-Families/ Plutocrat/Editor/ Dole Queuer	BARRY MARTIN
Floor Manager/Trust-me-Trust/ Plutocrat/Prison Warder/ Married Couple	RAYMOND BRODY
Cameraman/Plutocrat/Lord Helpass's Aide-de-Camp/Journalist	BRAD GRAHAM
Assistant Cameraman/Money Collector/ Plutocrat/Policeman/ Journalist	BOB APPLEBY
The Jolly Sisters/Plutocrats/ Dignitaries	CHARLOTTE AVERY DAWN HOPE, DEENA PAYNE
Serccio Formani/Lord Helpass/ Worshipful Cashier/Master of Ceremonies	MALCOLM RENNIE
Jean Metcalf/Money Collector/ Plutocrat/Dignitary/Journalist/ Married Couple	PIPPA BOULTER
Sharon Toogood/Money Collector/ Plutocrat/Dignitary/ Journalist/Girl	RACHEL IZEN
John Harris/Lord Helpass's Aide- de-Camp/Plutocrat/Journalist/ Ex-Bank Clerk	TREVOR JONES
Albert/Money Collector/Plutocrat/ Lady Mayor/Dole Queuer	DOUGAL LEE

Director	BRAHAM MURRAY
Designer	GERALD SCARFE
Technical design adviser	STEPHEN DONCASTER
Design consultant	JOHANNA BRYANT
Orchestrations and musical supervision	DAVID FIRMAN
Choreography	GILLIAN GREGORY
Choreography assistant	BRAD GRAHAM
Lighting	ROBERT BRYAN
Sound	PHIL CLIFFORD
Musical director	KATE YOUNG

12 September - 19 October 1985

HAY FEVER

by Noel Coward

Sponsored by

♻ National Westminster Bank

Sorel Bliss	LUCY ASTON
Simon Bliss	RICHARD McCABE
Clara	ANNA WELSH
Judith Bliss	DILYS HAMLETT
David Bliss	TERENCE FRISBY
Sandy Tyrell	ADEN GILLETT
Myra Arundel	MARSHA HUNT
Richard Greatham	BOSCO HOGAN
Jackie Coryton	VICTORIA HASTED

Director	JAMES MAXWELL
Set designer	CLARE BIRKS
Costume designer	JOHAN ENGELS
Lighting	GLYN PEREGRINE
Sound	ROSALIND ELLIMAN

"a production almost stolen by Johan Engels' – sometimes literally – dazzling costumes. *Hay Fever* emerges as a tougher play than we imagined, and durably funny"
Martin Hoyle *Financial Times*

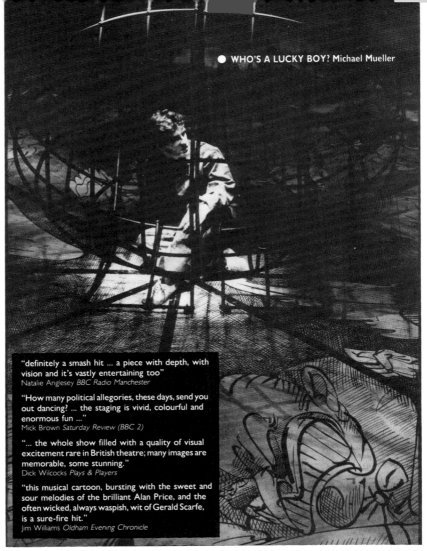

● WHO'S A LUCKY BOY? Michael Mueller

"definitely a smash hit ... a piece with depth, with vision and it's vastly entertaining too"
Natalie Anglesey *BBC Radio Manchester*

"How many political allegories, these days, send you out dancing? ... the staging is vivid, colourful and enormous fun ..."
Mick Brown *Saturday Review (BBC 2)*

"... the whole show filled with a quality of visual excitement rare in British theatre; many images are memorable, some stunning."
Dick Wilcocks *Plays & Players*

"this musical cartoon, bursting with the sweet and sour melodies of the brilliant Alan Price, and the often wicked, always waspish, wit of Gerald Scarfe, is a sure-fire hit."
Jim Williams *Oldham Evening Chronicle*

● HAY FEVER Lucy Aston

24 October - 30 November 1985

DEATH OF A SALESMAN

by Arthur Miller

Willy Loman	TREVOR PEACOCK
Linda	AVRIL ELGAR
Biff	RORY EDWARDS
Happy	COLUM CONVEY
Bernard	ROBERT CLARE
The Woman	CARMEN RODRIGUEZ
Charley	ARTHUR WHYBROW
Uncle Ben	JACK CARR
Howard Wagner	MARTIN OLDFIELD
Jenny	CECILIA EMERSON
Stanley	LORIN STEWART
Miss Forsythe	NANCY LIPPOLD
Letta	CECILIA EMERSON
Director	GREGORY HERSOV
Set designer	LAURIE DENNETT
Costume designer	STEPHEN DONCASTER
Lighting	GEOFFREY JOYCE
Sound	JULIAN BEECH
Fight adviser	MALCOLM RANSON

"a powerful production and a personal triumph for Peacock, who gave heart and soul back to what was threatening to become another theatrical pot-boiler" Patrick O'Neill *Daily Mail*

PREMIERE

5 December 1985 - 4 January 1986

Jack & the Giant

Book and lyrics by Trevor Peacock
Music by Chris Monks and Trevor Peacock
Sponsored by **Quicks for Ford**

Jack	JASON WATKINS
Mother/Giant's Wife/Figure	SALLY KNYVETTE
Tomboy/Bird/Figure	ROBIN McCAFFREY
Traveller/Butcher/Crone/ Knight	BRIAN HICKEY
Ivan/Gus/The Large Head/ Figure	MICHAEL MULKERRIN
Igor/Maurice/Giant/Fairground Person/Figure	NEIL DUNCAN
Sea Creature/Bearded Lady/ Villager/Figure	SIMON HARRISON
Dog/Stiltman/Villager/ Figure	CHRISTOPHER LEY
Singer/Foreman	HARRY BURTON
Musician/Hen	DIANNE ADDERLEY
Director	MERVYN WILLIS
Designer	DAVID SHORT
Composer and musical director	CHRIS MONKS
Choreography	GERALDINE STEPHENSON
Lighting	PAUL W JONES
Sound	TERRY JARDINE
Magic adviser	MATTHEW FREEMAN

● **DEATH OF A SALESMAN** Trevor Peacock

"Trevor Peacock is quite riveting from the very beginning, from the moment of his low key first appearance, through his frenzied journey along the roads of illusion and despair, right up to his suicide in a car crash, superbly simulated: he speeds to his doom in a bulbously large, stationary red period car swept by passing street lights, a powerful engine hammering away. The Royal Exchange's technical virtuosity is legendary."
Dick Wilcocks *Plays & Players*

79

"The Royal Exchange is stunningly good at creating the atmosphere of fantasy and magic without resorting to superficial tinsel effects. Director Mervyn Willis and designer David Short had me gasping and shrieking with delighted terror as winged statues came alive and the Giant's head swung through one entrance while his gleaming black fist shot through another and plucked his wife off the stage. Jason Watkins as Jack succeeded in evoking non-twee childhood, appealing to us to share his sense of wonder."
Charlotte Keatley *Financial Times*

● **JACK AND THE GIANT** Jason Watkins

9 January - 15 February 1986

As you like it

by William Shakespeare

Duke Senior	STUART RICHMAN
Duke Frederick	DAVID HOWEY
Amiens	WILLIAM OSBORNE
Jacques	RAAD RAWI
Le Beau	STUART RICHMAN
Charles	RICHARD FALLON
Oliver	JAMES WILBY
Jacques de Boys	WILLIAM OSBORNE
Orlando	DUNCAN BELL
Adam	DENIS CAREY
Dennis	WILLIAM OSBORNE
Touchstone	RICHARD McCABE
Sir Oliver Martext	DENIS CAREY
Corin	DAVID HOWEY
Silvius	GUY MANNING
William	RICHARD FALLON
Rosalind	JANET McTEER
Celia	SUZANNE BURDEN
Phebe	SARA SUGARMAN
Audrey	VICTORIA HASTED
Director	NICHOLAS HYTNER
Designer	DI SEYMOUR
Lighting	PAUL PYANT
Sound	JOHN A LEONARD
Music composed and arranged by	JEREMY SAMS
Fight arranger	MALCOLM RANSON

Following the run at the Royal Exchange *As You Like It* toured in the mobile touring theatre:
Lowton High School (7-12 April), Grimsby Leisure Centre (14-16 April), Newbiggin Sports and Community Centre (17-19 April), Huddersfield Sports Centre (21-23 April), Sands Centre, Carlisle (24-26 April), Whitehaven Sports Centre (28-30 April), Ellesmere Port Indoor Centre (1-3 May), Hudson Sports Centre, Wisbech (5-7 May), Bletchley Leisure Centre (8-10 May), Stratford Park Leisure Centre, Stroud (12-14 May), Crawley Leisure Centre (15-17 May)
with the following cast change:
Phebe   SARAH-JANE HOLM

"Nicholas Hytner's irresistible production, too, is brimful of vim and vigour. As we now expect of this gifted young director, it is superbly organised in this difficult but ever exciting Exchange arena ... Celia, superbly played by Suzanne Burden ... a superior Orlando to the RSC's in Duncan Bell, a truly promising young actor ... Stuart Richman is a sneering pragmatic Le Beau, one of the best I've seen ... Other knockout performances come from Raad Rawi and Richard McCabe ... (Miss McTeer's is) a performance not to be missed."
Michael Coveney *Financial Times*

"what lends the evening distinction is the unusual Rosalind of Janet McTeer. With the height and the intent, soul-searching gaze of a younger Vanessa Redgrave, this 24-year-old actress never lets us forget that being in love is a distressing plight. With her huge eyes and firm jaw, and her gift for speaking with a dazzling speed and spontaneity, her victory is always certain – except to her ... It is a bold concept, fascinating to watch because so beautifully realised." John Barber *Daily Telegraph*

"The Royal Exchange production opened in Manchester to unanimous critical acclaim. Now it takes to the road ... It is the casting of Janet McTeer and Suzanne Burden that gives it such unusually memorable freshness. As well as a strong young cast, the production is a visual gem."
Alan Jowett *Sunday Today*

● AS YOU LIKE IT Janet McTeer

RIDDLEY WALKER David Threlfall & David Meyer

"a splendid triumph of rich writing harnessed to theatrical technique. It was an inspiration to try to stage a book which fits so well with this company's concerns – with the essences of things beyond the external, with the triumph of the human spirit and with the healing magic of story telling ... Hoban succeeds brilliantly in retelling his story in dramatic, visual terms ... The visual realisation of his awesome vision is rivetting, as designer Johanna Bryant and the technical team spring on us a series of stunning surprises, from the swarming, near-naked bodies that make up the pack of dogs to superbly-crafted puppet figures for the Punch and Judy show that stands for culture. At the heart of it all is a commanding performance from David Threlfall"
Robin Thornber *The Guardian*

AN INSPECTOR CALLS Graeme Garden

"It is exactly 40 years since this play had its British premiere at Manchester's Opera House and anyone not familiar with the story has a delight in store. For everyone else there is the treat of renewed acquaintance with a superb piece of writing, thoughtfully presented with polished performances – an altogether stylish production."
Nick Nunn *Lancashire Evening Telegraph*

riddLey waLKƏR

by Russell Hoban

Riddley Walker	DAVID THRELFALL
Abel Goodparley	MALCOLM RENNIE
Erny Orfing	IAN HASTINGS
Granser	ARTHUR WHYBROW
Lissener	CYRIL NRI
Lorna/Mother Nite/Auntie	PAM FERRIS
Belnot Phist/Drop John	DAVID MEYER
Straiter Empy	EAMONN WALKER
Durster Potter	PAUL BRENNEN
Riser Partman	CARLTON CHANCE
Coxin Shoaring	HARMAGE S KALIRAI
Skyway Moaters	THOMAS BRANCH
Fister Crunchman/A Heavy	CON O'NEILL
Gerty Rundl	KATHRYN HUNTER
Minsy Wattl	LUCY SHEEN
Tangy Sasser	JOY RICHARDSON
Dissen Ants/Musician	AKINTAYO AKINBODE
Children	JASON BLOOR, DYLAN CONNOLLY
	ROBERT FENTON, SCOTT FLETCHER
	THOMAS GOODWIN, JO-ANNE GREEN
	EMMA LONGBOTTOM, LEE MILLWARD
	RACHEL TAYLOR, DAVID VICKERSTAFFE
	HELEN WILD

Director	BRAHAM MURRAY
Designer	JOHANNA BRYANT
Choreography and movement	FERGUS EARLY
Lighting	ROBERT BRYAN
Music	CHRIS MONKS
Sound	PHILIP CLIFFORD
Puppet advisor	KEITH HUBBARD
Fight arranger	MALCOLM RANSON

"An extraordinary theatrical event ... The play is harrowing, but Threlfall's vivid performance of humour and vulnerability makes it a production you must not miss."
Charlotte Keatley *Yorkshire Post*

"It's a show that will puzzle, irritate, and annoy"
Patrick O'Neill *Daily Mail*

"a triumph – I cannot recommend it highly enough"
Jim Williams *Oldham Evening Chronicle*

81

27 March - 3 May 1986

An Inspector Calls

by J B Priestley

Arthur Birling	RUSSELL ENOCH
Gerald Croft	STEVEN MANN
Sheila Birling	GERALDINE ALEXANDER
Sybil Birling	CAROL GILLIES
Edna	FLIP WEBSTER
Eric Birling	HUGH GRANT
Inspector Goole	GRAEME GARDEN

Director	RICHARD WILSON
Set designer	SAUL RADOMSKY
Costume designer	STEPHEN DONCASTER
Lighting	MICHAEL CALF
Sound	ROSALIND ELLIMAN

"The Royal Exchange production succeeds by taking the play emphatically at its own valuation. Saul Radomsky's naturalistic set – an oppressively opulent dining-room with massive mahogany table, cut-glass decanters and potted ferns – floats like a small, encumbered island adrift in space and time. Graeme Garden brings a drily meditative scepticism to the part of the Inspector, and maintains a tone of judicious thoughtfulness ... a memorably sombre production." Grevel Lindop *Times Literary Supplement*

MUMBO JUMBO Michael Grandage

PREMIERE
8 May - 31 May 1986

mumbo jumbo

by Robin Glendinning
Joint winner of the first Mobil
Playwriting Competition

82

The Dean	NIGEL STOCK
Mrs Howlett	RICHENDA CAREY
Bill Dunham	DENYS HAWTHORNE
Marion Dunham	ANNE LAWSON
Barry Dunham	MICHAEL GRANDAGE
Creaney	JOHN ELMES
Patterson	DAN GORDON
Brown	ANTHONY HEARNE
Butler	PETER RICHEY
Dunbar	DERMOTT GRAHAM

Lowry (Bobby)	DAVID ADAIR
McKenna	DAVID MICHAELS
Richards (Wombat)	MARCUS O'HIGGINS
Robinson	MAURICE DEE
Jameson	ADAM SUNDERLAND
	or JASON MOSS
Angela	SADIE FROST
Director	NICHOLAS HYTNER
Designer	MARK THOMPSON
Lighting	MARK HENDERSON
Sound	COLIN DUNCAN

"one of our most interesting new arrivals ... an original and buccaneering sensibility, full of dark humour and fearless common sense ... Glendinning writes like a cross between Wedekind and Joyce; like the best of Irish writing, his play is full of intellectual ferocity and withering humour. Nicholas Hytner's direction brings out all the strength of this tough, lithe text, the performance pulsates with adolescent puzzlement and adult rage. Nigel Stock and Michael Grandage lead an impeccable cast."
John Peter *Sunday Times*

"(An) honourable, witty, sadder and wiser new play ... Grandage and Elmes carry the weight of the play with marvellous and moving assurance"
Michael Ratcliffe *The Observer*

Mumbo Jumbo was subsequently produced at the Lyric Theatre, Hammersmith 15 May - 27 June 1987 with the following cast changes:

The Dean	ALAN McNAUGHTAN
Patterson	GERARD O'HARE
Butler	ROBERT PATTERSON
Dunbar	ALLEN McKELVEY
McKenna	JAMES DURRELL
Jameson	IAN TUCKER
Angela	KERRYANN WHITE

MUMBO JUMBO Nigel Stock

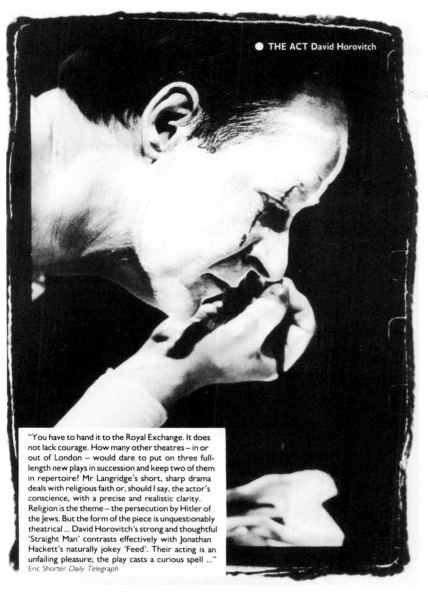

● THE ACT David Horovitch

TWO PREMIERES IN REPERTOIRE
4 June - 28 June 1986

BEHIND HEAVEN

by Jonathan Moore

Glass	JONATHAN MOORE
Speed	SHARON CHEYNE
Green	ROBERT GWILYM
Stimpson	JONATHAN STRATT
Moon	JAMES MAXWELL
Director	GREGORY HERSOV
Set designer	LAURIE DENNETT
Costume designer	GINNIE O'BRIEN
Lighting	MICHAEL CALF
Sound	CATHY DEVENISH
Assistant sound designer	NICKY MATTHEW
Technical music adviser	COLIN GODDARD
Whip instruction by	TOM CODY

The first performance of *Behind Heaven* was on Wednesday 4 June 1986

Behind Heaven transferred to the Donmar Warehouse Theatre, London 16 October - 8 November 1986

THE ACT

by Richard Langridge

Frink	DAVID HOROVITCH
Hansen	JONATHAN HACKETT
Steiner	RORY EDWARDS
Director	CASPER WREDE
Set designer	LAURIE DENNETT
Costume designer	GINNIE O'BRIEN
Lighting	MICHAEL CALF
Sound	CATHY DEVENISH
Assistant sound designer	NICKY MATTHEW
Music for the songs by	MICK WILSON

The first performance of *The Act* was on Thursday 5 June 1986

"It is a resonant piece, using powerful theatrical images – the European tradition of the socially subversive clown, the strong authoritarian imagery of the Third Reich – to telling effect. Casper Wrede's production reverberated through the big issues of church and state and race and individual responsibility" Robin Thornber *The Guardian*

83

"You have to hand it to the Royal Exchange. It does not lack courage. How many other theatres – in or out of London – would dare to put on three full-length new plays in succession and keep two of them in repertoire? Mr Langridge's short, sharp drama deals with religious faith or, should I say, the actor's conscience, with a precise and realistic clarity. Religion is the theme – the persecution by Hitler of the Jews. But the form of the piece is unquestionably theatrical ... David Horovitch's strong and thoughtful 'Straight Man' contrasts effectively with Jonathan Hackett's naturally jokey 'Feed'. Their acting is an unfailing pleasure; the play casts a curious spell ..."
Eric Shorter *Daily Telegraph*

● BEHIND HEAVEN Robert Gwilym

Behind Heaven is a black Grand Guignol for the 1980s. You don't have to be either a dogmatic anti-Thatcherite, or anti-anything, to enjoy this ebullient and uninhibited bed-sit fantasy about young drop-out couple (the author and Sharon Cheyne), transvestite policeman (Robert Gwilym) and fruity landlord (James Maxwell), spouting robust freemarket slogans. The characters talk with uninhibited relish, quoting Shakespeare and St Paul with equal facility. It's like a collaboration between Joe Orton and Rowan Atkinson." John Peter *Sunday Times*

"Director Gregory Hersov's production is sharply etched, neatly capturing the farce and the pain. All the performances are good but I particularly liked James Maxwell's immaculately groomed, wheelchair bound landlord, offering encyclopaedic knowledge and watching with cool detachment as his henchman gets to work with the drill and whip."
Alan Hulme *Manchester Evening News*

COURT IN THE ACT! Gabrielle Drake & Michael Denison

BRITISH PREMIERE
3 July - 9 August 1986

COURT IN THE ACT!

a farce by Maurice Hennequin and Pierre Veber translated and adapted by Robert Cogo-Fawcett and Braham Murray

Tricointe	MICHAEL DENISON
Pinglet/Marius	ARTHUR WHYBROW
La Moulain/Bienassis	COLIN PROCKTER
Bouquet des Ifs/Poche	TREVOR COOPER
Denise	MAGGIE O'NEILL
Aglae	AVRIL ELGAR
Sophie/Juliette	LISA HOLLANDER
Gobette	GABRIELLE DRAKE
Cyprien	LEE MONTAGUE
Octave	TERENCE WILTON
Francois/Dominique	ROY HEATHER
Angelina	MARGARET NORRIS
Workmen	DAN MAXWELL
	CHRISTOPHER SEED
Director	BRAHAM MURRAY
Set designer	STEPHEN DONCASTER
Costume designer	TERENCE EMERY
Lighting	GEOFFREY JOYCE
Song by	CHRIS MONKS

"even funnier (than *Have You Anything to Declare?*) ... an entertainment of classical complexity, clarity and breathless charm at which I laughed so much I nearly fell into the setting by Stephen Doncaster which fills this arena ingeniously ... the evening is a triumph of teamwork with just the right degree of intense anxiety in the playing ... Apart from the magnificent Mr Denison, there are richly observed performances from the delectable Miss Drake (flighty fugitive from the Moulin Rouge), Miss Elgar (dowdily devoted to polishing anything brass in sight), and Lee Montague (Parisian big-wig highly susceptible to women) ... it is too good to stay in Manchester." Eric Shorter *Daily Telegraph*

"From Pinero to Brighouse, the Royal Exchange Company have made several successful gambles on long-forgotten farces, and in this – their second flutter on the Parisian duo of Hennequin and Veber – they have again struck lucky." Irving Wardle *The Times*

Following a tour to the Yvonne Arnaud Theatre Guildford (21 January - 7 February), Theatre Royal Bath (9 - 21 February), Grand Theatre Wolverhampton (23 - 28 February), Theatre Royal York (2 - 7 March), Theatre Royal Brighton (9 - 14 March), New Theatre Hull (16 - 21 March), New Theatre Cardiff (23 - 28 March) and the Ashcroft Theatre Croydon (30 March - 4 April), *Court in the Act!* transferred to the Phoenix Theatre London 21 April - 29 August 1987 with the following changes:

Pinglet/Marius	DEREK SMITH
Denise	OONA KIRSCH
Workmen	JONATHAN PRINCE
	ANTONY ERSKINE

"Some of the best performed farce currently to be seen in London ... Mr Murray's exuberant treatment of this silly, entirely charming concoction is a model of verve and élan, tight, precise and fleet. Miss Drake's coquette is perfection, an enchanting combination of wide-eyed romance and practical lechery ... Mr Denison and Mr Montague, each jiggling on the spot in wretched little fandangos of anxious futility, extract each and every legitimate laugh with the assurance of many years experience. Miss Elgar is wonderful, and the rest of the cast support admirably." Robin Ray *Punch*

"Our great theatre companies normally do this sort of thing so clumsily that the chief pleasure of Murray's Royal Exchange production is that it is so fresh, fast, light and dry. Mugging is almost banished and sight-gags come second to sustaining the show's translucent buoyancy and speed. Denison of the anguished boom leads a first-rate ensemble." Michael Ratcliffe *The Observer*

COURT IN THE ACT! Gabrielle Drake

Photo: Zoe Dominic

"James Maxwell's tactic as director is the right one: let the villains be laughable and have Tim Healy play Zack as the untidy pony every little girl wants to comfort. He shuffles, he retreats, but the hint that there is some method in his slow-wittedness gathers the audience's affection."
Jeremy Kingston *The Times*

● ZACK Tim Healy

TENTH ANNIVERSARY PRODUCTION
11 September – 18 October 1986

ZACK
by Harold Brighouse

Mrs Munning	BRIDGET TURNER
Sally Teale	KAREN HENTHORN
Paul Munning	JOHN FLANAGAN
Virginia Cavender	KAREN DRURY
Zachariah Munning	TIM HEALY
Martha Wrigley	SARA RICHARDSON
James Abbott	MARK CHATTERTON
Joe Wrigley	JACK CARR
Thomas Mowatt	STUART GOLLAND
Harry Shoebridge	MARTIN OLDFIELD
Director	JAMES MAXWELL
Set designer	DAVID MILLARD
Costume designer	MICHAEL HOLT
Lighting	GLYN PEREGRINE
Dialect coach	IAN HASTINGS

"This engaging new production, directed by James Maxwell, has so much charm and polish ... The charm comes largely from Tim Healy's performance as the amiable buffoon Zachariah Munning ... The polish comes from a consistently strong company – especially Bridget Turner's glacial mother and a wickedly Fawlty brother from John Flanagan – and from meticulously evocative settings ... it's fun"
Robin Thornber *The Guardian*

23 October – 22 November 1986

EDWARD the second
by Christopher Marlowe

Piers de Gaveston	MICHAEL GRANDAGE
King Edward II	IAN McDIARMID
Edmund, Earl of Kent	PETER WIGHT
Lancaster/Abbot of Neath	MICHAEL HUGHES
Mortimer the Elder/	
Leicester	JOHN SOUTHWORTH
Mortimer the Younger	DUNCAN BELL
Warwick/Sir Thomas Berkeley	DAVID HOWEY
Pembroke/Rice Ap Howell	STUART GOLLAND
Bishop of Coventry/	
Spencer the Elder	LEONARD MAGUIRE
Archbishop of Canterbury/	
Arundel	GEOFFREY BANKS
Queen Isabella	BRID BRENNAN
Baldock	COLIN McFARLANE
Spencer the Younger	IAIN GLEN
Lady Margaret de Clare	KAREN HENTHORN
Prince Edward,	ALEX HAIG/
later King Edward III	ADAM SUNDERLAND
Matrevis/James	ADRIAN PALMER
Gurney/Levune	SEAN BLOWERS
Lightborn	LOUIS HILYER
Director	NICHOLAS HYTNER
Designer	TOM CAIRNS
Music	JEREMY SAMS
Lighting	MARK HENDERSON
Sound	COLIN DUNCAN
Italian Masque written and	
staged by	MARTIN DUNCAN
Fight arranger	MALCOLM RANSON
Assistant designers	NICKY GILLIBRAND
	JOHN LEDLEY

85

● EDWARD THE SECOND Ian McDiarmid & Michael Grandage

"McDiarmid's performance, steely, dignified and moving, shows us a kingly figure who is destroyed because he cannot choose. ... one of the finest performances I've seen in this theatre."
John Peter *Sunday Times*

"the most visionary theatre I have seen all year ... It is to the Royal Exchange's credit that they have created a team to rival anything in British theatre today." David Roper *Plays & Players*

"One of the year's outstanding theatrical events: a superb staging of the first English chronicle play that is as modern and outrageous as anything you might devise by mixing early Shakespeare with Joe Orton ... Designed by Tom Cairns and lit by Mark Henderson, Marlowe's world and this remarkable vision of it sucks us in, from the planetary sky hung like a huge tympanum from the roof (a descending lightbulb firmament and terrific rainstorm) to a muddy charnel house below, the grim vaults of Berkeley Castle where the skilled murderer Lightborn entwines his regal prey in a scene, unparalleled in British drama, of lewd murderousness ... This intelligent, brave and generous revival..."
Michael Coveney *Financial Times*

WOUNDINGS Reece Dinsdale & Leslee Udwin

27 November - 13 December 1986

WOUNDINGS≋

by Jeff Noon

Sponsored by M⊙bil

Sergeant-Major Taylor	GEORGE SWEENEY
Private Stanley Jardine	BRIAN BINNS
Private Douglas Briggs	BRENDAN PRICE
Private Jimmy Compton	REECE DINSDALE
Vivienne	LUCINDA CURTIS
Angela	MALINDI O'RORKE
Colonel Chadwick-Brown/	
Adam	MICHAEL GODLEY
Denise Jones	TRACEY WILKINSON
Kim Patterson	MAGGIE SAUNDERS
Louise Brooks	LESLEE UDWIN
The Prince	SIMON GREENALL
Soldiers	SIMON GREENALL, TOM BUTCHER
	WILLIAM IVORY, PETER FAULKENER
Dan	PETER FAULKENER
Benny	WILLIAM IVORY
Director	GREGORY HERSOV
Set designer	LAURIE DENNETT
Costume designer	ELLEN CAIRNS
Lighting	MICHAEL CALF
Sound	JULIAN BEECH
Fight arranger	MALCOLM RANSON
Army drill	DAVID WILLIAMSON

"Even if it was not a first play by a new writer, Jeff Noon's Mobil prize-winner would still be a startlingly original and powerful piece of theatre. In this context, it's sensational – a genuine discovery of a strong new talent ... His work has the fluid structure of a television or screen play – an epic scale, with 46 scenes and 25 characters, yet it's as emotionally intimate and intricate as a chamber concert ... It sounds, and is, strange but it all makes astringent sense. And it's vividly envisaged and realised in Greg Hersov's spellbinding production."
Robin Thornber *The Guardian*

"*Woundings* is set on an island garrison, where the ratio of 4,000 soldiers to 20 local girls is alleviated by a shipment of English roses. Mr Noon's island is bleak, a setting for warfare between the sexes, and his language is, therefore, blunt, characters speaking what would be subconscious in everyday courtship. ... This is writing of tremendous emotional honesty and ambitious imagination."
Charlotte Keatley *Financial Times*

18 December 1986 - 24 January 1987

the Country Wife

by William Wycherley

Mr Horner	GARY OLDMAN
A Quack	SEAN BLOWERS
A Boy	PATRICK HENRY
Sir Jaspar Fidget	DAVID HOWEY
My Lady Fidget	SHEILA BALLANTINE
Mrs Dainty Fidget	LINDA GARDNER
Mr Harcourt	DUNCAN BELL
Mr Dorilant	ADRIAN PALMER
Mr Sparkish	ALEX JENNINGS
Mr Pinchwife	IAN McDIARMID
Mrs Margery Pinchwife	CHERYL CAMPBELL
Mrs Alithea	KAREN DRURY
Mrs Squeamish	TRICIA MORRISH
Lucy (Alithea's Maid)	DELIA CORRIE
Old Lady Squeamish	ROSALIE WILLIAMS
Musicians	JULIA SINGLETON
	SANDY BURNETT
	NATASHA HOLMES
Director	NICHOLAS HYTNER
Designer	MARK THOMPSON
Music composed and arranged by	JEREMY SAMS
Lighting	PAUL PYANT
Sound	COLIN DUNCAN
Movement	LESLEY HUTCHINSON
Assisted by	WENDY HOUSTOUN

"There seems to be no holding Manchester's Royal Exchange Theatre Company ... an audacious, vital and abrasive production of Wycherley's comedy of cuckoldry that draws parallels between the Restoration and our own times. The result is engrossing, provocative and thoroughly exhilarating ... Gary Oldman is an intense Horner of repressed energy and pent-up intensity ... Cheryl Campbell's lovably bucolic Margery is an innocent sensualist, as

THE COUNTRY WIFE Linda Gardner, Tricia Morrish, Sheila Ballantine & Gary Oldman

● THE COUNTRY WIFE Cheryl Campbell & Ian McDiarmid

yet lacking Horner's cunning but his match in physical energy ... Ian McDiarmid's virtuoso comic performance prances, coos, snarls, snaps at the audience and leaves one uncomfortably aware that Margery is lumbered with a bully as well as a buffoon." Martin Hoyle *Financial Times*

"Cheryl Campbell gives a hair-raising display of rustic innocence igniting like a bonfire. She has an extraordinary repertory of growls, squawks, and involuntary sensual gurgles conveying each new discovery of the town's delights. But she still has her toys; taking out her frustration on a rag doll, and lining up a table full of soft animals for Pinchwife to dismember at the height of his fury. There are some great comedies that kill laughter stone dead." Irving Wardle *The Times*

"Cheryl Campbell as Margery Pinchwife, flops, flutters, gurgles and bounds in a full chintzy dress like a delicious silly doll ... Campbell's gorgeously funny and sexy performance manages the brief pathos of the moment as securely as every other aspect of the role – enthusiasm, impetuousness, honesty, indignation and sheer fun." Michael Ratcliffe *The Observer*

"Magical too are the choreography, the scene changes, the music; the play is charged with eroticism and wit by a production which, for all the mixing of registers, anachronisms and cuts, is as true as can be to the themes and language of the original ... a wicked, wonderful evening."
Michael Schmidt *The Independent*

● A WHOLLY HEALTHY GLASGOW Tom Watson & Gerard Kelly

PREMIERE
29 January - 14 February 1987

A WHOLLY HEALTHY GLASGOW

by Iain Heggie

Donald Dick	TOM WATSON
Charley Hood	GERARD KELLY
Murdo Caldwell	PAUL HIGGINS
Director	RICHARD WILSON
Designer	SUE PLUMMER
Lighting	PAUL PYANT
Sound	ROSALIND ELLIMAN

A Wholly Healthy Glasgow transferred to the Church Hill Theatre, Edinburgh 10-22 August 1987 as part of the Edinburgh International Festival and to the Royal Court Theatre, London 28 January - 27 February 1988. A BBC Scotland television production with the same cast and director was shown on BBC1 on 16 February 1988

"Iain Heggie's rich, unpredictable comedy was a Mobil prize winner in 1985 ... original inventive and joyful ... the funniest play I have seen for months." Jeremy Kingston *The Times*

"a comedy that is sharp with Glesca atmosphere, exuberant with street corner wit and guile ... a highly individual, bold play, from a very assured new writer." Mary Brennan, *Glasgow Herald*

"a sensual celebration of the richness and vitality of the tough, telling Glaswegian way with English. Iain Heggie revels in a heightened form of the low language of the back alley, which might be upsetting to those of a delicate disposition, but its vigour is irresistible." Robin Thornber *The Guardian*

"One of the funniest plays of recent years ... Heggie assimilates the Chicago techniques of David Mamet and turns them to gloriously Glaswegian effect. The language is extraordinary: not for its violence, which is not exceptional, but for its subtlety and its insanely expressive syntax, which are. An apparently blunt instrument, the dialogue cuts into paradox, swagger and self-defence as keenly as a surgeon's knife ... The play is acted to blistering and sly perfection." Michael Ratcliffe *The Observer*

"The Mobil Playwriting Competition has struck oil again ... a funny as well as a rude play; it signals the arrival of a highly individual new voice." Martin Hoyle *Financial Times*

19 February - 28 March 1987

The Alchemist

by Ben Jonson

Sponsored by PRUDENTIAL

Face	JONATHAN HACKETT
Subtle	MICHAEL FEAST
Dol Common	ALYSON SPIRO
Dapper	TERENCE BEESLEY
Abel Drugger	IAN HASTINGS
Epicure Mammon	NICK STRINGER
Surly	RORY EDWARDS
Ananias	MATTHEW ZAJAC
Tribulation	ROY SAMPSON
Kastril	LOUIS HILYER
Dame Pliant	SALLIE-ANNE FIELD
Lovewit	MICHAEL GODLEY
Neighbour/Officer	MICHAEL CHRISTOPHER
Neighbour/Parson	MARK ALEXANDER

Neighbours also played by about 20 amateur actors

Director	GREGORY HERSOV
Set designer	LAURIE DENNETT
Costume designer	DAVID SHORT
Lighting	MICHAEL CALF
Sound	TERRY JARDINE
Fight arranger	MALCOLM RANSON

The Alchemist subsequently went on a tour, sponsored by Prudential, in the mobile touring theatre to:
Broomfields Leisure Centre, Warrington (31 March - 2 April); Ellesmere Port Indoor Centre (3 - 7 April); Whitehaven Sports Centre (8 - 11 April); Huddersfield Sports Centre (13 - 16 April); Carn Brea Leisure Centre, Redruth (24 - 28 April); Herringthorpe Leisure Centre, Rotherham; (30 April - 2 May); Grimsby Leisure Centre (5 - 8 May); Washington Leisure Centre (9 - 13 May); Newbiggin Sports and Community Centre (14 - 16 May); Hudson Sports Centre, Wisbech (18 - 19 May); Bunyan Recreation Centre, Bedford (20 - 23 May)

---

2 April - 16 May 1987

THE MERCHANT OF VENICE

by William Shakespeare

Antonio	MALCOLM RENNIE
Salerio	SIMON GREENALL
Solanio	CHRIS LANG
Bassanio	ALAN PARNABY
Lorenzo	GERARD LOGAN
Gratiano	MICHAEL CROMPTON
Portia	HARRIET WALTER
Nerissa	DONA CROLL
Shylock	ESPEN SKJØNBERG
Prince of Morocco/Balthasar	TONY PORTACIO
Launcelot Gobbo	RENNY KRUPINSKI
Old Gobbo/Duke of Venice/Tubal	ROGER SWAINE
Jessica	JOANNA FOSTER
Prince of Arragon/Stephano/ Gaoler	DAVID BECALIK

Director	BRAHAM MURRAY
Designer	DI SEYMOUR
Lighting	PAUL PYANT
Music	CHRIS MONKS

"The Big Bang meets the Bard head-on in this quality updating; business suits and word processors are the trappings of Braham Murray's minimalist production. Espen Skjønberg's Shylock is remarkable; avoiding caricature despite accentuating the moneylender's more despicable facets ... a production not to be missed." Guy Nelson *The Independent*

"The remarkable Norwegian actor Espen Skjønberg plays Shylock as an urbane, jovial old gentleman who at first sight seems to ooze with charm. But this is not simply a mask which he drops in private: this man has clearly absorbed and withstood a lot of hostility and he has built himself a core of confidence, even dignity, which stays with him to the end. And his great duel with Walter's sombre, steely Portia is among the most thrilling I have seen."
John Peter *Sunday Times*

● THE ALCHEMIST Michael Feast & Jonathan Hackett

"One of the best performances of a Ben Jonson play I've ever seen. Hersov's production brings it off superbly. He has a first class Epicure Mammon in Nick Stringer, a gross middle-aged cherub; and Face and Subtle are played by Jonathan Hackett and Michael Feast with athletic force and a chameleon range of impersonation. Laurie Dennett's set is simple, flamboyantly imaginative and functional. This is work on National Theatre level, both in content and standard." John Peter *Sunday Times*

"Fast, furious, physical and funny, Gregory Hersov's production of *The Alchemist* continues the Royal Exchange's run of hits." Martin Hoyle *Financial Times*

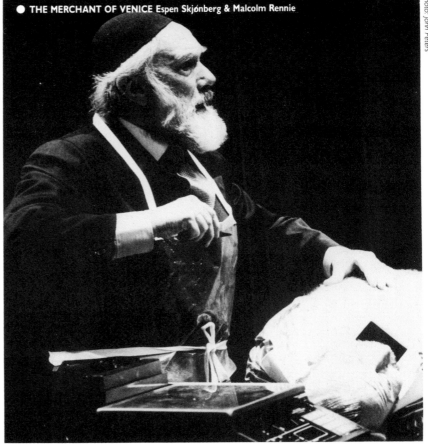

● THE MERCHANT OF VENICE Espen Skjønberg & Malcolm Rennie

Photo: John Peters

● OEDIPUS AT COLONUS Rohan McCullough & Eleanor Bron

Photo: Ian Woollams

● OEDIPUS AT COLONUS David Threlfall & Espen Skjønberg

Photo: Ian Woollams

100TH PRODUCTION

PREMIERE OF NEW TRANSLATION
21 May - 20 June 1987

OEDIPUS

Sophocles' *Oedipus the King* and
Oedipus at Colonus
translated by Christopher Stace

OEDIPUS THE KING
Oedipus, King of Thebes	DAVID THRELFALL
Creon	MICHAEL N HARBOUR
Tiresias	CHRISTOPHER GOOD
Boy	DANIEL LOWE/ANNA GOODERE
Jocasta, Queen of Thebes	ELEANOR BRON
Messenger from Corinth	MALCOLM RENNIE
Old Shepherd	ESPEN SKJØNBERG
Antigone	KIMBERLEY WALKER/ ANNA SOUTHWARD
Ismene	DANIEL LOWE/ANNA GOODERE

OEDIPUS AT COLONUS
Oedipus	DAVID THRELFALL
Antigone	ROHAN McCULLOUGH
A Stranger	MALCOLM RENNIE
Ismene	ELEANOR BRON
Theseus, King of Athens	ESPEN SKJØNBERG
Creon	MICHAEL N HARBOUR
Polynices	CHRISTOPHER GOOD

In both plays:
Leader of the Chorus	JOHN WATTS
Chorus	SUSANNE FORSTER, JULIAN FORSYTH ELAINE HALLAM, SEETA INDRANI COLIN MARSH, DAVID J NICHOLLS CAROL NOAKES, KAREN PARKER DAVID STRAUN, LEONARD WEBSTER
Soldiers	SUSAN CLEAVER STEPHEN COOGAN MILES HARVEY NICK MAYNARD
Musicians	CHRIS MONKS AKINTAYO AKINBODE JOHN O'HARA
Director	CASPER WREDE
Designer	JOHANNA BRYANT
Music	CHRIS MONKS
Choreography and movement direction	FERGUS EARLY
Lighting	JEFFREY BEECROFT
Sound	PHILIP CLIFFORD

89

"Something remarkable is currently happening at the Royal Exchange: a powerful and moving Sophoclean double-bill presented under the title of *Oedipus*. At a time when so many regional theatres, fatally under-subsidised; are forced to play safe, it is exhilarating to find the Royal Exchange celebrating its 100th Production by offering us a pair of downright masterpieces ... It is a thrilling production that reminds us of the indispensability of the Royal Exchange." Michael Billington *Country Life*

"a triumphant Oedipus ... Christopher Stace's new translation dusts down the text and makes it bright, brisk, strong and accessible ... the director and his production team succeed in creating an intensely vivid, primitive world of myth ... David Threlfall's performance as Oedipus carries the audience on to levels of thought and emotion that most of us, without this spellbinding shared experience of sensuality, might shy away from. He ranges through the extremities of existence, the heights of anger and depths of despair, and takes us with him until we too are drained." Robin Thornber *The Guardian*

Casper Wrede's magnificent production ... No other production has showed me so clearly that Greek tragedy was both a local and a communal event. The Chorus sing and dance, and Fergus Early's choreography is clearly based on Greek village dances without being fake folklore. The atmosphere is both primitive and poetic: we are in simple communities, not far from savagery, where the presence of the supernatural is immediate and intensely felt. The constant interaction of song and the spoken word emphasises the ritual quality of the plays". John Peter *Sunday Times*

● THE BLUEBIRD OF UNHAPPINESS Trevor Peacock & John Bennett

Photo: Donald Cooper

"A slickly presented series of Woody Allen off-cuts from the New Yorker and elsewhere, featuring the familiar Allen anxieties about sex, death, religion and culture." Robert Hewison *Sunday Times*

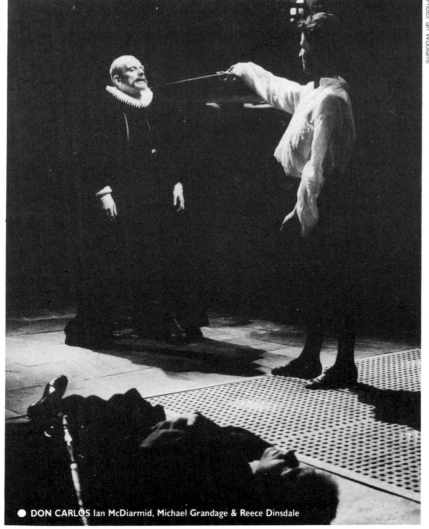

Photo: Ian Woollams

● DON CARLOS Ian McDiarmid, Michael Grandage & Reece Dinsdale

30 June - 8 August 1987

THE BLUEBIRD OF UNHAPPINESS

A Woody Allen Revue
adapted by John Lahr
Music by Stanley Silverman

Ben Kaddish, Executioner, Virgil Ives, Rabbi, Cezanne, Kugelmass, Death, Father, Rabbi, Rapkin, Rabbi Wiseman, Sgt Reed   JOHN BENNETT
Flossie, Sarah, Mrs Rifkin, Jewish Lady, Daphne, Emily, Lady Critic   PAM FERRIS
Kaiser Lupowitz, Agathon, Gauguin, Rabbi, Father O'Brien, Maitre d', Shirt Seller   DEREK GRIFFITHS
Sherri, Emma Bovary, Connie, Heather Butkiss, Claire Rosenweig   HAYDN GWYNNE
Sgt Holmes, Messenger, Guard, Scholar, Dr Mandel, John Chasen, Narrator, Chicago Phil, 2nd Mafia
       IAN HASTINGS
Salesman, Simmias, Isaac, Lautrec, Harold Cohen, Plotkin, Sony seller, Manager, 1st Mafia
       TEDDY KEMPNER
Word Babcock, Orthodox Rabbi, Socrates, Abraham, Van Gogh, Persky, Nat, Actor, Uncle Marty, Schwartz, Pope   TREVOR PEACOCK

Director	BRAHAM MURRAY
Lyrics	JOHN LAHR
Set designer	JOHANNA BRYANT
Costume designer	TERENCE EMERY
Musical director	MICHAEL DIXON
Movement	ANTHONY VAN LAAST
Lighting	MICHAEL CALF
Sound	PHILIP CLIFFORD

"its jokes tend to fall into one of four categories. The first is the Jewish joke, the second the psychoanalyst joke, the third the death joke, and the fourth the joke in which the opposed excitements of intellectual and sexual discovery are piquantly equated. In all these, the adapter, John Lahr, has come up with some lovely pieces ... so much is hilarious ... Braham Murray has directed such versatile performers as Trevor Peacock, John Bennett, Haydn Gwynne and Derek Griffiths with unremitting verve."
Francis King *Sunday Telegraph*

"Brilliant stuff, and brilliantly staged."
Eric Shorter *Daily Telegraph*

10 September - 10 October 1987

DON CARLOS

by Friedrich von Schiller
translated by James Maxwell

Supported by the Goethe-Institut, Manchester

Don Carlos	MICHAEL GRANDAGE
Domingo	PETER LAIRD
Marquis of Posa	REECE DINSDALE
Elisabeth of Valois	VIRGINIA GREIG
Princess of Eboli	MELINDA McGRAW
Marchioness of Mondecar	MELANIE THAW
Duchess of Olivarez	DELIA CORRIE
King Philip II of Spain	IAN McDIARMID
Duke of Alva	PETER CARTWRIGHT
Count of Lerma	JOHN SOUTHWORTH
Duke of Feria	JOHN PICKLES
Don Raimundo da Taxis	RON McCORMICK
Henarez	ADRIAN ROSS-MEGENTY
Prior of the Carthusian Monastery	
	ANTHONY WINGATE
Duke of Medina Sidonia	RANDAL HERLEY
Prince of Parma	TOM HIGGINS
Don Luis Mercado	ANTHONY WINGATE
The Grand Inquisitor	JAMES MAXWELL
Soldiers/Monks	NICHOLAS GLEAVES
	JONATHAN PEMBROKE

Director	NICHOLAS HYTNER
Designer	RICHARD HUDSON
Music	JEREMY SAMS
Lighting	NICK CHELTON
Sound	PHILIP CLIFFORD
Wigs/Make-up	MICHAEL WARD
Assistant to the director	TOBY JONES

"a blazing majestic production of Don Carlos by Nicholas Hytner. It unfolds with a sense of high, flamboyant theatricality." John Peter *Sunday Times*

"In James Maxwell's unobtrusively brilliant new translation, it emerged as a very great play indeed ... Mr Maxwell himself supplied a towering, chillingly implacable Inquisitor ... an absolutely riveting evening in the theatre." Rodney Milnes *Opera*

"One performance in particular rises heroically to the challenge: Ian McDiarmid's Philip II. Mr McDiarmid is a technically astonishing actor who sometimes seems a little enthralled by his own Olivier-like virtuosity. But here he creates a real character – a lonely autocrat surrounded by yea-sayers and plotters – who makes every line he utters cut like acid through metal ... a memorable piece of acting." Michael Billington *Country Life*

"*Don Carlos* is a long play with-out a single longueur. McDiarmid has the dramatic and vocal range to open every irony in Schiller's text and he retains the essential formal majesty of the role even in the harrowing scenes of recognition and defeat. At the end of the evening, I was convinced that one destiny of the Royal Exchange is to rescue Schiller from the opera house. I hope this wonderful production will lead to others." Michael Schmidt *The Independent*

Photo: Ian Woollams

● DON CARLOS Virginia Greig & Ian McDiarmid

15 October - 14 November 1987

A DOLL'S HOUSE

by Henrik Ibsen
translated by Michael Meyer

Week of 2-7 November sponsored by IBM United Kingdom Trust IBM

Nora Helmer	BRENDA BLETHYN
Porter	TOM HIGGINS
Torvald Helmer	DAVID HOROVITCH
Helen, the maid	DEBBIE BOWERS
Mrs Linde	ANGELA MORANT
Nils Krogstad	STRUAN RODGER
Dr Rank	DAVID ALLISTER
Anne-Marie, the nurse	ANNA WELSH
Children	BEN CHOYCE, KRISTIAN BENTHAM
	DAVID LLOYD, WARREN BENTHAM
	AMY SCRZPAZAK, JOANNE BURGESS

Director	GREGORY HERSOV
Designer	MICHAEL HOLT
Lighting	GLYN PEREGRINE
Sound	NICKY MATTHEW
Movement director	JACKY LANSLEY
Music adviser	PATRICK BRIDGMAN

"Brenda Blethyn's Nora is an irresistable, glittering portrayal. She gives Nora a teasing blend of naivety, cunning, innocent selfishness and impulsive warmth: we are constantly fascinated by her mobility of countenance, the guileless way emotions follow each other across her face, as she first tries to conceal, and then comes to boast about, the debt she has contracted for her husband's sake, keen to preserve her dignity but longing to impress Christine Linde, who seems to know so much more about the 'real' world." Grevel Lindop *Plays & Players*

"Gregory Hersov's fine revival ... very moving." Eric Shorter *Daily Telegraph*

● A DOLL'S HOUSE Brenda Blethyn

Photo: John Peters

"Brenda Blethyn's performance as Nora triumphantly overwhelms ... Effectively she performs two roles. Her performance as the pampered bride and as the born-again new woman are breath-takingly convincing ... She dances the Tarantella with a panic-stricken energy like a newly caged bird discovering the bars."
Ian Williams *The Independent*

19 November - 12 December 1987

LOOT

by Joe Orton

McLeavy	BERNARD GALLAGHER
Fay	SUSAN TRACY
Hal	STEPHEN McGANN
Dennis	PATRICK FIELD
Inspector Truscott	PATRICK BARLOW
Meadows	ADRIAN LOCHHEAD
Director	PAUL UNWIN
Designer	DAVID MILLARD
Lighting	JOHN A WILLIAMS
Sound	ROSALIND ELLIMAN
Music	STEPHEN WARBECK
Fight arranger	NICHOLAS HALL

"Patrick Barlow as the abrupt Inspector Truscott, sloping about the stage, serves Orton well. ... his movement and his variable diction, mixing accents and registers, are masterly. Susan Tracy as Fay, the murdering Irish nurse, comely in her late patient's black dress, is plausible and seductive."
Michael Schmidt *The Independent*

17 December 1987 - 30 January 1988

The Cabinet Minister

by Arthur Wing Pinero
Supported by the Angels of the Royal Exchange

Brooke Twombley	CHRIS LANG
Probyn	RANDAL HERLEY
Hon. Mrs Gaylustre	HAYDN GWYNNE
Valentine White	DAVID MORRISSEY
Lady Euphemia Vibart	ABIGAIL BOND
Rt. Hon. Sir Julian Twombley GCMG MP	FRANK THORNTON
Lady Kitty Twombley	SUSAN FLEETWOOD
Imogen Twombley	MELANIE THAW
Dowager Countess of Drumdurris	DILYS HAMLETT
Egidia, Countess of Drumdurris	SUSANNAH HITCHING
Keith, Earl of Drumdurris	BILL BRITTEN
Lady Macphail	JULIA McCARTHY
Sir Colin Macphail of Ballocheevin	MALCOLM RENNIE
Mr Melton	TIMOTHY DYNEVOR
Angele	DANIELLE ALLAN
Joseph Lebanon	PHILLIP WALSH
The Munkittrick	RANDAL HERLEY
Miss Munkittrick	DANIELLE ALLAN
Director	BRAHAM MURRAY
Set designer	JOHANNA BRYANT
Costume designer	TERENCE EMERY
Lighting	ROBERT BRYAN
Sound	PHILIP CLIFFORD
Choreography	SUZANNE HYWEL

"it is a lovely, funny play, while its craftmanship, swagger and cut are superb ... Clothes are always important here, and in plays of this kind. Terence Emery sets up clashing vulgarities in silk shades of summer pudding, mulberry tartan, cinnamon, peacock and gold lace, above which feathered aigrettes tremble like the antennae of society dowsing for rich prospects, a fat marriage and, at least, a bearable man. Braham Murray directs with secure lightness and Susan Fleetwood invests the hysterical Kitty with single-minded energy and zeal."
Michael Ratcliffe *The Observer*

"Here is a real find: a vintage Pinero farce of manifest financial topicality, relaunched in what seems to be its first major revival since 1890. Braham Murray has directed a winner." Irving Wardle *The Times*

Photo: John Peters

● LOOT Patrick Barlow

"Patrick Barlow's portrayal of the demon investigator, Inspector Truscott, is a masterpiece of comic movement, all stiff shoulders, glaring eyes and twitching moustache ... Catch it if you can; its wicked, but very funny." Judy Meewezen *Yorkshire Post.*

● THE CABINET MINISTER Susan Fleetwood & Frank Thornton

Photo: Ian Woollams

● AMERICAN BAGPiPES Tom Mannion & Eliza Langland

Photo: Ian Woollams

"a savagely Beano comedy of manners and mores ...
it is a startling, sparkling piece about the way that
fractured language reflects fractured relationships —
and it's given a sparky production here, with cannily
knowing performances." Robin Thornber *The Guardian*

PREMIERE
4 February - 20 February 1988

AMERICAN BAGPIPES

by Iain Heggie

Sandra Michigan	ELIZA LANGLAND
Rena Nauldie	EILEEN NICHOLAS
Patrick Nauldie	TOM MANNION
Willie Nauldie	CAMPBELL MORRISON
Director	CASPER WREDE
Designer	GEOFF ROSE
Lighting	VINCENT HERBERT
Sound	PHILIP CLIFFORD
Fight arranger	NICHOLAS HALL

"a powerful, quirky, funny and virtually Euripidean
domestic comedy that surprises as much as it delights
... *A Wholly Healthy Glasgow* is a ripe but entirely
invigorating play. In following it with a play such as
American Bagpipes, Iain Heggie advertises both his
innate talent and a determination to develop through
experiment. The production is beautifully acted,
maintaining a fine balance between absurdity and
truth, and is most skilfully designed by Geoff Rose
as a suburban battlefield of pale blue carpet squares
and proliferating newsprint."
Michael Coveney *Financial Times*

"In its discovery of new writers the Royal Exchange,
Manchester is now unrivalled ... the acting is
wonderfully well-timed. The quartet of Scottish
players could not be bettered; and Casper Wrede's
direction is masterly." Eric Shorter *Daily Telegraph*

● ALL MY SONS Paul Wood & John Thaw

Photo: John Peters

24 February - 9 April 1988

93

ALL MY SONS

by Arthur Miller

Joe Keller	JOHN THAW
Dr Jim Bayliss	WILLIAM HOYLAND
Frank Lubey	MICHAEL PACKER
Sue Bayliss	CLARE TRAVERS-DEACON
Lydia Lubey	WENDY MILLER
Chris Keller	MICHAEL MALONEY
Bert	PAUL WOOD/
	ADAM IRVING/
	JONATHAN OWEN
Kate Keller	LYNN FARLEIGH
Ann Deever	JOANNA FOSTER
George Deever	JONATHAN BARLOW
Director	GREGORY HERSOV
Designer	MICHAEL HOLT
Lighting	GLYN PEREGRINE
Sound	TIM McCORMICK
Dialect coaches	JOAN WASHINGTON
	CHARMIAN HOARE

"... would effortlessly hold its own against any
competition ... This is a blazing production, deeply
moving, entirely unsentimental. John Thaw portrays
Joe Keller with the simplest means. His posture, the
angle of his head, the odd glance, suggest a lion in
autumn: the appearance of a relaxed strength
conceals a nagging fatigue. There's a scorching
performance from Michael Maloney as his son."
John Peter *Sunday Times*

"Gregory Hersov's new production at the Royal
Exchange is a high-water mark in the theatre's
history." Michael Schmidt *The Independent*

"Gregory Hersov's *All My Sons* is marvellously cast
throughout and achieves an all-round cohesion and
energy which makes it the best thing I have seen this
year. Lynn Farleigh copes with the arguably potty and
certainly distrait Kate Keller without apparent
effort; if John Thaw finally stands out from his
colleagues as Joe it is because of what he can do with
the space between the words and the sudden shifts
from confident bonhomie to fiery accusation and
then to bewildered incomprehension. I'm sorry
London's missing it." Paul Allen *New Statesman*

Photo: Ian Woollams

● DON JUAN Jonathan Kent

Photo: Ian Woollams

● DON JUAN Bernard Bresslaw

"The real joy of the production is Bernard Bresslaw's Sganarelle. He is a hypnotic presence, radiating genial ineptness and childlike naivety, dwarfing his master in height and bulk, manoeuvring about the stage like an elephant on tiptoe. Bresslaw makes his cowardly, simple-minded goodness both ludicrous and appealing." Grevel Lindop *Times Literary Supplement*

14 April - 7 May 1988

don JUAN

by Molière
translated by John Fowles

Don Juan da Tenorio	JONATHAN KENT
Sganarelle, his servant	BERNARD BRESSLAW
La Ramee	DARRYL KNOCK
Don Luis	RANDAL HERLEY
Donna Elvira	KATHERINE O'TOOLE
Gusman	JOHN PICKLES
Don Carlos	JOHN ELMES
Don Alonso	MARK AIKEN
Charlotte	MICHELLE FAIRLEY
Martha	MARY BRENNAN-MOORE
Peter	JOHN ELMES
A Pauper	MARCUS HUTTON
Dimanche	JOHN PICKLES
Don Pedro da Solva,	
The Commander	PAUL RATTEE
Musicians	EVELYN PRESTON
	JANE SEBBA
Director	IAN McDIARMID
Set designer	JULIAN McGOWAN
Costume designer	MARTIN CHITTY
Lighting	NICK CHELTON
Sound	JOHN A LEONARD
Music	JEREMY SAMS
Fight arranger	MALCOLM RANSON
Masque and movement	
devised and staged by	MARTIN DUNCAN
Wigs & Make-up	MICHAEL WARD

Don Juan subsequently toured in the mobile touring theatre to:
Lowton High School (10 -14 May); Whitehaven Sports Centre (16 - 19 May); Newbiggin Sports and Community Centre; (20 - 24 May); Huddersfield Sports Centre (25 - 28 May); Mansfield Sports Centre (30 May - 2 June); Riverside Ice and Leisure Centre, Chelmsford (3 - 7 June); Grimsby Leisure Centre (9 - 11 June); Stour Centre, Ashford (13 - 15 June); Kingsbridge Sports Centre (17 - 20 June); Alexander Sports Centre, Bedford (22 - 25 June)

Late-night performances of Marivaux's one-act comedy SLAVE ISLAND, translated by Nicholas Wright and directed by Ian McDiarmid were also given at eight of the venues.

"Jonathan Kent is a libertine of uncompromising and carnivorous ferocity and Bernard Bresslaw a Sganarelle of stature, delicacy and style ... This dark, splendid and hell-steaming production ..."
Michael Ratcliffe *The Observer*

"Ian McDiarmid's intelligent production enjoys Baroque visual flourishes that fleetingly recall Fellini's *Casanova*, Losey's *Don Giovanni* and Cocteau's *La Belle et La Bête*. Julian McGowan's set is well in the proud Royal Exchange tradition: a black platform from whose uneven surface smoke rises from the play's start, *a memento averini*. Fluted pillars are suspended in mid-air, their charred bases melted and blistered to a sharp point; they hang over the action like daggers poised. Nick Chelton's lighting, the dripping water and swelling organ tone of Jeremy Sams's music make the mausoleum superbly dramatic ... Don Juan is played by Jonathan Kent in grey silk and a braided pigtail, his cherub face puffy and pallid, his principal boy stance is as apt as his impeccable delivery of John Fowles' translation. No dullness here, from the whispering statue's self-raising visor through the frenetic Baroque musical jangle to the clockwork parade of mourners, dipping and bowing in unison. Could someone tell our two national companies how it's done?" Martin Hoyle *Financial Times*

"Jonathan Kent's Juan incarnates the vision of joyless experience. With a sneer permanently fixed in his parchment face, every turn of the head and hands and legs is measured and artificial. A master of the contemptuous snarl, Kent is once or twice so elegantly overcome by *ennui* that his voice expires on a whisper. This is a continuously fascinating performance." Jeremy Kingston *The Times*

12 May - 25 June 1988

TWELFTH NIGHT

OR WHAT YOU WILL

by William Shakespeare

Supported by the Angels of the Royal Exchange

Orsino, Duke of Illyria	TIM McINNERNY
Viola	SASKIA REEVES
Olivia	HARRIET BAGNALL
Malvolio	GARY WALDHORN
Maria	NIMMY MARCH
Sir Andrew Aguecheek	IAN HASTINGS
Sir Toby Belch	TREVOR COOPER
Feste	DEREK GRIFFITHS
Sebastian	JOHN WAGLAND
Antonio	ROY HEATHER
Fabian	COLIN PROCKTER
Sea Captain/Priest	OLIVER BEAMISH
Valentine	ANDREW MACKINTOSH
Curio	MICHAEL O'CONNOR
Musicians	AKINTAYO AKINBODE/CHRIS MANNIS
	IAN FORGRIEVE
	IAN MORRIS

Director	BRAHAM MURRAY
Designer	JOHANNA BRYANT
Lighting	ROBERT BRYAN
Sound	PHILIP CLIFFORD
Music	CHRIS MONKS
Movement and choreography	FERGUS EARLY

"Murray has given us a largely compelling and complete *Twelfth Night* in which the themes of kinship, love in its myriad combinations and confusions, and vanity and its consequences, are inventively explored." Michael Schmidt *The Independent*

30 June - 6 August 1988

★ BORN ★ Yesterday

by Garson Kanin

Helen	REGINA REAGAN
Paul Verrall	TERENCE WILTON
1st Bellhop	TOM BUTCHER
2nd Bellhop	TOBE ROTHWELL
Assistant Manager	GLYN MORROW
Eddie Brock	GEORGE SWEENEY
Harry Brock	DERRICK O'CONNOR
Billie Dawn	BRENDA BLETHYN
Ed Devery	TOM WATSON
Manicurist	KATHRYN GEORGE
Barber	JIM MARSH
Bootblack	MIKE RITCHIE
Senator Norval Hedges	TONY BROUGHTON
Mrs Hedges	NANCIE HERROD
Waiter	MIKE RITCHIE

Director	GREGORY HERSOV
Set designer	MICHAEL HOLT
Costume designer	ANTHONY WARD
Lighting	GEOFFREY JOYCE
Sound	NICKY MATTHEW
Fight arranger	MALCOLM RANSON
Voice coach	KATHY BRINDLE

"It's amazing that a 1940s Broadway comedy hit should seem so refreshing – and even dangerous – in 1988 ... the bimbo is beautifully played by Brenda Blethyn ... Greg Hersov's production brilliantly re-creates that edgy world, with a luxury hotel suite designed by Michael Holt and pointedly lit by Geoffrey Joyce and forties-feel costumes by Anthony Ward." Robin Thornber *The Guardian*

Photo: John Peters

"a production of *Twelfth Night* stands or falls by its Malvolio. Gary Waldhorn rises to the challenge in grand style. His Malvolio, a sour-faced Puritan in stiff black and white is thoroughly traditional but none the worse for that. There is immense gusto here, under the tightly irritable manner, and Waldhorn is an expert at manipulating an audience, timing his lines and looks so that every egocentric blunder falls with excruciating aptness."
Grevel Lindop *Times Literary Supplement*

● TWELFTH NIGHT Gary Waldhorn

● BORN YESTERDAY Brenda Blethyn & Terence Wilton

Photo: Ian Woollams

"Marvellous ... the set and costumes were terrific ... her costumes were vulgar in exactly the right way ... it all worked fabulously well. Brenda Blethyn's is a remarkable performance ... there are some magic moments which had the audience absolutely on the edge of their seats."
Hermione Lee *BBC Radio 4 – Kaleidoscope*

● A MIDSUMMER NIGHT'S DREAM Peter Lindford & Kenneth Cranham

Photo John Peters

15 September - 29 October 1988

A MIDSUMMER NIGHT'S DREAM

by William Shakespeare

Theseus, Duke of Athens	STUART RICHMAN
Hippolyta	ANNA SAVVA
Egeus	ROY HEATHER
Hermia	CAROLINE MILMOE
Lysander	ADAM KOTZ
Demetrius	ROBERT CLARE
Helena	SUSAN SPIEGEL
Philostrate	DAVID KIERNAN
Oberon, King of the Fairies	KENNETH CRANHAM
Titania	FIONA VICTORY
Puck	PETER LINDFORD
Peaseblossom	ANNA SAVVA
Cobweb	JOHN BATEMAN
Moth	GILLIAN WINN
Mustardseed	DAVID KIERNAN
Other Fairies	GILLIAN WINN, JOHN BATEMAN, DAVID KIERNAN, ANNA SAVVA
Peter Quince	DAVID ALLISTER
Nick Bottom	GRAHAM SINCLAIR
Francis Flute	DAVID KEYS
Tom Snout	PHILLIP WALSH
Snug	ROY HEATHER
Robin Starveling	STEPHEN BOYES
Director	GREGORY HERSOV
Set designer	LEZ BROTHERSTON
Costume designer	DAVID SHORT
Music written and recorded by	MARK VIBRANS
Choreography	STUART HOPPS
Lighting	RICK FISHER
Sound	TIM McCORMICK

A Midsummer Night's Dream opened at the Assembly Hall, Edinburgh on 15 August and ran until 3 September as part of the 1988 Edinburgh International Festival.

"The design cleverly transports us from the classical pre-nuptial skirmishes of Theseus and Hippolyta to a cobwebbed fairy world derived in equal measure from the visual imaginations of Richard Dadd and Arthur Rackham ... a dramatic feast"
Michael Coveney *Financial Times*

"In its visual sophistication and conceptual intelligence Gregory Hersov's production is streets ahead of recent offerings at the Assembly Hall"
Michael Billington *The Guardian*

● A MIDSUMMER NIGHT'S DREAM Fiona Victory

Photo John Peters

"Gregory Hersov has come up with a Dream which is securely in the company tradition: exploring that other world beyond the real, it's filled with sensual delights ... There are spell-binding performances, too, from Kenneth Cranham's regal Oberon and Fiona Victory's sensuous Titania, a mercurial Puck from Peter Lindford, and some classic clowning from the mechanicals, crowned by a mighty Bottom—as commanding in ass's head as in makeshift armour—from Graham Sinclair." Robin Thornber *The Guardian*

3 November - 17 December 1988

MACBETH

by William Shakespeare

Macbeth	DAVID THRELFALL
Lady Macbeth/Third Witch	FRANCES BARBER
Duncan/Old Man/Siward English Doctor/Lord	JOHN WATTS
Macduff/Messenger	IAN HASTINGS
Banquo/Seyton/Messenger	WYLLIE LONGMORE
Malcolm/First Murderer	JOHN HANNAH
Lady Macduff/Second Witch	TILLY TREMAYNE
Ross/Messenger	PETER RUMNEY
Angus/Third Murderer/Servant	STEPHEN LIND
Donalbain/Second Murderer/ Menteith	JAMES CLYDE
Porter/Sergeant/Caithness	ANDY SERKIS
Lennox/Servant	DAN MAXWELL
Fleance/Boy Macduff/ Young Siward	RICHARD HENDERS
First Witch/Gentlewoman	SANDY McDADE
Director	BRAHAM MURRAY
Designer	JOHANNA BRYANT
Music	CHRIS MONKS
Movement	FERGUS EARLY
Lighting	ROBERT BRYAN
Sound	PHILIP CLIFFORD

"a magnificent, breathtaking experience . . . a production that grabs you from the opening moments, leads you by the hand through an immaculately sustained leap of the imagination, and churns your insides in a way that only daring, soaring, doubt-defying live theatre can do . . . what performances! The inspired casting that couples David Threlfall and Frances Barber as Lord and Lady Macbeth produces a high-octane chemistry that boots the production into another realm."
Robin Thornber, *The Guardian*

● MACBETH Frances Barber & David Threlfall

Photo Ian Woollams

■ **UNCLE VANYA** 1977
Leo McKern as Ivan Petrovich Voinitsky
Eleanor Bron as Elena Andreyevna
Alfred Burke as Aleksandr Vladimirovich
Photo: Brian Linney

■ **PRESENT LAUGHTER** 1977
Albert Finney as Gary Essendine
Photo: Brian Linney

THE DRESSER 1980
Tom Courtenay as Norman
Freddie Jones as Sir

MUMBO JUMBO 1986
Nigel Stock as The Dean

ALL MY SONS 1988
Lynn Farleigh as Kate Keller
John Thaw as Joe Keller
Photo: John Peters

Contemporary PLAYS

All but four of the productions detailed in this section comprise a series of one-act plays – the majority with contemporary themes or settings and all by contemporary writers – staged within the theatre at lunchtime, early evening or late-night performances under the direction of assistant directors at the Royal Exchange. [These year-long positions have been funded by the Arts Council Trainee Directors Scheme or by other organisations such as Manchester Polytechnic or Theatre Ontario.]

The exceptions are Stoppard's short comedy *Albert's Bridge*, a project initiated by the acting company for 'The Skin of Our Teeth' and performed by them outside the auditorium on the girders of the theatre, and the three full-length plays *Cock Ups, Street Captives* and *Masterpieces* which were part of the Company's 'Festival 83' in the mobile theatre at the Corn Exchange.

More recently, a series of play readings by professional actors under the directorship of the company's first Literary Manager Michael Fox and a new series of Sunday performances with limited decor has introduced the work of new writers.

1977

8, 10 and 11 February 1977

ALBERT'S BRIDGE

by Tom Stoppard

Bob	JULIAN EVANS
Charlie	CHRISTOPHER MILES
Dad	JOHN BOSWALL
Albert	IAN HASTINGS
Chairman	JOHN ROGAN
Committee	BARRY PURVES, PENELOPE POTTER
	JULIAN EVANS, CHRISTOPHER MILES
Fitch	DAVID HUSCROFT
Albert's Mother	LINDSAY DUNCAN
Kate	JENNIE McGUSTIE
Voices in the	
Darkness	JULIAN EVANS, JOHN ROGAN
	CHRISTOPHER MILES
Albert's Father	BARRY PURVES
Fraser	KEVIN MOORE
Director	TAYLOR McAULEY
Lighting	MICHAEL SWEETLAND
	& GEOFFREY JOYCE
Sound	GEORGE GLOSSOP

This production was performed on the girders of the theatre module

17, 19, 20 January 1978

LAST RESORT

by Peter Flannery

Septimus	ENN REITEL
May	ROSALIND KNIGHT
Wyn	SALLY WATTS
Cuthbert & The Man	CLIVE PANTO
The Girl	LINDSAY DUNCAN
The Puppeteer	MICHAEL COLYER
Director	MICHAEL CAMERON
Designer	LIZ DA COSTA
Lighting	DEBORAH GOODKIN
Sound	DAVID EASTERBROOK

14, 16, 17 February 1978

IT'S A WHORE'S WORLD

by Taggart Deike

Big E	JOHN CHURCH
Alec	MICHAEL COLYER
Bea	CARYN HURWITZ
The Lady	ELAINE IVES-CAMERON
Beatrice	ALISON LEE ROSE
Alistair	JOHN WATTS
Director	MICHAEL CAMERON
Designer	DAVID WHETTON
Lighting	GEOFFREY JOYCE
Sound	DAVID EASTERBROOK

1978

25, 26, 28 April 1978

LIKE DOLLS OR ANGELS

by Stephen Jeffries

Zuki	SHARON BOWER
Hannigan	GEOFFREY McGIVERN
Director	MICHAEL CAMERON
Designer	CLARE BIRKS
Sound	DAVID EASTERBROOK
	and COLIN GODDARD
Lighting	DEBORAH GOODKIN

5, 7, 8 December 1978

LOVE LETTERS ON BLUE PAPER

by Arnold Wesker

Victor Marsden	MORRIS PERRY
Sonia	ANGELA ROOKS
Maurice Stapleton	PETER GUINNESS
Trade Union Official	PAUL CLAYTON
Director	PAT TRUEMAN
Designer	TRICIA MOHAN
Lighting	DEBBIE GOODKIN
Sound	COLIN GODDARD

STREET CAPTIVES Jonathan Stratton, Albert Welling & Breffni McKenna

Contemporary

PLAYS

1979

● MASTERPIECES

Shirley Dixon, Kathryn Pogson & Patti Love

6, 8, 9 March 1979

TO THE CHICAGO ABYSS

by Ray Bradbury

Old Man	ALAN ALDRED
Woman in the Park	JOYCE GRUNDY
Young Man	PAUL BRADLEY
Stranger	PETER SETTELEN
Wife	FIONA GRAY
Policeman	PAUL BRADLEY
Boy	MARK ROGERS
Director	PAT TRUEMAN
Designer	PETER SKERRETT
Lighting	DEBBIE GOODKIN
Sound	DAVID EASTERBROOK
	and COLIN GODDARD

7, 8, 12 June 1979

PHILIPP HOTZ'S FURY

by Max Frisch
translated by Michael Bullock

Philipp Hotz	CHRISTOPHER BRAMWELL
Dorli	MOIRA BROOKER
Old Removal Man/ Foreign Legionnaire	DON TROEDSON
Young Removal Man/ Customs Officer	PAUL BRADLEY
Wilfrid	ROBERT DUNCAN
Clarissa	ROSEMARY KINGSTON
Director	PAT TRUEMAN
Designer	PETER SKERRETT
Lighting	GEOFFREY JOYCE
Sound	DAVID EASTERBROOK
	and COLIN GODDARD

10, 12, 13, 14 July 1979

A TRIBUTE TO RIO MARCONI

devised by Pat Trueman, Chris Walton & Colin Goddard

In this tribute the stars are portrayed by the following
Compere	ALAN McMAHON
Rio Marconi	DAVID TYSALL
Herman Pyle/Al Fresco/ Johnny Babble/Rob Ferris/ Marc Pikleson/Ron Ramage/ Reporter	KEITH VARNIER
Cindy McGear/Journalist/ Susan Derbyshire/Linda Ramage/ TV Advertising Model	JENNY HOWE
Festival Compere/ TV Advertising Man	JON GLENTORAN
The Band	CHRIS WALTON
	COLIN GODDARD, JON GLENTORAN
	GRAEME MORGAN
Tribute staged by	PAT TRUEMAN
Convention designed by	PETER SKERRETT
Gig lit by	GARY BROWN
Sound mixed by	BAZ EASTERBROOK
Gear by	GINNIE O'BRIEN and IRENE ETEL

1980

12, 14, 15, 16 February 1980

FEIFFER'S PEOPLE

Sketches and observations
by Jules Feiffer

The cast:
JONATHAN BARLOW	BARBARA SHELLEY
CLARE HIGGINS	ANTHONY WINGATE
ANNE ROGERS	
Director	DION McHUGH
Designer	SALLY COX
Lighting	GLYN PEREGRINE
Sound	DAVID EASTERBROOK
	and COLIN GODDARD

20, 22, 23, 24 May 1980

THE TECHNICIANS

by Olwen Wymark

Starr	ALAN PARNABY
Jordan	JOHN WATTS
Mrs Rust	JUDITH BARKER
Mr Rust	STUART RICHMAN
Roland Cat	RON EMSLIE
Director	DION McHUGH
Designer	JUDY DEANEY
Lighting	GLYN PEREGRINE
Sound	DAVID EASTERBROOK
	and COLIN GODDARD

3, 5, 6, 7 June 1980

CHAMBER MUSIC

by Arthur Kopit

Mrs Mozart	LESLEY NICOL
Osa Johnson	SHIRLEY CASSEDY
Gertrude Stein	LISA TRAMONTIN
Pearl White	LINDSAY BLACKWELL
Amelia Earheart	VIVIENNE RITCHIE
Queen Isabella	JOHANNA KIRBY
Joan of Arc	CLARE HIGGINS
Susan B Anthony	JUDITH BARKER
Man in White	RON EMSLIE
Director	DION McHUGH
Set and costume design	BARRY JARVIS
	GLORIA MULQUEEN, DION McHUGH
	STEPHEN DONCASTER
Lighting	BILL SMITH
Sound	DAVID EASTERBROOK
	and COLIN GODDARD

1981

PREMIERE
24, 27, 28 February, 3, 6, 7 March 1981

PHILBY – GOING HOME

by Roger Stennett

Harold 'Kim' Philby	MILES ANDERSON
Director	GREGORY HERSOV
Designer	JUDY DEANEY
Lighting	JACQUI LEIGH
Sound	DAVID EASTERBROOK
	and COLIN GODDARD

PREMIERE OF NEW VERSION
30 April, 1, 2, 5, 7, 8, 9 May 1981

WILL

devised by Gregory Hersov

PROLOGUE	
Shakespeare	ALAN PARTINGTON
LOVE – PLAY	
Man	RICHARD REES
Woman	VIVIENNE RITCHIE
COMEDY – LAUGHTER	
1st Comic	ROY SAMPSON
2nd Comic	COLIN PROCKTER
3 – AUTHORITY	
Merchant	COLIN PROCKTER
Beggar	RICHARD REES
Elizabeth	VIVIENNE RITCHIE
Court Official	ROY SAMPSON
Actress	VIVIENNE RITCHIE
Actor	RICHARD REES
1st King	ROY SAMPSON
2nd King	COLIN PROCKTER
Beggar	VIVIENNE RITCHIE
Director	GREGORY HERSOV
Designer	ELLEN CAIRNS
Sound	DAVID EASTERBROOK
	and COLIN GODDARD
Lighting	GLYN PEREGRINE

16, 18, 19, 20 June 1981

PRIVATE WARS

A black comedy in one act
by James McLure

Gately	TIM McINNERNY
Silvio	IAN HASTINGS
Natwick	GEOFFREY BATEMAN
Director	GREGORY HERSOV
Designer	MIKE HUBBARD
Lighting	CLIVE ODOM
Sound	DAVID EASTERBROOK
Music	COLIN GODDARD

MASTERPIECES

by Sarah Daniels

Rowena	KATHRYN POGSON
Yvonne/Hilary	PATTI LOVE
Jennifer/Judge/Irene Wade	SHIRLEY DIXON
Trevor	GERARD MURPHY
Ron/Man in Street/Man in Tube/ Prosecutor	EAMON BOLAND
Clive/Prologue/Policeman/Teacher/ Man in Tube/Judge	WILLIAM HOYLAND
Director	JULES WRIGHT
Designer	DI SEYMOUR
Lighting	NIGEL WALKER
Sound	CHRIS COXHEAD

Masterpieces was subsequently produced with the same cast and director at The Royal Court Theatre Upstairs (11 October - 5 November 1983) where it won the Plays & Players Most Promising Playwright Award for Sarah Daniels.

21, 22, 28, 29, 30 July 1983

SEXUAL PERVERSITY IN CHICAGO

by David Mamet

Dan Shapiro	ANDREW KAZAMIA
Bernard Litiko	IAN HASTINGS
Deborah Soloman	TINA MARIAN
Joan Webber	MELANIE KILBURN
Director	CHRISTINA BURNETT
Set designer	HEATHER HIGTON
Costume designer	FRAN CARROLL
Lighting	JASON TAYLOR and NIGEL WALKER
Sound	JOHN DEL'NERO

1982

21, 22, 23, 26, 29, 30 January 1982

THE SOUL OF THE WHITE ANT

by Snoo Wilson

Edith	MELANIE KILBURN
June	CHERYL PRIME
Mabel de Wet	BERNICE STEGERS
Pieter de Groot	GEOFFREY BATEMAN
Eugene Marais	NORMAN ESHLEY
Julius	WILLIAM HOPE
Director	GREGORY HERSOV
Designer	SUE PEARCE
Lighting	JOHANNA TOWN
Sound	CHRIS COXHEAD
Song composed by	COLIN GODDARD

4, 5, 6, 9, 12, 13 March 1982

PAINTING A WALL

by David Lan

Willy	IAN HASTINGS
Sampson	CHRISTOPHER BRAMWELL
Peter	NIVEN BOYD
Henry	COLIN PROCKTER
Director	GREGORY HERSOV
Designer	CHRISTOPHER A TANDY
Lighting	CHRISTINE STEELE

8, 10, 11, 12 June 1982

THE UNSEEN HAND

by Sam Shepard

Blue Morphan	IAN HASTINGS
Willie	GEOFFREY BATEMAN
Cisco Morphan	PHILIP BARNES
The Kid	TIM McINNERNY
Sycamore Morphan	ROY SAMPSON
Director	GREGORY HERSOV
Designer	ALAN MURRAY
Lighting	PAUL W JONES
Sound	DAVID EASTERBROOK
Music	COLIN GODDARD

PREMIERE OF REVISED VERSION
19-30 April 1983

COCK UPS

by Simon Moss

Joe Orton	RON COOK
Kenneth Halliwell	PATRICK MALAHIDE
Inspector Truscott	COLIN McCORMACK
Watson	MAX GOLD
Russel	TOM COTCHER
Genziani	CHRISTOPHER HANCOCK
Smart	SEAN CHAPMAN
Miss Milligan	JEAN RIMMER
Director	GREGORY HERSOV
Designer	CAROLINE McCULLOCH
Lighting	PAUL W JONES
Sound	JOHN DEL'NERO and JENNY HISLOP

10-21 May 1983

STREET CAPTIVES

by Jonathan Moore

Charles	ALBERT WELLING
Jim	BREFFNI McKENNA
Stranger	JONATHAN STRATTON
Director	TIM FYWELL
Designer	DAVID SHORT
Lighting	JET TOWN
Sound	JOHN DEL'NERO
Special sequences by	NICK HALL

● COCK UPS Ron Cook & Patrick Malahide

1985

21, 22, 23 February, 1 March 1985

FEN

by Caryl Churchill

Val/Ghost	ROBERTA KERR
Nell/Businessman/Mavis/May	SARA SUGARMAN
Shirley/Shona/Miss Cade/ Margaret	CAROL NOAKES-GORMAN
Boy/Angela/Deb/ Mrs Finch	CHARLOTTE PLOWRIGHT
Mrs Hasset/Becky/Alice/Ivy	ROSALIND KNIGHT
Wilson/Frank/Mr Tewson/ Geoffrey	RORY EDWARDS
Director	ELIZABETH LAWLESS
Designer	MIKE HUBBARD
Lighting	TARAS KOCHAN
Sound	ROSALIND ELLIMAN
Music	AKINTAYO AKINBODE and STEPHEN WARBECK
Fight arranger	RORY EDWARDS
Dance arranged by	ROSALIND KNIGHT
Dialect coach	ALEX TAYLOR

2, 3, 4, 11 May 1985

DEREK

by Edward Bond

Derek	MARK ADDY
Julie	CHERYL PRIME
Mother	ROSALIND KNIGHT
Biff	ADRIAN PALMER
Foreman/Doctor	ROY HEATHER
Director	ELISABETH LAWLESS
Designer	ALAN MARSHALL
Lighting	TARAS KOCHAN
Music	AKINTAYO AKINBODE

A ★ W ★ A ★ R ★ D ★ S

1976

MANCHESTER SOCIETY OF ARCHITECTS PRESIDENT'S AWARD
- to the TRUSTEES OF THE ROYAL EXCHANGE THEATRE for their outstanding contribution to the artistic and social life of Manchester and the North West, in creating the Royal Exchange Theatre

BRITISH TOURIST BOARD 'COME TO BRITAIN' TROPHY
- Special Commendation awarded to the ROYAL EXCHANGE THEATRE COMPANY for outstanding tourist enterprise

Tom Courtenay & Freddie Jones in *The Dresser*

1977

ROYAL INSTITUTE OF BRITISH ARCHITECTS
- North West Regional Award
presented by Sir Hugh Casson on 27 April 1978

Lynsey Baxter in *The Lady from the Sea*

1980

EVENING STANDARD DRAMA AWARDS
- VANESSA REDGRAVE/*The Lady from the Sea*
Best Actress

PLAYS & PLAYERS AWARDS
- LYNSEY BAXTER/*The Lady from the Sea*
Most Promising New Actress

1981

EVENING STANDARD DRAMA AWARDS
- TOM COURTENAY/*The Dresser*
Best Actor
- RONALD HARWOOD/*The Dresser*
Best New Play

BRITISH THEATRE ASSOCIATION 'DRAMA' AWARDS
- TOM COURTENAY/*The Dresser*
Best Actor
- RONALD HARWOOD/*The Dresser*
Best New Play

VARIETY CLUB OF GREAT BRITAIN AWARDS
- HELEN MIRREN/*The Duchess of Malfi*
Best Stage Actress

1982

MANCHESTER EVENING NEWS THEATRE AWARDS
- ROBERT LINDSAY/*The Beaux' Stratagem* & *Philoctetes*
Best Actor

1983

PLAYS & PLAYERS AWARDS
- ALAN PRICE & TREVOR PEACOCK/*Andy Capp*
Best New Musical

MANCHESTER EVENING NEWS THEATRE AWARDS
- CHARLIE DRAKE/*The Caretaker*
Readers' Performance of the Year

1984

MANCHESTER SOCIETY OF ARCHITECTS PRESIDENT'S AWARD
- for the set in Michael Elliott's production of *Moby Dick*

A ★ W ★ A ★ R ★ D ★ S

ASSOCIATION OF BRITISH THEATRE TECHNICIANS
■ Golden Hook Clamp Award for *Moby Dick*

PLAYS & PLAYERS AWARDS
■ SARAH DANIELS / *Masterpieces*
Most Promising Playwright

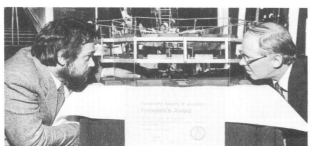
Laurie Dennett & the President of the Manchester Society of Architects, Robert Stones, looking at the model of the award-winning set for Moby Dick

MANCHESTER EVENING NEWS THEATRE AWARDS
■ TOM COURTENAY / *Jumpers*
Best Actor
■ TRACIE BENNETT / *Carousel*
Best Actress
■ LIAM NEESON / *The Plough and the Stars*
Best Supporting Actor
■ MICHAEL ELLIOTT (awarded posthumously)
Horniman Award for outstanding services to theatre

Espen Skjønberg in *Three Sisters*

Liam Neeson

1985

BRITISH THEATRE ASSOCIATION 'DRAMA' AWARDS
■ ESPEN SKJØNBERG / *Three Sisters*
Best Supporting Actor

MANCHESTER EVENING NEWS THEATRE AWARDS
■ SYLVIA SYMS / *Entertaining Mr Sloane*
Best Actress
■ RENNY KRUPINSKI / *Great Expectations*
Best Supporting Actor
■ *Three Sisters* (Director Casper Wrede)
Best Production
■ DI SEYMOUR / *Great Expectations & Three Sisters*
Best Designer

BUSINESS SPONSORSHIP INCENTIVE SCHEME
■ £20,000 for the Mobil Playwriting Competition

1986

MANCHESTER EVENING NEWS THEATRE AWARDS
■ AVRIL ELGAR / *Death of a Salesman & Court in the Act!*
Best Actress

1987

MANCHESTER EVENING NEWS THEATRE AWARDS
■ MICHAEL GRANDAGE / *Edward the Second*
Best Supporting Actor

BUSINESS SPONSORSHIP INCENTIVE SCHEME
■ £6,666 for the Prudential Tour of *The Alchemist*

1988

MANCHESTER EVENING NEWS THEATRE AWARDS
■ IAN McDIARMID / *Don Carlos*
Best Actor
■ *Don Carlos* / (Director Nicholas Hytner)
Best Production
■ IAIN HEGGIE / *American Bagpipes*
Best New Play
■ JOHN THAW / *All My Sons*
Readers Performance of the Year

FUNDRAISING AND DEVELOPMENT
AT THE
ROYAL EXCHANGE THEATRE

The Royal Exchange came into existence through the vision and foresight of a small group of enthusiastic individuals. Fundraising and the generosity of the local community played a vital role in realising their dream. Nearly five hundred companies throughout the North West and thousands of individuals, many of whom are acknowledged on the following pages, contributed to the massive fundraising appeal which raised a quarter of a million pounds towards building the theatre.

After the theatre opened in 1976, despite very generous subsidies from the Arts Council, Greater Manchester Council (as it was then) and other local government authorities, substantial additional funding was required and approximately £60,000 has been raised every year through fundraising efforts of every description as well as a number of very successful sponsorships. Of the latter, the Mobil Playwriting Competition has been, arguably, the most notable to date, achieving wide-spread and sustained publicity for both the sponsor and the Royal Exchange, whilst providing a fund of new writing which will enhance the theatre's repertory for several years to come. Touring has been made possible by sponsorship from the Prudential and sponsorship in kind has also made an important contribution, with many companies providing goods and services free of charge or at greatly reduced rates, in exchange for appropriate benefits.

In 1985, in response to Government's stated objective of encouraging subsidised arts organisations to take greater responsibility for their own funding, the Royal Exchange appointed its first Development Director. A Development Committee of leading professionals and industrialists was formed at the same time and the task of setting up a new, full-scale development programme began.

The first vital step in the programme has been to encourage commercial and industrial support for the Royal Exchange. This has been achieved through establishing a Corporate Membership Scheme which offers subscribers an attractive package of ticket, advertising and entertaining privileges. Corporate Members are entitled to use the exclusive and specially-created Taittinger Bar, sponsored by Taittinger Champagne, to entertain their clients and friends. Scaled-down versions of the scheme are also available for the benefit of smaller companies.

The recently inaugurated Angels' Scheme offers both private individuals and smaller companies a unique opportunity to be involved with a specific production, combining a closer relationship with the company with an inexpensive way of supporting it. Our experienced Benefit Committee helps to ensure that various fundraising functions during the year raise vital funds for the theatre, whilst offering the widest possible range of supporters an enjoyable means of giving.

As a registered charity the Company is able to advise potential donors of the most tax-efficient means of making donations. Major sponsorships for productions remains a prime objective and the Company has never been better placed in its ability to respond to the requirements of sponsors, large or small. The cost of play sponsorship is entirely dependent on the size and scale of the production, although it is almost always possible to provide a package suitable to the sponsors' requirements once these have been identified. The benefits to both parties can also be enhanced if the sponsor is eligible for an award from the Government under the Business Sponsorship Incentive Scheme (BSIS).

As the Royal Exchange looks forward to the 1990s new and ambitious plans for the Company's future are on the drawing board. They will not come to fruition without large-scale public support to equal that which helped to create the Theatre in the first place.

Pierre Emmanuel Taittinger with Braham Murray and Cheryl Campbell at the opening of The Taittinger Bar *Photo: Mike Frisbee*

These are the ways in which companies and individuals can support the Royal Exchange Theatre

▶ **ENROL** as a Corporate Member

■ **SPONSOR** a season, a production or a performance

● **HELP REFURBISH** the Royal Exchange – a listed building

▶ **SPONSOR IN KIND** the materials we need for productions and refurbishment

■ **JOIN** the Friends of the Royal Exchange

● **BECOME** a season ticket holder

▶ **SPONSOR** a special event, concert or recital

■ **ADVERTISE** in theatre programmes

In return we offer:

■ Special ticket arrangements for performances

● Extensive and prestigious publicity

▶ Exclusive opportunities for private entertaining

■ Unique links with the Theatre Company

The Royal Exchange Theatre is a registered charity. Consequently, we are able to derive maximum benefits from Donations, Covenants and Legacies.

DEVELOPMENT COMMITTEE

Paul A Lee *Chairman*
Christopher Attrill
Barrie Bernstein
Mrs Rayna Dean
James Dunlop
Richard Fildes
Tom Finnigan
Peter Folkman
David Kaye
Ted McMahon
Paul Mitchell
Tim O'Brien
John Parsons
Philip Ramsbottom
Bernard Terry

BENEFIT COMMITTEE

Brenda Brown
Christine Brown
Susie Diggines
Jennifer Dunlop
Sue Holman
Morag Leech
Bernice Lieberman
Helen O'Brien
Elizabeth Taylor
Cathy Wills
Josie Wilson

DEVELOPMENT STAFF

Charlotte Bowen
Development Officer
061-833 9333 ext 235

Sue Lawton
Development Officer
061-833 9333 ext 256

MAJOR SUPPORTERS

Granada Television
Marks & Spencer plc
Mobil Oil Company Limited
National Westminster Bank plc

Prudential Assurance Co Ltd
H & J Quick Group plc
Taittinger Champagne
Tom Garner Motors

CORPORATE MEMBERS
PAST & PRESENT

Addleshaw, Sons & Latham
ADS Group Ltd
AMI Alexandra Hospital
Alsop Wilkinson
Arthur Andersen & Co
Arthur Young
Barclays Bank plc &
  Barclays de Zoete Wedd Ltd
BBA Group plc
Binder Hamlyn
Bowden Dyble Hayes & Partners
British Gas (North Western)
British Telecom
Citibank
Coats Viyella plc
Cobbett Leak Almond & Partners
Kooltherm Insulation Products
Leach Rhodes & Walker
MBS Combro Ltd
Mobil Oil Company Limited
Morgans Timber Group
National Westminster Bank plc
North Western Postal Board
Pakcel Ltd
Peat Marwick McLintock
Presbar Diecastings Ltd
Price Waterhouse & Co Ltd
Production Steel & Metals Group plc
Refuge Assurance plc
Rickitt, Mitchell & Partners Ltd
W H Robinson & Co
N M Rothschild & Sons Ltd

Coloroll Group plc
Computerland
Connell & Finnigan Ltd
Co-operative Bank plc
Coopers & Lybrand
Ernst & Whinney
Granada Television
Grant Thornton
Halliwell Landau
Henry Cooke, Lumsden Ltd
H & J Quick Group plc
ICL (UK) Ltd
James Chapman & Co
The Royal Bank of Scotland plc
Shell UK Limited
Slater Heelis
Swiss Bank Corporation
The Mynshul Trust Ltd
T & N plc
C Topham & Sons
Touche Ross & Co
Trowers & Hamlins
TSB England & Wales plc
United Biscuits (UK) Ltd
West Pennine Trucks Ltd
Whitbread Chesters

ASSOCIATE CORPORATE MEMBERS

Allied Lyons National Sales
BBC North West

SPONSORS
PAST AND PRESENT

The Advertising Unit
Angels of the Royal Exchange
APW (Associated Perforators and
  Weavers) Ltd
Batchelors Foods Limited
Binatone International Limited
Bruntwood Estates
BSR (Housewares)
Chris Benson Signs Limited
Diners Club International
The Drawing Room
Edwards Chartered Accountants
Focus Marketing Limited
Friends of the Royal Exchange
Fuji Professional
Tom Garner Motors
Goethe-Institut, Manchester
Granada Television
Holbrook Printing Company Ltd
Hong Kong and Shanghai Banking
  Corporation
IBM (United Kingdom) Limited
IBM United Kingdom Trust
ICI plc
ICL (UK) Ltd
Investors In Industry plc
Irish Tourist Board
Keith Johnson & Pelling Ltd
Key 103
Kimberly-Clark
F H Lee (Paper Convertors) Ltd
Makro plc (with support from more
  than 60 individual companies)
Marks & Spencer plc
Megson Stationery Ltd
Memorex UK Ltd
Mobil Oil Company Limited
National Westminster Bank plc
Nikon UK Ltd
Piccadilly Radio
Prudential Assurance Co Ltd
H & J Quick Group plc
Royal Doulton Limited
Shell (UK) Limited
Simon Engineering plc
David Sleap Machinery Ltd
Smiths Food Group
Systime Limited
Taittinger Champagne
Thornton Baker
Thorntons Limited
3M UK Limited
Whitbread Chesters
Whitehead Bros (Manchester) Ltd

Brenda Blethyn and David Horovitch receive the keys of the theatre's new van from Mr Ivan Wallis of Tom Garner Motors

The Royal Exchange Theatre Trust has received many covenants and donations since the Building Appeal was launched in 1972. Major financing of the project was made by the Arts Council of Great Britain, the Greater Manchester Council and Manchester City Council, but a large proportion of the money came from companies and individuals:

104

MAJOR DONORS

£2,000 AND ABOVE

Granada Foundation
Granada Television
Courtaulds
Mr & Mrs Fred Dawes
Mr & Mrs John Doggart
Finnigans
Thomas French & Sons
L Gardner & Sons
General Electric Company
Martin Green
William Hare Ltd
Imperial Chemical Industries

Thomas Markland
Marks & Spencer
Michael Meyer
National Westminster Bank
Northern Commercial Trust
The Pilgrim Trust
Prudential Assurance
H & J Quick Group
Shell UK Ltd
Simon Engineering
Raymond Slater
Ward & Goldstone

COVENANTS

COVENANTS TAKEN OUT BY COMPANIES

Allied Breweries (UK) Ltd
Anchor Chemical Co Ltd
K O Boardman International Ltd
Boddingtons' Breweries Ltd
Bodycote International Ltd
British Engine Boiler & Electrical
  Insurance Co Ltd
British Gas plc
Brooke Bond Liebig
Matthew Brown & Co
N Brown Investments
Burns Anderson (Northern) Ltd
Edwin Butterworth & Co Ltd
Carlton Holdings Ltd
The Clayton Aniline Co Ltd
Connolly's Cables
Co-operative Wholesale Society Ltd
Courtaulds Ltd
Customagic Manufacturing Co Ltd
W H Dean & Son Ltd

Development Associates Ltd
G Dew & Co Ltd
Dolland & Aitchison (Property) Ltd
Dunlop Ltd
Elkos (Manchester) Ltd
EVA Industries Ltd
Ferranti Ltd
Finnigans Ltd
Fothergill & Harvey Ltd
S Frankenhuis & Son Ltd
Thomas French & Sons Ltd
Friedland Doggart Group Ltd
L Gardner & Sons Ltd
Glazebrook Steel & Co Ltd
Guardian Assurance Co Ltd
Arthur Guiness Son & Co (Park Royal) Ltd
Halon & Co Ltd
Hambro Life Assurance Ltd
William Hare Ltd
Harp Lager Breweries (Northern) Ltd

Harrods Ltd
Henderson Holmes & Reiss Ltd
P Q Henriques Charitable Trust
Imperial Chemical Industries Ltd
Jessel Securities Ltd
Johnson & Firth Brown Ltd
Johnson & Nephew
John Kennedy (Civil Engineering) Ltd
William Kenyon & Sons Ltd
Kodak Ltd
Lankro Chemicals Group Ltd
Lex Service Group
Lindsay & Williams Industries Ltd
Lloyds Industries International Ltd
Manchester Steel Ltd
Marks & Spencer Ltd
Mather & Platt Ltd
Michael Meyer Bland Trust
W M Miller & Co Ltd
John Myers & Co Ltd
National Vulcan Engineering Group
National Westminster Bank Ltd
Pifco Ltd
Platt Clothiers Ltd
Price Waterhouse Associates
The Prudential Assurance Co Ltd
H & J Quick Group Ltd
Reacro Rubber Co Ltd
Readson Ltd
Reed Rains Ltd
Refuge Assurance Ltd

Refuge Securities Ltd
Reynold Ltd
Samuel Renshaw & Sons Ltd
Frederic Robinson Ltd
Alexander Ross (Textiles) Ltd
Royal Insurance Group
Royds Manchester Ltd
Ernest Scragg & Sons Ltd
Singer & Friedlander Ltd
John Singleton Ltd
Smallmans Ltd
Spicer & Pegler Service Co Ltd
Stenhouse Northern Ltd
Stonegate Securities (Properties) Ltd
Stonegate Securities Ltd
Stone-Platt Industries Ltd
Maurice Sugar (Linings) Ltd
Sun Alliance Insurance Co Ltd
Francis Sumner (Holdings) Ltd
Tootal Ltd
Turner & Newall Ltd
United Dominions Trust
Vantona Group Ltd
Voltdene Ltd
Ward & Goldstone Ltd
Westerley Foods Ltd
Whitecroft Ltd
Williams & Glyn's Bank Ltd
M & C Winer & Co Ltd
Victor Wolf Ltd

COVENANTS TAKEN OUT BY INDIVIDUALS

Addleshaw Sons & Latham
M L Alexander
Arthur Llwellyn Armitage
Stella D Austin
Catherine Mary Bagnall
David Baldwin
Raymond Whittier Baldwin
Geoffrey Frederick Barratt
Leah Barron
Paul Karfoot Berry
C E Bloodworth
Barbara Catherine Boone
Joan R Borin
Susan Boyson
Mary L Brierley
Eric Bentley Brogan
William Arthur Bromley-Davenport
A C Bubb
Roy Buckle
Dorothy Carlile
Thomas Douglas Carnworth
Bernard Cassel
Derek Castle
Rita Cohen
John Bernard Coleman
Philip Julian Conn
Harold Cotton
T Coxon
Roger M Dauncey
Isabella Morrison Davidson
Mona Davies
Ryhs Everson Davies
John D Davison
Frederick Richard Dawes
Phyllis Dawes
Jane Devaney
John Doggart
James Peter Douglas
Janet Everiss
Emily Fender
Albert Finney
Neil James Fitton
Elizabeth M I Foot
Roy Forrest
Dianne Garstang
Alan M Gent
Thea Goldschmidt
John Kennedy Goody
Wilfred Hall
Peter Pakenham Hamilton
Henry David Stewart Hardle
Derek Hartle

James Dunsford Hemsley
H Alastair Hetherington
Gordon Ernest Higginson
Nicholas John Higham
Mr & Mrs F H C Hitchcock
June Irene Hill
John Holden
Raymond Honeyford
George Malcom Fleming Humble
David Ian Hunter
Edward A Hurst
Flora Hurtley
Martin Isba
Peter Darrell Jackson
Susan E Jackson
George Marcus Komrower
Cyril Kringer
D M Landau
Bryan James Leatherbarrow
Dennis Isambard Lever
Mrs S Levy
Rolf Lindemann
Andrea Lord
Anthony John McCrorie
Veronica McGourley
Manchester Ship Canal Company
F L Marshall
David Martin
Sir William Mather
Murial G Montague Meyer
P A J Milligan
Robert David George Milner
David Edward Montgomery
Judge Sir William Morris
Jessie Moston
Bernice Northen
Harold Ottman
CPS Parkes
Clifford James Paterson
Marjorie Helen Pott
Marjorie Priestley
Charles Redmond
Frank Robinson
Brian T Robson
Gerhart Martin Schaefer
Laurence P Scott
Joan Skelton
David S Southern
Roy M Southern
Barry Spiero
F M Stansfield
Edna Strivens

Mr Thompson
Jack Thornley
Thornton Baker & Co
D L Uttley
Harold Bertram Vanstone
Michel Vercambre
John Peter Wainwright
John Gordon Watkin
James Andrew Waller

David E Weissand
William Jeffry Alexander Wickham
Alice A Wilkinson
Geoffrey G Williams
Ruth Ann Williams
Alma Marian Willink
Jack Wrightson
Basil Alexander Young

DONATIONS

Dave Allen
Davoud Alliance
Allied Polymer Ltd
Altrincham Grammar School Staff
Arbuthnot Chancery Trust
Tom Arnold
Sir Richard Attenborough
ATV Ltd
Mr & Mrs H Baker
Bank of England
Barclays Bank Ltd
P W Barkworth
H Barnes
Alan Bates
Sir Jacob Behrens & Sons Ltd
Sir Leonard & Lady Behrens
J C Bell
David Bentley Ltd
Barrie Bernstein
S E Bernstein
Alexander Bird
Lionel Black
Honor Blackman
Katharine Blake
Maurice Blank
Boots
Mrs Johanne Brookes
Brown, Shipley & Co Ltd
Jo Burge
Alfred Burke
Arnold Burlin
Burnley Building Society
J Butterworth
Mrs C J Canner
H E Canner
Cannon Assurance Ltd
Carrington Viyella Ltd
Roy Castle
Castlemere Properties
A Cattan
Chancery Trust Ltd
Cheadle Hulme School
Chloride Group Ltd
Ciba – Geigy
R N B Clegg Esq
Michael Codron
Colgate Palmolive Ltd
Commercial Union Assurance Co Ltd
Sean Connery
Cook & Thorp Ltd
Henry Cooke, Lumsden & Co
J Copeland & Son (Textiles) Ltd
Ronnie Corbett
Mrs Joe Cox
Bernard Cribbins
Joy Crowther
Constance Cummings
Michael & Carol Cummings
Larry Dalzell
Danish Food Centre
Joanna David
Irene Z Dawkins
Dawson & Forbes Ltd
Debenham's Charitable Trust
Deering & Miuikin
Vernon Dobtcheff
Nigel Douglas
D R M Industrial Fabrics
Peter Eade Ltd
Eagle Star Insurance Group
Jack Eastwood
Louis C Edwards & Son (Manchester) Ltd

Avril Elgar
E E P Elliot
J M Elliot
E M I Ltd
Experimental Theatre Club (Manchester)
Ronald Eyre
Fenchurch Group
The Filten Trust
D Forster
R Forsythe
Fothergill & Harvey
Edward Fox
J Foy
Mrs S Freedman
Mrs J Freeman
Gall & Eke
Gallaher Ltd
Alan Garner
Ian Andrew Gatt
Mrs J Gaymond
General Electric Co Ltd
General Surety & Guarantee Co Ltd
Félicité Gillaham
Dr A Glass
Iain Glidewell
Mr & Mrs A S Goode
J Gradel
Granada Foundation
Granada Television Ltd
Mr & Mrs Charles Green
Martin Green
Greenall Whitley Group
Joyce Grenfell
Peter Grimshaw Esq
Guardian Newspapers
Guardian Royal Exchange Assurance Group
Guide Bridge Theatre
Halliday Simpson
Roger Hammond
C J Hampton
Ronald Harwood
G E & J Heald
H J Heinz Ltd
K A Henderson
Lord Hewlett
Hill Samuel & Co Ltd
Dame Wendy Hiller
Dr & Mrs Edmund Hine
Sheila Hine
Sir Kenneth Hollings
Anthony Hopkins
Miss Margaret I Hopwood
Frankie Howerd
M G Howarth
R D Howgate
Roy Hudd
Hulme Hall Schools
Mrs Joyce Hytner
IBM (United Kingdom) Ltd
Illingworth & Henriques
J Jarvis & Sons
Jasolyne Layton Bennett & Co
Mr & Mrs C F Jeanes
Beryl Jones
William C Jones Ltd
Albert Joseph
Lennard Joseph
Kendal Milne & Co
Keyser Ullman Ltd
Harry Kingsley
Mark Kingston
Esmond Knight

A H Knowles
Knutsford U D C
Dr F H Kroch
Lancashire & Cook
I L Lander
Councillor B S Langton
Linda Langton
Mrs Meg Langton
Patti Langton
Henry Laniado
The Last Drop
J M Leach
Rosemary Leach
Lead Industries
Raymond Leppard
Harold Lever
Basil J Levy
Ralph Levy
Ralph Levy Charitable Trust
The Sarina Levy Trust
C I Linder
Lloyds Bank Ltd
London & Yorkshire Trust
J & N Loughran
Arthur Lowe
Mrs G L McCallum
Ian McKellen
Leo McKern
Charles S Madan & Co Ltd
Manchester Central Area Sports &
    Social Club
Manchester & Salford Trustee Savings
    Bank
Manchester Evening News
Manchester Liners Ltd
March Pearson & Skelton
Thomas Markland Ltd
Mrs H Marples
David Marshall
James Mason
James Maxwell
Mr & Mrs Nicholas May
Memorial Enterprises
Metal Box Ltd
Mrs D Meyer
Richard Meyer
Midland Bank Ltd
Sir Richard Miller
Hayley Mills
Juliet Mills
Major L G Minton
Samuel Montagu & Co Ltd
Christopher Morahan & Anna Carteret
Councillor J H Morris
Miss Margaret Motley
Magnus Mowat
J J Mundle
George A Needham
Isaac Neild & Co
Borough Of Nelson
New Day Holdings Ltd
Peter Nichols
Nickerson Investments Ltd
Mrs Berry Northen
Northern Commercial Trust
North West Arts Association
Orlando Oldham Discretionary Trust
Peter O'Toole
Daphne Oxenford
Miss Marjorie Peel
Wm Pickles & Co Ltd
The Pilgrim Trust
Dr L H A Pilkington Charity Trust
Platt International Ltd
Christopher Plummer
Elaine Taylor Plummer
Robert Powell
Leon Presser
Proctor & Gamble Ltd
The Publishers Association
R L S Raffles
Rank Charitable Trust
Rank Hovis McDougall Ltd
Rank Strand
Mrs C H Rayman

Refuge Assurance Co Ltd
Harry Rose
B M Ross Charity Trust
Stanley Ross Ltd
Leslie Rostram
N M Rothschild & Sons Ltd
Round House Trust Limited
Patricia Routledge
Mr & Mrs F Savage
Rev E & Mrs Saxon
George H Scholes & Co Ltd
Scholfields Ltd
Mrs Maurice Sciama
Sir David Scott & Lady Scott
The Scott Trust
H D Seddon
Sedgley Park Academy of Speech & Drama
Peter Sellers
Barbara Sharples School of Dancing
Glen Byam Shaw
Shell Mex & BP Ltd
D Sidi
Mr & Mrs J Edward Sieff
C G H Simon
Simon Engineering
Miss R A Sisson
Ronald Skermer
John Slater Foundation
Slater Walker Ltd
G Smethurst
H M Solomans
Soroptimist International of Radcliffe
    & District
Marian Spencer
Dudley A C Spensley
Miss Ana Steiger
Mr & Mrs Rod Steiger
Margaret C Stevens
Clare Stewart
Stockpack Ltd
Mr & Mrs R B Stoker
Stretford Borough Council
Stretford Children's Theatre
G H Sugden
Sun Alliance & London Insurance Group
David Swift
Nora Swinburne
Tarmac Ltd
Emma & Sophie Thompson
Thrells Ltd
Tottington UDC
Wendy Toye
Turquands Barton Mayhew & Co
Vale Mill (Rochdale) Ltd
Anthony Valentine
Harold Vanstone
Miss E V Veevers
Wilfred Verber
Vernons Pools
H R H The Prince of Wales
Dr A H C Walker
D N Walton
Tom Walton Charity Fund
Bernard Wardle & Co
Price Waterhouse & Co
Gwen Watford
Weatherogue Ltd
Whinney Murray & Co
Caspar Wickham
Jeffry Wickham
Rupert Wickham
Saskia Wickham
David William
Victoria Williams
Willis Faber & Dumas Ltd
Eunice E Woodfield
Edward Woodward
Worsley U D C
W S G Productions
Michael York
Mrs W J M Ziegler

**In addition the Trust received hundreds
of donations under £50.00 from generous
individuals**

The Mobil Playwriting Competition

New plays are the lifeblood of the theatre, but good new plays are unfortunately too scarce to sustain that life at the level required for growth and development. That was the view held by the artistic directors for the first few years of the Royal Exchange's life but one which they fervently hoped circumstances would make them alter. Although around a dozen unsolicited playscripts would arrive at the theatre each week, very few showed any promise. The dearth of good new work meant that Royal Exchange premieres were usually commissioned – many were either adaptations of novels or musicals. Only one, *The Dresser* by Ronald Harwood, had national and international success.

It was not until 1983 that Casper Wrede floated the idea of a major national playwriting competition to find the new writers so desperately needed. Nothing on such a scale had been attempted since Kenneth Tynan ran a major competition for *The Observer* in 1957. And the only way to ensure its success was to find an enlightened sponsor to put up sufficient prize-money to act as a spur.

Early negotiations with a potential sponsor came to nothing but in May 1984 Alex Bernstein, Chairman of the Theatre and of the Granada Group, wrote to John Lowein, his counterpart at Mobil, to ask if Mobil would be interested in sponsoring such a competition. The response was both swift and encouraging. Within a few weeks agreement was reached: Mobil not only became sponsors of this major project, they also suggested a substantial increase in the prize-money being offered and that they play a major role in the promotion of the competition. Both decisions were pointers to their enthusiasm for the venture and were a foretaste of their committment to what was a potential risk: what would happen if none of the entered plays were considered worthy of prizes, let alone production?

Casper Wrede was determined that new writers should not receive any less consideration in the judging than established playwrights – the competition was, after all, a search for fresh talent. The rules drawn up over the following weeks reflected the importance of this; all plays had to be entered under a pseudonym (with the author's actual name and address in a sealed envelope to be opened only when the jury had reached its final decision) and anonymity had to be strictly maintained until the prize ceremony. Otherwise the competition was open to *anyone* regardless of age, nationality or country of residence. The only other stipulations were that each play had to be original, full-length and written in English, and not previously produced or offered for production.

An eminent band of theatre people readily agreed to act as judges. Writer and broadcaster Melvyn Bragg as Chairman of the Panel was joined by two distinguished playwrights Alan Bennett and Willy Russell, West End producer Michael Codron, actress Joan Plowright and, representing the Royal Exchange Theatre, James Maxwell. The closing date for entries, 31 August 1985, was set to give writers the maximum possible time, and four prizes totalling £21,000 (the greatest amount of prize money ever offered for a literary competition) were created including a special prize for North West writers in memory of Michael Elliott.

The Competition was launched at a press conference in October 1984, held at the Savoy Hotel in London. The venue was chosen because of the need to secure the highest possible profile for the competition, and the guests, who included the then Minister for the Arts Lord Gowrie, dramatists like Harold Pinter and leading members of the profession, were treated to a specially-commissioned cocktail, *Writer's Cramp!*

Mobil publicised the competition through advertisements in the national press. Although leaflets were widely distributed to theatres, playwrights' agents, universities, colleges and libraries all over the country, such was the power of the advertising campaign and press coverage that there were 6000 additional requests (for leaflets) from 32 countries round the world.

The first entry (a nine-page handwritten first play by a young boy!) arrived within a fortnight of the launch, but the bulk of the 2000 entries from 14 countries were received in the final month of the competition's duration. A team of 37 outside readers, the Royal Exchange's artistic directors, and two full-time staff ensured that every play was read and assessed by at least two people. Literary Manager Michael Fox reckoned that he read around 700 plays that year, undoubtedly a world record! Two months after the closing date a short list of 33 plays, each of which had been read by five or more pairs of eyes, was despatched to each of the six judges.

The adjudication meeting at Mobil House in November 1985 was fairly short; the list was quickly whittled down to six but then a problem was encountered. James Maxwell, on behalf of the jury, later announced: "The breadth and quality of the short-listed entries had so impressed the judges that they were keen to award six prizes instead of the four originally intended. Mobil responded very generously by increasing the amount of prize money to £23,000 to make that possible."

Willy Russell receiving a *Business Sponsorship Incentive Scheme Award* on behalf of the Royal Exchange – a cheque for £20,000 – from the then Arts Minister, Lord Gowrie, at a presentation in the theatre on 29 March 1985. The money was used in the further promotion of the *Mobil Playwriting Competition.*

The prize ceremony was held in the Royal Exchange Theatre on 6 December. Some 200 distinguished guests, many of whom had flown up from London for the occasion, heard anecdotes about the 'Problems of a Dramatist' compiled by Michael Meyer and performed by Dame Wendy Hiller, Alec McCowen and Freddie Jones before the awards were presented.

Joint winners, who each received cheques of £7,500 from Joan Plowright, were a Belfast schoolteacher, Robin Glendinning for *Mumbo Jumbo* and 'Coronation Street' script-writer Tony Perrin, from Newcastle-under-Lyme, for *War Pictures*. The third prize of £3,000 was presented by Tom Courtenay to 28-year-old Jeff Noon from Manchester. His first play *Woundings* was written when he was unemployed earlier that year. The Michael Elliott Prize for the best play set in the North West of England by a writer resident in the North West was awarded to the only well-established playwright amongst the winners, Liverpool-based Nigel Baldwin. His play *Insolent Confessions*, set in a women's prison in the Lake District, also won for its author £3,000. Two additional prizes of £1,000 each went to the London Scot Iain Heggie for *A Wholly Healthy Glasgow* and to a 73-year-old Californian, Herbert Finn, whose previous writing credits had ranged from material for Bob Hope to the television cartoon 'The Flintstones', for *The Almoster*. Both were first efforts at stage plays and both were comedies.

The judging panel had also expressed the wish that several other plays should receive public commendation. They were: *Traitor's Gate* by Canadian Jim Fox, *Tilting Ground* by Guy Hibbert, Michele Celeste's *Obeah*, *Scout's Honour* by Christopher Douglas, and, in the North West Category, *In Mr Singh's Kitchen* by the poet Tony Connor.

James Maxwell summed up the importance of the competition to the Royal Exchange: "Mobil's sponsorship was a remarkable act of faith in an initiative to support today's playwrights and to stimulate tomorrow's. I am delighted to tell you that their faith has been amply justified. For the first time in years the Royal Exchange Theatre Company's artistic directors have found a number of new plays they are excited about. We will be taking options on several plays which we hope to perform in the next few seasons and many others I am sure will be produced elsewhere. The underlying objective – that of finding new writers with whom the theatre can work over a number of years – has also been achieved."

Photo: Alistair McDavid

The Judging Panel: Alan Bennett, Michael Codron, James Maxwell, Willy Russell, Joan Plowright and Melvyn Bragg.

The truth of his words was borne out within a few months. The company mounted the joint first prizewinner *Mumbo Jumbo* in May 1986 with the late Nigel Stock leading a strong cast under Nicholas Hytner's direction. Robin Glendinning's sensitive, disturbing and amusing play about the pain of adolescent sexual awakening set against the background of the passion and violence of present-day Northern Ireland was very well received. And the following month Casper Wrede directed another short-listed play *The Act* by BBC television script editor Richard Langridge.

Shortly thereafter the artistic directors decided to stage two more of the prize-winners, *Woundings* (the production of which was subsequently sponsored by Mobil) and *A Wholly Healthy Glasgow,* during the Tenth Anniversary Season in 1986/87. Oberon Books agreed to

Winners of the first *Mobil Playwriting Competition* left to right: Herbert Finn, Iain Heggie, Nigel Baldwin, Jeff Noon, Tony Perrin and Robin Glendinning

publish both plays to coincide with their productions. Jeff Noon and Iain Heggie were also appointed writers-in-residence for the season (the former with the support of the Peter Q. Henriques Trust, the latter with funding from the Arts Council) and commissioned to write their second plays for the Royal Exchange. Two new playwrights were launched on their careers and Casper Wrede's underlying objective in initiating the whole venture – that of nurturing talented new writers once they had been found through the competition – was about to be realised. Heggie received further commissions from the Royal Court, Liverpool Playhouse and BBC Television. To cap it all, on 27 November 1986, the same night that *Woundings* opened in Manchester, Mobil was presented with an ABSA Award (prestigious awards made annually by the Association for Business Sponsorship of the Arts) for Best Single Project – just recognition of the project's success and of Mobil's central role in it.

Since then at least twenty five plays from the first competition have been performed, some in major productions by companies like the Royal Shakespeare Company (*Indigo* by Heidi Thomas) or major theatres such as the Lyric Hammersmith *(Scout's Honour* by Christopher Douglas), others in fringe venues or in playreadings. In the autumn of 1986 the New Victoria Theatre at Newcastle-under-Lyme produced the other joint first prize-winner *War Pictures* by Tony Perrin.

Photo: Mike Arron

The Royal Exchange's Mobil productions have been seen elsewhere too: Nicholas Hytner restaged *Mumbo Jumbo* at the Lyric Hammersmith in May 1987 under the banner of Avalon Productions and it was published simultaneously by Chappell Plays and later broadcast, albeit with a partly altered cast, on BBC Radio 4; Frank Dunlop invited the company to make its debut at the 1987 Edinburgh International Festival with *A Wholly Healthy Glasgow*, and, in January 1988, Heggie's comedy transferred to the Royal Court Theatre for a 4½ week run. It was published by Methuen, and a television version of the play (using the same cast and director but filmed in a Glasgow studio) was seen on BBC 1. The other plays were soon to receive productions elsewhere: *Woundings* was staged at RADA, and *The Act* at the Belgrade Theatre, Coventry, Nottingham Playhouse and the Offstage Theatre in London.

Photo: John Peters

Mobil Playwriting Competition 1988 Awards Ceremony left to right: Josephine Hart, San Cassimally (Special Prizewinner), Tom Courtenay, Eleanor Bron, Gabriel Gbadamosi (Special Prizewinner), James Maxwell, Lucy Gannon (Special Prizewinner), Ronald Harwood, Alex Finlayson (Special Prizewinner) and Michael Frayn.

Photo: John Peters

Mobil Playwriting Competition 1988 Awards Ceremony left to right: Tom Courtenay, Michele Celeste (International Prizewinner), Albert Finney, Michael Wall (First Prizewinner), Rod Williams (Joint Second Prizewinner), Geraldine McEwan and Keith Wood (Joint Second Prizewinner).

The overwhelming success of the competition, even at an early stage when only one or two of the plays had been produced, made it inevitable that another would be held. Launched in London in March 1987 with a closing date of 16 January 1988, the second Mobil Playwriting Competition promises to be just as valuable – in fact, rather more so if prize money is the only criterion! Mobil increased the prizes on offer to £25,000 (including first, second and third prizes of £10,00, £5,00 and £3,000) and, significantly, added a bursary of £8,000 to provide a writer-in-residence for one year at the Royal Exchange Theatre. Another innovation was the International Prize for the best play by a foreign writer, reflecting the considerable interest from abroad in the first competition. The jury was again a distinguished one, chaired by Ronald Harwood. Other members were his fellow playwright Michael Frayn, actress and writer Eleanor Bron (replacing the broadcaster Joan Bakewell whose commitments forced her to withdraw), London producer Josephine Hart, and the actors and Royal Exchange directors James Maxwell and Ian McDiarmid.

Sixteen hundred entries were received from 25 countries, about a quarter of the plays being in the International category. The majority came from America but others arrived from Canada, Australia, the Far East, India and most European countries. Following the judging, Literary Manager Michael Fox revealed that "the average standard was higher that that of the previous competition but, as one of the jury remarked, there was very little joy or celebration in any of the plays. The 'tough' school of English writing was predominant, with the best plays demonstrating a gritty honesty in coming to terms with life as it is currently lived."

Nevertheless the jury had no difficulty in selecting prizewinners. At the prize ceremony (in the Royal Exchange on 17 May 1988) James Maxwell spoke on behalf of the jury: "The quality of the short-listed plays so impressed the judges that they wished the talent of eight writers to be recognised." The number of prizes was increased from six to eight, with no prize in the North West category but three additional 'special' prizes. The international appeal of the competition was underlined by the nationalities of the winners – an American, an Irish Nigerian, an Italian and a Mauritian as well as four Britons.

The first prize was won by London-based writer Michael Wall for *Amongst Barbarians*, a play about two young Englishmen under sentence of death in a Malaysian prison for drug smuggling and the effect on their families. Wall was already established as a writer with four stage plays, a television play and eleven radio plays (including 'Hiroshima: The Movie' which won the Sony and Giles Cooper Awards in 1985) to his credit. Like Albert Finney, who presented the cheque for £10,000 to him, Wall lived in Salford as a child.

Joint second prizes of £4,000 cash were awarded to two young English writers for their first stage plays. Rod Williams, from London,

won with *No Remission* about three lifers confined to one cell during a prison riot and Keith Wood, from Bristol, with *Assuming The Role*, in which an apparent innocent migrates South and becomes a ruthless exploiter of other's weaknesses.

The recipient of the International Prize of £3,000 was Michele Celeste, an Italian living in London who had been commended in the first Mobil competition. His play *Hanging the President* brutally exploits the dramatic possibilities of an Afrikaaner prison in which two murderers await execution in the company of a black freedom fighter.

Four Special prizes of £1,000 each were won by San Cassimally, a Mauritian now teaching mathematics in Dunstable, for a comedy about Nigerian business corruption *Acquisitive Case*, Alex Finlayson, an American from Richmond, Virginia, for her 'divine comedy' *Winding The Ball*, Lucy Gannon from Derby (winner of the first Richard Burton Award in 1986 and the author of plays staged by the RSC and the Bush Theatre) for a play about mental patients' release into the community *A Dog, Barking*, and Gabriel Gbadamosi, an Irish Nigerian, also living in London for *Shango*, which poetically evokes a West African courtship and marriage, with shades of Lorca's 'Blood Wedding'.

Chairman of the Royal Exchange Alex Bernstein summed up the results: "We are confident that this second competition, which has attracted some remarkable talent, will amply repay Mobil's faith in supporting the search for new writing for the theatre." Of course, only time, production of the plays, and the judgements of others will tell if the jury chose wisely. The first major test will come when the first prize-winner *Amongst Barbarians* is premiered in Manchester in February, 1989 but one of the second prize-winners *Assuming The Role* was premiered in October 1988. Two performances with limited decor were given on Sunday evenings as part of a new initiative to increase the amount of new work produced by the Theatre. Other plays are also scheduled for production next spring and winner of the first Mobil bursary Gabriel Gbadamosi should, as writer-in-residence at the Royal Exchange Theatre, be writing a new play – another new play!

Since the inception of the Royal Exchange Theatre Company, one of its policies has been to make its work as widely seen as possible. One third of the 69 Theatre Company's productions transferred to London or toured elsewhere in England and the value of such exposure quickly became apparent. No fewer than 23 productions of the Royal Exchange's have been enjoyed by audiences outside Manchester, from Edinburgh to Bucharest – despite the fact that the company is firmly rooted in the North West.

The first tour, the result of an invitation from the British Council, was in the autumn of 1979, the year of the company's two foreign visits. The initial foray was a brief but highly successful appearance at the Festival of Arena Theatre at Münster in Germany in May that year with Michael Elliott's production of *Crime and Punishment*, but the second was a major European tour. For five weeks, following visits to Cardiff and Oxford, the company toured *The Winter's Tale* in a highly complex operation through seven countries.

Opening performances at the Shakespeare Festival at the Thalia Theatre in Hamburg were followed by appearances in Holland (in Rotterdam, Arnhem and Eindhoven), Belgium (as part of the Flanders Festival in Louvain and at The Royal Flemish Theatre in Brussels), Luxembourg, West Germany (Cologne, Ludwigshafen and Frankfurt), Switzerland (Basle), Hungary (as part of the major annual festival Budapest Arts Week) and Romania.

THE ROYAL EXCHANGE ON TOUR

■ Transfers and pre-London touring

● On tour with the mobile theatre

THE MOBILE THEATRE

THEATRE DESIGN	Alan Broadhurst of Broadhurst & Goodwin, Consulting Structural Engineers, Manchester
PROJECT MANAGER	Clive Odom
ACOUSTIC DESIGN	D K Jones
TECHNICAL DESIGN	Production Departments of the Royal Exchange Theatre Theatre Construction, front of house, and back stage provisions carried out by the staff of the Royal Exchange Theatre Company
FABRICATION	James Thomas Engineering Ltd, Pershore, Worcs.
ACOUSTIC COVERING	Mitco Peck Tarpaulins, Wigan
SEATS	G & C Home & Leisure Supplies Ltd, Pershore, Worcs
SEATING ROSTRA	Richard Welding Services, Worthing

It was built with the financial support of the following organisations:

The Granada Foundation

Arthur Andersen & Co Foundation
The Arts Council of Great Britain
Friends of the Royal Exchange Theatre
Gibbs Sage Ltd
Granada Television
The Heinz & Anna Kroch Foundation
The Leche Trust
National Westminster Bank
The New Moorgate Trust Fund
Reeds Rains
Harry Whittaker Ltd

The Royal Exchange Theatre Trustees

An exhausted company flew back from Bucharest – only to go straight into rehearsals again so that the production, which had been playing in proscenium arch theatres throughout Europe, could be adapted to 'in-the-round' for its Manchester performances two weeks later.

The tour highlighted the main problem the Royal Exchange has in transferring its work – the 'orientation' of productions. In the following two years when six Royal Exchange successes were taken to the Round House at Chalk Farm in London, the company constructed its own seven-sided seating arrangements in the auditorium and was able to stage the shows exactly as in Manchester.

Thereafter the decision was made that when the company ventured outside its own theatre, it should, wherever possible, play in a seven-sided round stage configuration. At the same time the desire to produce more work by new writers and develop a new play policy in a space similar to the main auditorium became evident. *Creating* a structure which would fulfil both roles was the only straightforward solution to the artistic directors' problem: a structure that had exactly the same stage size, seating on seven sides and an audience capacity large enough for economic touring but sufficiently intimate for new work. The idea of the mobile theatre was born.

The theatre was designed and constructed during 1982 and the early part of 1983. Following Richard Negri's blueprint, the structure was designed by Alan Broadhurst of Broadhurst & Goodwin, Consulting Structural Engineers based in the Corn Exchange in Manchester. The brief required that the theatre would be assembled and dismantled quickly and easily and that it could be packed, along with sets, costumes and all technical equipment, into three 40' articulated lorries. Not an easy brief but one that was realised superbly!

By the spring of 1983 the Royal Exchange had a second auditorium costing £90,000, practically all of which was raised privately. Although the overall structure is smaller than the parent theatre – it is on only one level – the stage area follows the same dimensions. Seating 403 people, the theatre itself is a framework made from 42 sections of lightweight aluminium tubing. Each section is light enough and small enough to be carried through a standard doorway by only two people. The framework forms a seven-sided cone rising 12 feet from floor level, and is covered with Ny-tarp, a flame-retardant PVC coated nylon, which forms an acoustic barrier over and around the auditorium. During construction the roof is winched up from the floor on seven 10 foot high towers (using hand-operated 'turfor' winches) – but only after the lighting bars, ready-rigged with lanterns, speakers, house-lights and cables have been hung from underneath. The seven blocks of seats, when assembled inside the structure, leave a central stage floor area measuring 30 feet in diameter. The outer walls, also made of Ny-tarp, and the seven doors (hung on lift-off hinges) are the final parts of the structure to be installed.

The complete theatre can be erected in as little as 8 hours and taken down in 5. All that is required to accommodate it is an unobstructed space of 80' x 80' x 25' minimum (25m x 25m x 7.5m), in order to conform with safety and fire regulations, and a power supply (a three-phase mains input of 100 amps per phase). Thus the fully equipped theatre can fit easily into the space available in most sports and community halls, and it has the important advantage that, whatever the venue, the same relationship between actors and audience and the same high standard of lighting, sound and acoustics is maintained. Artistic and technical standards need not be sacrificed when the Royal Exchange is on tour, all audiences should see *exactly* the same production.

The first use of the new theatre was not on tour, however, but for *Festival '83*, a festival of new writing held from mid-April to mid-June in the Corn Exchange in Hanging Ditch, only a couple of minutes walk from the Royal Exchange. Planned by Gregory Hersov, the festival presented the work of three young writers, Simon Moss, Jonathan Moore and Sarah Daniels, as well as shows by visiting companies, the Black Theatre Co-operative, the People Show, the National Theatre of Brent and Paines Plough. All three of the company's productions – Moss's *Cock Ups*, seen in a specially revised version, *Street Captives* by Jonathan Moore and the only premiere *Masterpieces* by Sarah Daniels – showed what could be achieved when new young writers, directors, designers and technicians are given the time and the space to develop their skills. The season was made possible by a special projects grant from the Arts Council and funding from North West Arts. Despite the success of *Festival '83*, lack of revenue funding prevented the staging of further seasons of new writing in the same venue, and also stymied plans, which were worked on up to 1987, to convert the Corn Exchange hall into a *permanent* second theatre space for the company.

The second function of the mobile theatre, that of touring, came to fruition in 1984. In April a company led by Robert Lindsay, Alison Fiske and Philip Madoc began a nine-week, eleven-venue tour of *Hamlet*. Braham Murray's production had packed the Royal Exchange for eight weeks the previous autumn, and it played to capacity audiences from Newbiggin-by-the-Sea to Crawley. The tour ended up with a three-week season on the roof of the Barbican Centre in London, the only occasion on which the structure has been used out of doors. An extra Ny-tarp cover was made to shield the theatre from the elements but the actors were frequently caught in the rain as they waited outside to go on stage!

Actors Edward Fox, Alfred Burke and Ursula Smith are shown the mobile theatre by project manager Clive Odom, while Michael Elliott and James Maxwell look on.

Subsequent tours have been equally successful. In 1986 Nicholas Hytner's production of *As You Like It*, with Janet McTeer as Rosalind, also toured to eleven venues but five of them were new. The following year Ben Jonson's comedy *The Alchemist*, directed by Gregory Hersov, took to the road with sponsorship from Prudential, and in 1988 Ian McDiarmid directed Molière's *Don Juan*, with Bernard Bresslaw and Jonathan Kent, for another barnstorming tour.

All the tours have been funded by the Touring department of the Arts Council, and have played 'non-theatrical' venues (i.e. school halls or sports halls in leisure centres) in towns with no major resident theatre company or proscenium touring venue. The Royal Exchange, by its ability to take its own theatre on tour, can give the public in these areas the opportunity to see live theatre of a quality and scale not locally available.

TOUR ● ON TOUR ●

Photo: Clive Totman

Robert Lindsay with the mobile theatre under construction on the roof of the Barbican in 1984.
Below: a series of photographs taken in Huddersfield Sports Centre showing the mobile theatre being constructed.

Local authorities also play a crucial role in the funding of these tours. District, Borough and County Councils, various local arts support groups and Regional Arts Associations may be approached for financial assistance towards a touring package so that the Royal Exchange is paid a per performance fee in each town visited. In each venue one of these organisations, usually the Leisure Services department of the local authority itself, acts as promoter liaising with the company over the provision of facilities at the sports centre, marketing and box office services and so on.

The Royal Exchange's Tour Manager co-ordinates all aspects of the venture from the selection of venues and financial negotiations to transport, insurance and accommodation, and ensures that everything runs smoothly and morale remains high. With continual travelling (the company usually plays three towns in every two-week period) and limited facilities (dressing rooms are often the changing rooms of sports halls and technicians, wardrobe and stage management staff may be squeezed into some storage room with accompanying equipment) touring can be a difficult, trying and certainly very tiring way of life.

Free time is limited further by the number of events the company offers to the public. Besides eight full performances each week, there are open days, after-show discussions, technical talks, educational workshops given by actors, production staff and the education director, and sometimes a late-night show as well. During the *Don Juan* tour, for instance, most of the company was involved in staging late-night performances of Marivaux's one-act comedy *Slave Island*. In the whole seven-week tour in 1988 over 100 events or performances were presented. Such a schedule undoubtedly fulfils the company's aim of making its work accessible but it also explains partly why only one tour of this nature is arranged each year!

Photos: John Woods

Notes from the Front: Memories of The Winter's Tale

As I put pen to paper in the comfort of my own home in SW9 it seems purely fantasy that the Manchester Royal Exchange White Elephant, sometimes known as *The Winter's Tale*, ever managed to flap its dumboesque ears, take off, land in time and receive a standing ovation in Hamburg's Thalia Theatre. How the technical crew ever managed this "almost miracle" we shall never know. All we do know is that it happened – not just once but again and again right across Europe. Towns, theatres, even countries merge. If its Tuesday it *must* be Ludwigshafen. Where?

Certain details of course stand out – the total comprehension of the German Audiences. Sharper and more alert to verbal humour in Cologne than in Cardiff. The stage-hands who talked incessantly and the electricians who plunged us into a Stygian gloom undreamed of even by Michael Williams, the veritable Prince of Darkness. All this was the revenge of Leuven for our daring to speak in French, a language they abominate. The curtain calls in Germany, protracted until the last solitary clapper has packed up and decided he has had enough. The slow hand claps in Budapest – a sign of approval. The Theatrical Experience, the play, its performance, its audience, remain constant from Bolton to Bucharest.

A theatrical company on tour, such as ours, is subject to extreme emotional and physical pressures. We were an ill-assorted bunch, our only common factor being the play. No-one can imagine the hidden strengths and weaknesses that would be revealed. The strain was at times unbelievable, although most of us found some life-line. One thing is certain: no-one who landed at Heathrow on the 27th October had remained unaffected by the experience.

If the memories of the performances have become blurred, many sights and sounds stand out in sharp relief. The clamour of bells on a Sunday morning in Basle. A secretive city, its rose-coloured cathedral perched high above the Rhine, its myriad fountains, its beauties revealed slowly but with quiet certainty. The cracked pavements and gaping holes of earthquake stricken Bucharest. The slow-moving canals of The Dead City – Bruges. Old Heidelberg prettier than any cut-out setting for 'The Student Prince'. The ostentatious affluence of Frankfurt – gross and overpowering like its sausages and its men. The sad, begrimed delapidation of Budapest. Imperial magnificence tottering on crumbling foundations. We will all have our own memories. They will endure.

There was enough time for many extra-mural activities. Four intrepid travellers set out for The Reeperbahn, Hamburg's Golden Mile of Sin. Good German Deutschmarks were paid out, watered down. Schnapps imbibed, grotesque fumblings observed, hysteria set in, intrepid foursome feel obliged to leave. Rembrandts in The Hague, the Bejart Ballet in Brussels, a grotesque *Cosi fan Tutte* in Bucharest, Botanical Gardens everywhere.

Five weeks and seven countries later The White Elephant landed at Heathrow to be met by an industrial dispute. The resilient company, bruised but still game for the next hurdle – the production must be refashioned for the Royal Exchange Theatre. A new challenge. Shakespeare will survive and so, I am sure, will the Company, after its baptism of fire across Europe.

Knight Mantell (A member of the cast of *The Winter's Tale* writing on return from the tour)

Return to Arden

It was a long hard winter in Manchester. The production may have been *As You Like It*, the weather was most definitely not. In the 'green room' the talk would turn from time to time to 'the tour'; which was to begin in April.

I would describe with great enthusiasm to my colleagues the delights of Northumberland; its coastline and castles, its market towns and moorlands and its lush green valleys; infinite in its variety, its views and its history. All this I painted in the rose-tinted hues of a Coquet Valley childhood.

Well, it gave them something to look forward to, but ask them now what they remember of Newbiggin and Northumberland and the answer you'll get is the Rex Hotel, Whitley Bay and an Italian restaurant in Morpeth. Touring is hard work.

Visiting two venues, performing eight shows and presenting two workshops every week for six weeks is exhausting. When you've seen one leisure centre you've seen them all.

When you've performed for three and a half hours one bar is as good as another if it's open; and even those with the stamina to rise before mid-day and venture out would find winter still on the doorstep. It's still there now isn't it?

I did, however, leave one vital element out of my tourist board eulogy to Northumber-

Rigging lanterns in the mobile theatre

land; the people. As a result the Company were able to discover for themselves, like all visitors before them, the friendliness and humour of the people of the North East.

Accommodating and adaptable like nowhere else we visited they came into their own when gathered together as an audience. There was a freshness and generosity of response that can only come from going to the theatre with open-minded anticipation; without the pre-conceptions of the 'theatre-goer', the voyeurism of the tourist or the stubbornness of the 'punter'.

It was the people who made the Company's visit to Northumberland different and memorable. I am proud to be one of them; if I can still lay claim to be so.

In spite of close family ties, the years spent at Durham University and the Flora Robson Playhouse, I still feel something of an alien when returning to the North East.

It has to do with 'leaving home' and entering a world as far removed from farming as the theatre is; and I've lived in London now for twenty years. To come up for Christmas is one thing; to come as an actor entirely another. To stay with my family and go out to work is a curious contradiction. It's a contradiction that resolved itself in Newbiggin in a way that demonstrates the truth of *As You Like It* and the power of the theatre. To be on stage as Duke Frederick was to be a representative of that alien world of which a Northumberland audience were as naturally suspicious as they are of their own seat of government and contemporary metropolitan values.

To be on stage as Corin was to be one of the audience and to share their instinctive understanding of the world and values of Arden; no rose-tinted rural life but a place of hardship, hard work, honesty and humour where my family had lived and worked for generations.

It was a joy to represent that on stage and to feel the two worlds finally connect. Like the characters in the play, my true feelings have been released and my perceptions sharpened by a brief visit to Arden.

David Howey (A member of the cast of **As You Like It** writing shortly after the tour)

Photo: John Woods

MOUNTING A PRODUCTION

Planning the Season

The artistic directors decide on the plays to be produced throughout the season. Together with the administrator they co-ordinate the time-scale and establish the opening dates for each production as early as possible. They also decide who will direct each play. They consult the administrator and the financial controller who, together with the production manager, draw up the budgets for the season. The heads of each department cost out their individual requirements within this overall figure.

Planning a Production

The director selects a designer (possibly two or three, for sets, costumes and lighting) and together they discuss the manner in which the production is to be presented. The director and casting director cast the production, initially approaching any performers the director has in mind. Auditions are held to find the right actors for the remaining characters and the cast is contracted as quickly as possible. The Royal Exchange does not employ understudies so the director is only looking for the specific characters in the play.

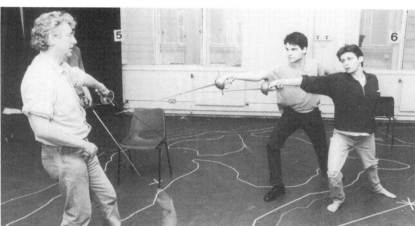

Malcolm Ranson arranging the fights for Don Juan with Mark Aiken and Darryl Knock

Rehearsals

Rehearsals generally start four or five weeks prior to the opening date. A production meeting is held on the first day of rehearsals, at which the director introduces the cast to each other and to the theatre staff: the meeting is usually attended by all the heads of department. The director then talks about the play and his interpretation of it, and the designer explains his model of the set and costume drawings.

The director rehearses the company every day (excluding Sunday), at the end of each day's work deciding which scenes he will concentrate on the following day. The stage manager posts the company's 'calls' on the notice board, so that each actor knows what time they are needed.

Up to the final week, rehearsals are held in the rehearsal room, which has been 'blocked'

to resemble the stage, as it will be when the set is complete. During the last week all rehearsals are held on stage so that the actors become accustomed to the space. This is particularly important as the Royal Exchange is very different from traditional proscenium stages. The close proximity of the audience, completely surrounding the performance area, may be daunting to actors appearing there for the first time!

During the rehearsal period, weekly production meetings are held to monitor the progress of the production and to deal with any technical problems as they arise. These are attended by the production manager, director, designers, heads of sound, lighting, wardrobe, props and wig departments and the stage management team.

The Eleventh Hour

The last few days before a play opens are extremely busy for every department. The director and actors do 'technical' and dress rehearsals on stage, whilst final touches are added to the set and costumes, and the electricians and technicians adjust the sound, lighting and mechanics. During the final rehearsals, production photographs are taken for front-of-house displays and for the press. There is also a photo-call for all members of the press to take their own shots.

Amanda Donohoe, Hugh Quarshie and other members of the Cymbeline cast in rehearsals.

The First Night

The First Night or Press Night of a production, is always at 7.00pm, even though most evening performances start at 7.30 or 8.00pm. This is to allow the critics time to meet their printing deadlines.

In Performance

The Half

For all performances, actors are required to be in the theatre 35 minutes before curtain-up. This is a standard theatre requirement which is known as 'the half', and ensures that there can be no confusion as to when performers are called.

Controls

Due to the shape of the theatre module the control desk cannot be hidden (as it is in most theatres) and therefore all the cues are given by the DSM (deputy stage manager) in a control area on the second gallery, amongst the audience.

Sara Richardson in her dressing room preparing for a performance of ZACK

Dressing Rooms

Actors use dressing rooms to prepare for the performance and also to relax, both before and during a show, when they are not on stage. The theatre has 4 single dressing rooms, 2 for four people and 1 for six. There are also quick-change dressing rooms situated at the back of the foyer for occasions when actors do not have time to get back to their own dressing rooms for costume changes. Experienced dressers are needed, particularly for quick changes, to help artists into, and out of, costumes swiftly and silently.

As there are always two acting companies working in the theatre, the rehearsing company cannot get access to the dressing rooms until the production week, after the previous show has ended and that cast has left. In the meanwhile they keep their belongings in lockers close to the rehearsal room.

Green Room

The Green Room is a théâtre 'common room' – a room which everyone working in the theatre can use to buy hot drinks and food, or simply as a sitting room. Traditionally it was used primarily for actors to relax between rehearsals and whilst waiting to go on stage; it was painted green as this was considered the most restful colour – hence the name. This is rarely the case these days and the Royal Exchange's is, in fact, cream and blue!

THE PRODUCTION TEAM

Design

The director and designer discuss the concept of the production a long way in advance. The designer then makes a model of the set and prepares costume designs (sets and costumes are often done by different designers) for an initial production design meeting. The meeting will be attended by the production manager, stage management team, workshop and technical staff. It is important to discuss all aspects of the designs in order to establish how the set will be constructed and operated, and to allow sufficient time to modify designs if necessary in the light of budgetary, technical or potential sight-line problems.

Settings and Props

Because the theatre is in-the-round, there are no traditional sets – which consist of 'flats' (flat pieces of scenery slid or lowered on to the stage to form a backdrop to the action) – and no 'wings' for stage entrances. Instead the actors enter and exit through all the six doors used by the audience and by two others which are often used to bring on parts of the settings or props. Use is also made of the 'flying' equipment and productions may include major elements (sometimes actors!) being flown on stage.

The lack of scenery encourages a strong emphasis on stage flooring and props. The theatre employs a props buyer to hire or purchase props for each production but the majority of props, and all the floor coverings, are constructed in the workshop. This is situated at stage level so that large items can be transported easily into the theatre. Designs for both sets and props have to take into account the shape and size of the auditorium and its entrances, and they must be made to very high standards because the audience is close enough to see minute details.

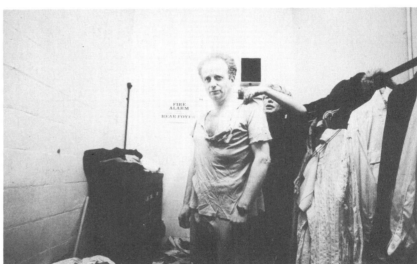

Top: Nicholas Hytner (director), Mark Thompson (designer) and members of the production team for The Country Wife *in a design production meeting. Above: Ian McDiarmid being fitted for one of his costumes in* Edward II. *Below: members of the Props Department in the workshop.*

Costumes

For the same reason particular attention is paid to detail in designing and creating the costumes. The costume designer and wardrobe supervisor usually go shopping together for fabrics and for any costumes that are to be bought or hired. Once costumes have been cut and partially made, actors' costume fittings are held, attended by the designer, supervisor and costume cutter, so that any alterations or changes can be made at this stage. A second fitting session will usually take place before the final touches are added, to check for fit and comfort.

Once the production has opened, costumes are laundered and mended on a regular basis, many items needing daily washing and ironing. It is essential that costumes are well-maintained throughout the production, both for the good of their appearance and for the comfort of the actors.

Costumes and props are housed in the theatre's stores in Piccadilly, as there is no storage space in the theatre. The stores are currently the headquarters of the theatre's hire department, which supplies costumes and props to theatre companies – both amateur and professional – and individuals, from a large and varied stock.

Wigs and Beards

Wigs used at the theatre are all handmade from natural hair, in order to recreate a realistic head of hair for the artist. Again the close proximity of the audience dictates the importance of high quality workmanship and authenticity. Once the wig has been made it is cut and dressed to the required style, which will have been previously decided between the designer, actor and wig-maker. Facial hair is made along the same lines as a wig. A pattern is taken of the artist's beard growth, and hair matched to the colour. Once knotted, the beard, sideburns etc are dressed with fine, old-fashioned tongs.

Lighting

Each show has a different lighting rig, consisting of an arrangement of individual lighting units, known as lanterns. After each production about 10 lighting personnel (many of whom are casual workers brought in especially) dismantle the rig from that show and set up the new one in an overnight session, following a plan created by the lighting designer. The following day a crew of about 4 'focus' the rig with the designer present to supervise the positioning of each lantern. Once the rig has been focussed the director, designers (lighting and set) and lighting-board operator go through the play and gradually create the lighting effects required. These are programmed into the computer-controlled lighting-board, cue by cue.

Sound

The limited use of scenery provides an opportunity to take advantage of the exceptional acoustics of the Royal Exchange building. The theatre itself has a relatively clear and intimate sound, whilst the hall has an extremely reverberant one, and exploiting both these acoustics, simultaneously or alternately, produces notable results.

The unusual number of entrances and possible sound sources mean that substantial equipment is permanently in use. The work of the sound department consists of the preparation of material for performances of all kinds, recording magnetic tape – the theatre possesses 13 tape recorders – and maintaining a routine that checks the performance very thoroughly. Consistency of operation from one performance to the next is essential. It is particularly demanding because, like all routines, it can become tedious and therefore neglected, if its importance is not completely understood by the sound operator.

Stage Management

The stage management team (company manager, stage manager, deputy stage manager, assistant stage manager) is involved with the production from the beginning of rehearsals, throughout the rehearsal and playing period. One member of the team, usually the DSM, is 'on the book', i.e. attends all rehearsals and writes all the stage directions and cues into the prompt copy of the script. The stage management liaise between all departments in the theatre, ensuring that everyone and everything is in the right place at the right time, and that all information relating to the production is disseminated throughout the theatre to the relevant departments.

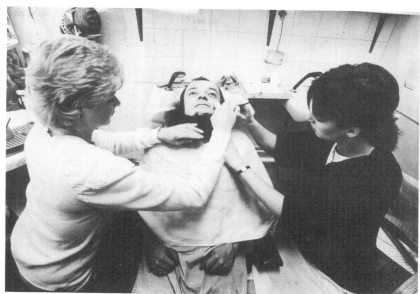

Members of the Wig Department fitting Tim Healey's wig for Zack.

The lighting-board operator at work

Members of the Stage Management team at work

PROMOTING THE PRODUCTION

Box Office

Tickets are on sale from between one and two months before a production opens, so that the box office may well be selling tickets for three main house productions and perhaps a dozen 'special events' at any one time. All tickets are sold via the RITA (Real-Time Integrated Ticketing and Administration) computer system, developed by the Royal Shakespeare Company and British Telecom specifically for theatre box offices. Seating plans showing seat availability for each date can be viewed on the screen and information is keyed in on the keyboard to effect the sale, which automatically appears on the screen. Tickets are sold to personal callers, by phone with a credit card and by post using a cheque or credit card; also through ticket agents around the North West. Apart from ticket sales for individual shows, the theatre operates a successful season-ticket scheme, whereby theatregoers can buy tickets for the season at great discounts in advance of the general public.

Publicity

The publicity department devises and puts into operation all the marketing schemes – such as the season ticket scheme, and the discount schemes for groups or the 'disadvantaged' – to 'sell' the theatre's productions to the public, and produces all the printed material promoting either the theatre itself or specific events. The publicity staff discuss the concept of each production with its director and then brief a freelance graphic designer who designs a poster for the show. Several sizes of posters are printed and distributed, for display in a variety of places, in time for the start of rehearsals. The poster design is used for the front cover of the programme, which is complied, edited and printed during the rehearsal period. At the same time display advertisements are placed in appropriate publications and up to 800 press releases are sent out to local and national press and media. Interviews with actors or others involved with the production are sought from newspapers and magazines, radio and television. As the first night approaches critics are telephoned to check that they can come to review the production, maximising press coverage at the beginning of the run. Promotion of the production does not end with its opening, however. Box office 'returns' (analyses of sales figures) are compiled daily so that the publicity department can respond to sales trends and ensure that the high box office income targets are met.

OTHER FACILITIES FOR THE AUDIENCE

Café Bar

The café is open from 10.00 in the morning until the start of the evening performance, with a wide range of food from snacks to complete meals, and the bar is open during normal licensing hours. The relaxed atmosphere encourages people to use these facilities whenever they are in town, even if they aren't coming to see a performance, and there is always a lively mix of theatre personnel and members of the public.

Top: The Café Bar
Bottom: The Box Office

Craft Centre and Foyer Art Exhibitions

The craft centre, conveniently positioned in the theatre foyer, next to the café-bar, is open from 11.00 every morning until the start of the first performance. First opened in 1981 and extended in size five years later, it has a wide and unusual stock from the best of British craftsmen, with items at all prices. Every month the centre exhibits shows by professional craftworkers so there is always a wide variety of styles. Together with the art exhibitions (of paintings, prints, photographs or even jewellery) around the foyer, which also change on a monthly basis, there is plenty to look at – and buy – whether you're going to see a performance, buying tickets, or just popping in for a coffee while you're out shopping.

From when it first opened, the Royal Exchange Theatre was interested in developing an education programme alongside its main-house activities. It soon became clear that the ad hoc after-show discussions and occasional workshops, which represented the extent of the Company's initial educational work, were inadequate. A greater commitment to the existing arts and educational policies in Greater Manchester was required if people were to be encouraged to learn about theatre through the Royal Exchange.

As the only leading theatre company without any kind of formal programme for young people or theatre-in-education company, there was no doubt that the funding bodies – the Arts Council and local authorities – would approve any such development. Through discussions with representatives from the Arts Council, North West Arts, educationalists and other theatres and arts bodies, the company began to familiarise itself with what other people were already doing, while identifying the gaps in its own area. As a result of this research, the Royal Exchange demonstrated its commitment to providing a comprehensive education service with the appointment of a full-time Education Director early in 1987. In attempting to exploit to the full the enormous potential of the Royal Exchange as a learning source, Education Director John Butterly developed a programme of activities to complement the existing drama education policy in the ten districts of Greater Manchester. His work ranges from creating links with schools and colleges and organising workshops, talks and career sessions to initiating and administering training courses, theatre days and summer schools, as well as running a Young Exchange Club. All this comes under the umbrella of EXCHANGE EDUCATION, the aims of which are:

a) to make theatre more accessible – by demystifying and clarifying the processes of theatre, to make its work more widely understood;
b) to promote an understanding of good theatre practice – through contact with theatre personnel, educators and students are encouraged to develop their own knowledge and skills;
c) to enrich the work of the Royal Exchange – contact with the educational community is seen as a necessary adjunct to the Royal Exchange's own work, increasing its value to the community;
d) to promote equality of opportunity – Exchange Education is committed to equal rights for all, irrespective of race, gender, nationality or disability.

The first few months of Exchange Education were spent on an initial period of contact and research, during which time the Education Director consulted the Ten Districts' Drama Advisors to assess local education authority needs in each of the districts. Discussions with drama and English teachers invited suggestions for possible content of Exchange Education projects and created useful links for the future. By viewing a wide variety of workshops and school productions, John Butterly was able to gauge current provision standards and identify potential difficulties with the change-over to GCSE syllabus.

When devising the Royal Exchange's programme and policy, the Education Director had to balance work in schools with special projects. Although he has had back-up support from all departments of the Royal Exchange, John Butterly has had to work within the limitations of being a one-person operation – a fact which makes it impossible to service all ten districts properly at the same time. The answer to this problem has been found in the implementation of a rolling prog-

Brenda Blethyn taking time between performances of *Born Yesterday* to lead an improvisation workshop at the annual Summer School

Photo: John Peters

Photo: John Peters

Director, Braham Murray, discussing his production of *Macbeth*

ramme of work for Exchange Education, concentrating initially on 14 to 18 year olds, with each district benefitting over a period of two years, every two years. Each year, the majority of activities is focussed on 2-3 districts, with a further 2-3 receiving follow-up attention from the previous academic year ie.

1987/88 Rochdale, Tameside, Trafford
1988/89 Manchester, Wigan
(Rochdale, Tameside, Trafford)
1989/90 Bury, Oldham, Salford
(Manchester, Wigan)
1990/91 Bolton, Stockport
(Bury, Oldham, Salford)

All special projects outside the schools programme, however, are open to the ten districts at all times.

While schools' work represents a major part of the Education Director's time, there are several other areas (briefly mentioned earlier) in which Exchange Education plays a significant role.

One of these is in-service training courses for teachers, a facility made all the more valuable by the new GCSE drama syllabus which requires teachers to be equipped to teach students about set design, lighting, props, costume, make-up and sound etc. The courses are aimed at teachers with a basic knowledge of the subject and comprise talks, practical workshops and "hands-on" learning experience led by members of the Royal Exchange's professional staff. Of course, it is not only teachers who can impart information and, from a group of students on a short-term work experience placement, Exchange Education devised a *Passing-On Project*. Thus a group of sixth formers from Stockport spent two weeks in four departments at the Royal Exchange – sound, lighting, production and box-office and followed this with a 45-minute multi-media presentation entitled *Behind the scenes at the Royal Exchange*.

Pre-production workshops and post-production analysis involve various members of the Theatre's creative team in exploring, with the participants, issues related to a particular production including cast, design, technical work, rehearsals etc.

Each year Exchange Education plays an important role on the Theatre's national tour. For the 1987 tour of Ben Jonson's *The Alchemist* Butterly produced a special education supplement combining background details on Jacobean society with some of the creative thinking behind the Royal Exchange production. On the 1988 tour of Molière's *Don Juan* Exchange Education organised a series of workshops in tour venues throughout the country, often involving actors in school visits which offered pupils the stimulus of both discussions and practical participation.

The same degree of physical involvement and exchange of ideas occurs during the annual Summer School which caters for around thirty students aged 16 to 19 who attend a week-long course at the Royal Exchange. During this time they are tutored in improvisation sessions, play-readings and discussions, technical talks and demonstrations and the administrative side of the theatre, gaining an invaluable insight into behind the scenes and enhancing their understanding of good theatre practice at first-hand. Every department in the company is included from the artistic directors to some of the visiting actors and most of those involved on the company's side would profess to finding the summer school extremely refreshing and rewarding.

A similar though less intense experience is offered through Young Exchange, a group of students aged in their late 'teens who meet fortnightly for acting and technical workshops and talks and demonstrations from the resident creative team. There are other exciting projects planned for the future but many of these are dependent on commercial sponsorship so that, together with the Development Department, the Education Director is constantly reviewing alternative sources of funding in order that the Royal Exchange's education programme remains a challenging and worthwhile area of the company's work.

Musicians of the Royal Exchange

It was a special pleasure to be invited by James Maxwell in late 1977 to form a chamber ensemble to give an annual series of concerts in the Royal Exchange Theatre, both because of my long association with Manchester and because the theatre is so perfectly designed in scale and shape for intimate communication between a small group of musicians and their audience. The first notes of Mozart's wonderful *Trio for clarinet, viola and piano* at 3.30pm on Sunday 1 October 1978 announced the beginning of an ever closer relationship between the Musicians of the Royal Exchange (the name, dubbed an awful mouthful at first, has now long been accepted) and their public, exchanging its after-lunch snooze three or four Sundays a year for a second, musical feast which usually contains an appetising *hors d'oeuvre*, a satisfying main course, a piquant side-dish or two and more often than not a delicious trifle.

Since then the ensemble has grown from its initial number of five, three of whom, Angela Malsbury, Moray Welsh and myself, remain, to the stage where the December 1986 concert – admittedly a special event – featured eleven people and included *Carnival of the Animals* with

"A valuable addition to the musical life of Manchester"
Gerald Larner The Guardian

Caroline Clemmow joining me as a two-piano team. A very important policy has always been to avoid any possible barriers by introducing the music informally from the arena; in addition, successive seasons have gradually taken on their own linking musical motifs, three of the most recent being: less familiar works by Beethoven, instrumental music by Italian opera composers, and Weber/European romantics. Weber joins Bach, Handel, Scarlatti, Schumann, Brahms, Bloch, Messiaen and several others in having had an anniversary commemorated, and a perusal of the list of composers represented reveals quite a few lesser known and unjustly overlooked composers to

"The Royal Exchange Theatre where this group resides is obviously blessed" The Times

have been brought to light, often with exciting results.

The Musicians have steadily widened their horizons, with many London concerts, festival appearances and broadcasts to their credit, but the heart of their activities continues to be the Royal Exchange season. A most felicitous symbiotic relationship has been formed, providing a marvellous spiritual and physical home for the group, while we try our best to repay the enlightened patronage of the Royal Exchange with imaginative and stimulating programmes drawn from all corners of an incomparably rich chamber-music repertoire.
Anthony Goldstone

"An exceptionally talented group of performers" The Guardian

Artists who have performed with the Musicians of the Royal Exchange

ATAR ARAD viola
ALEXANDER BALANESCU viola
NORBERT BLUME viola
TIMOTHY BROWN horn
PETER BUCKOKE double bass
JOAN BUSBY* mezzo soprano
DAVID CAMPBELL* clarinet
JENNIFER CAWS oboe
CAROLINE CLEMMOW piano
MICHAEL COLLINS clarinet
MARCIA CRAYFORD violin
ANDREW CROWLEY* trumpet
PHILIPPA DAVIES flute
PHILIP EASTOP horn
PAUL EDMUND-DAVIES flute
CHRISTOPHER ELTON* piano
CSABA ERDÉLYI viola

IAN FORGRIEVE percussion
ANTHONY GOLDSTONE piano
JOANNA GRAHAM* bassoon
BARRY GRIFFITHS violin
ANTHONY HALSTEAD horn
GARETH HULSE oboe
CARMEL KAINE violin
FRANCES KELLY harp
ELIZABETH LAYTON* violin
RICHARD LESTER cello
FRANK LLOYD horn
CORIN LONG double bass
ANGELA MALSBURY clarinet
PAUL MARRION double bass
JAMES MAXWELL speaker & baritone
SUSAN MILAN flute
KRYSTYNA OSOSTOWICZ violin
DAPHNE OXENFORD presenter
ELISABETH PERRY violin
MELISSA PHELPS cello

JONATHAN REES cello
SIMON ROWLAND-JONES viola
CHRISTIAN RUTHERFORD* horn
BRIAN BANNATYNE SCOTT* bass singer
GRAHAM SHEEN bassoon
PAUL SILVERTHORNE* viola
RICHARD SKINNER* bassoon
RALPH DE SOUZA violin
JONATHAN SPAREY violin
CAROLYN SPAREY* viola
DAVID THEODORE oboe
RONALD THOMAS* violin
JOHN TRUSLER violin
JOHN WALLACE* trumpet
RAPHAEL WALLFISCH cello
MORAY WELSH cello

*Artist who has not performed in the Royal Exchange Theatre

SPECIAL EVENTS

From the very first season, the Royal Exchange has presented a programme of extra events to attract non-theatregoing members of the public. On these pages is a selection of the many hundreds of these special presentations.

Alan Price

Popular Concerts

Alan Price, Albert Finney, Hazel O'Connor, Gordon Giltrap, Barbara Dickson, Georgie Fame, Peter Skellern, The Joeys, BLAH, Victoria Wood, Maria Muldaur, The Flying Pickets, Sad Cafe, Billy Jo Spears, Donovan, Swingle II, Dean Friedman, Carmel.

Stephane Grappelli

Jazz/Blues

Sonny Terry & Brownie McGhee, American Blues Legends, Barney Kessel & Sacha Distel, Ronnie Scott, Humphrey Lyttleton, Art Blakey, George Melly, Stephane Grappelli, Jimmy Witherspoon, Wild Bill Davison, Johnny Griffin, Chris Barber, Stan Tracey Quartet with Donald Houston (narrator), Benny Carter, Teddy Wilson, Dutch Swing College Band, Midnite Follies, Alex Welsh Band with George Chisholm, *Fascinatin Rhythm* with Marian Montgomery & Richard Rodney Bennett.

Loudon Wainwright III

Folk Concerts

Jake Thackray, Vin Garbutt, Martin Carthy, Tom Paxton, Bert Jansch, Liverpool Poets, Ralph McTell, De Danann, Christy Moore, The Boys of the Lough, June Tabor Band, The Albion Band, Loudon Wainwright III, Maddy Prior Band, The Corries, Robin Williamson, Fairport Convention, Julie Felix, Mike Harding, Ewan MacColl & Peggy Seeger, The McCalmans, Jeremy Taylor, Bernard Wrigley, Battlefield, Mary Coughlan.

The Joeys

Talks & Other Lunchtime Events

Jonathan Miller; Writers at One – John Arden & Margaretta D'Arcy, George MacBeth, Paul Bailey, David Hare, Ian McEwan, James Berry and Peter Flannery; Writers on Tour – Margaret Drabble, D M Thomas, Marina Warner and Rose Tremain; Joyce Grenfell, Adrian Henri; Opera Lectures by Sir Michael Tippett, Lord Harewood, Pauline Tinsley and others; John Lahr, Michael Frayn, Arnold Wesker, Alan Garner, Brigid Brophy, John Schlesinger, Desmond Wilcox, Patrick Nutgens and Platform Performances by the National Theatre. *The Write Stuff:* 12 five minute plays, Simon Callow, Arthur Miller, Irina Ratushinskaya with Ian McDiarmid, Alan Bennett.

Michael Frayn

Late-Night Events

Les Clowns du Prato, Ra Ra Zoo, *Hawk Moon* by Sam Shepard, *Awakening* by August Stramm, *Agamemnon* adapted from the Aeschylus version by Steven Berkoff, *The Diary of Samuel Pepys, An Evening with Lord Byron,* The Great Romantic, *The Small Zone* – The Life and Poetry of Irina Ratushinskaya devised by Michael Fox, An Evening with Paul Scofield and Joy Parker, Roger McGough.

Esmond Knight in Agincourt

Dance

Ballet Rambert, Hungarian Folk Ensemble, Junction Dance Company, Northern Dance Theatre, Stroller In The Air, Danceabout, Százszorszép Dance Group of Martonvásár.

Paul Tortelier

Other Events

International Days, Open Days, Snooker & Pool Tournaments, Puffin Book Carnival, Cricket Spectacular with Clive Lloyd, The Liverpool Poets, Mermaid Puppet Theatre Shows: *Caliph Sherbet, The Boggarts of Boggart Hole Clough, The Enchanted Island, The Golden Bird* and *The Wizard of Oz, Rogues & Vagabonds* with Dame Wendy Hiller, Edward Fox and Frank Muir, Julian Chagrin and Friends in *Hello Socks!,* John Bardon in *Here's A Funny Thing,* Alec McCowen's *St Mark's Gospel, The Wizard's Hat* performed by members of the Royal Exchange Staff, *Agincourt – The Archer's Tale,* presented by Esmond Knight, *He & She* with Frank Muir, Alan Bates and Helen Ryan, Manchester Youth Theatre, Amateur Theatre & Arts Festivals, Brass Band Concerts, An Antiques Workshop with Arthur Negus, Carousel Band. Prunella Scales – *An Evening with Queen Victoria,* Revelations of Black, Hale & Pace, 'Bad Language' workshop.

Orchestral Concerts

Manchester Camerata with Sir Charles Groves, Anthony Hose, Nicholas Braithwaite, Moura Lympany, Sir Clifford Curzon, Peter Frankl, Fou Ts'ong, Stephen Bishop-Kovacevich, Manoug Parikian, Marisa Robles, Kantamanto, Bernard Cribbins and others; The Northern Chamber Orchestra with Nicholas Smith, Jack Brymer and others; The Academy of Ancient Music with Christopher Hogwood, Emma Kirkby and others; The English Consort with Trevor Pinnock; The Northern Sinfonia with Jean-Bernard Pommier and the Scottish Chamber Orchestra with Jacek Kaspryck and Christopher Lee.

120

SPECIAL EVENTS

Chamber Music Concerts

Musicians of the Royal Exchange, The Nash Ensemble with narrators Richard Baker, Eleanor Bron and Fenella Fielding, Deime String Quartet, Landini Consort, Delphonic Ensemble Japan, Chilingirian String Quartet, Contrapuncti, Chetham's School of Music, Allegri String Quartet with Eleanor Bron & Clive Swift.

John Williams

Playreadings

Race Across Antarctica by Norman Leach, *All the Way* by Michael Feast, *Great Dreams from Heaven* by Nick Dear, *In Mr Singh's Kitchen* by Tony Connor, *Monopoly* by Nicholas McInerny, *Peace Play* by Norman Leach, *Sacred Hearts* by James Hogan, *The Wild Hunt of the Autumn Wind* by Kevin Mandry, *Conquistador* by David Calcutt, *Only Science* by Michael Fox, *The Morris Dancers* by Taylor Lovering, *Merlin* by Tankred Dorst. Fassbinder's *The Bitter Tears of Petra von Kant, Hannah Smith's Casket* by Adele Geras, Simon Callow in *Embracing the Enemy* by Philip Clapson.

Edith Sitwell by Cecil Beaton

Manchester Midday Concerts

More than 300 concerts (many of which have been broadcast live on Radio 3) have been given on Thursday lunchtimes under the auspices of the Manchester Mid-Day Concerts Society. *Artists include:* John Williams, Paul Tortelier, The King Singers, John Lill, George Malcolm, Medici String Quartet, Bernedette Greevy, Heinz Holliger, Felicity Palmer, Pierre Amoyal, Walter Klein, Anthony Goldstone, Peter Donohoe, Ann Murray, Peter Katin, Barry Tuckwell, Richard Rodney Bennett, Benjamin Luxon, Fitzwilliam String Quartet, Neil Mackie, Emanuel Ax, Joaquin Achucarro, Pascal Rogé, Anna Markland, Anthony Rolfe Johnson, Michael Collins, Kathryn Stott, Yossi Zivoni, Philip Fowke, Nigel Kennedy, Emma Johnson, Imogen Cooper, Alberni String Quartet, Erich Gruenberg, John McCabe, Felicity Lott, Ronald Stevenson, Steven Isserlis, Janet Hilton, BBC Northern Singers, Philip Jones Brass Ensemble, Howard Shelley, Raphael Wallfisch, Ian & Jennifer Partridge, Stuttgart Piano Trio, Goldberg Ensemble, Gyorgy Pauk, Domus, Marius May, Alan Brind, Ronan O'Hora.

One-act Plays

Duck Variations by David Mamet, *Politics in the Park* by Iain Heggie, *Katie Crowder* by Renny Krupinski, *Lone Star* by James Mclure.

Exhibitions

DAZZLE, Cecil Beaton Photographs, Gerald Scarfe, Theatre Photography by Nobby Clark and Kevin Cummins, Scottish and Lakeland Landscapes by Paul Windridge, Screenprints by Guy Vaesan, Monotypes by Jean Fletcher, Paintings by Michael Goddard & Colin Jellicoe, Batiks on Paper by Miranda Leonard, Etchings & pastels by Derek Wilkinson, Printmakers Council, Photographs by Mike Harding, Craft Market/Fairs, Craft Centre: Wooden Ducks by Guy Taplin, Puppets by Jan Zalud, Ceramics by Nancy Angus and Ivo Mosley, Glass by Lindean Mill, Deborah Fladgate and Margaret Alston, Jewellery by Jolene Smith, Joanna Morgan, Rowena Park and Kiran Singh, Textiles by Paul Emmerson, Georgina Cardew, Janet Hutchinson and Lindy Richardson.

121

FRIENDS OF THE ROYAL EXCHANGE THEATRE

Patron: Tom Courtenay

Prior to the Royal Exchange Theatre's opening in 1976, a veritable army of people gave voluntarily of their time, effort, and indeed their money, to help realise the vision of the artistic directors. So much did the theatre owe to these people, that in 1981 it was decided to launch the 'Friends of the Royal Exchange Theatre' as a way of re-establishing contact with old and valued friends, and of encouraging new members of the audience to become more closely involved with the life of the company. Seven years later, the Friends organisation is firmly established as an important and integral part of the life of the theatre.

In return for the 'Friendship' members are offered a variety of benefits both social and financial, details of which are announced in regular newsletters. The advantages to the company of having such an organisation are many: it provides the opportunity to have a more realistic and informal contact with the public; it is an invaluable source of voluntary help to various areas of the theatre – Friends help the Publicity and Front of House Departments and operate the Costume and Props Hire business; and, as an informed and interested group, members are capable of supporting and advocating the good of the theatre.

The events programme, which is organised by a Committee of Friends and Company staff, consists of at least two events every month – talks on the productions from directors and actors, trips to other theatres and places of interest (including in recent years Paris, Dublin, and London), occasional parties and fund-raising events, back-stage tours and a myriad of other events, most, although by no means all, theatre-related.

Benefits of membership include Priority Booking before the general public and a popular reduced-price First Night Ticket Scheme; reduced prices on certain special presentations, generous discounts from a number of city centre shops, restaurants and leisure centres and, perhaps most importantly, the opportunity to improve the quality of theatre-going by attending talks on productions.

FRIENDS COMMITTEE (at October 1988)

Noel Pilling	**Mrs Mary Evans**
Chairman	**Val Hodgkinson**
Dr Gillian Bates	**Rosalind Knight**
Social Secretary	**Sue Lawton**
Mrs Julia Pilling	Friends Organiser/
Membership Secretary	Development Co-Ordinator
John Brooks	**Mrs Sheila Lord**
Mrs Susan Evans	**Joseph Morley**
Minutes Secretary	**Mrs Pat Myers**

MEMBERSHIP RATES (at October 1988)

Single £6.00	Student £4.00
Joint £10.00	Company £40.00

WHO'S WHO

Winter 1988

BOARD OF DIRECTORS

Alex Bernstein Chairman
Bernard Terry Deputy Chairman
Cllr W Brogan
Cllr Mrs M Connell
Mrs Rayna Dean
Sir William Downward
Jack Goldberg
Anthony Goldstone MBE
Cllr M Harrison
Cllr A E Hatton
Mrs Sara Henriques
Cllr S G W Jacobs
Christopher Kenyon
Cllr J King
Paul A Lee
James Maxwell
Braham Murray
Richard Negri
John Parsons
Robert Scott
Cllr Mrs S V Shaw
Paull Tickner
George Wedell
Casper Wrede

Honorary Associate
G. Laurence Harbottle
(Chairman 1968-83)

THE ROYAL EXCHANGE THEATRE TRUST LIMITED

DIRECTORS
Alex Bernstein Chairman
Bernard Terry Deputy Chairmen
Cllr W Brogan
Sir William Downward
Cllr D Ford
Jack Goldberg
Cllr M Harrison
Mrs Sara Henriques
Cllr Mrs J D W Hill OBE
Cllr J King
J M Leach
Paul A Lee
Sir William Mather OBE MC
Canon G O Morgan
Cllr P M Morrison
Braham Murray
Robert Scott
H B Vanstone
Cllr A S Wood
Bill Dickson Secretary
Addleshaw Sons & Latham
Honorary Solicitors
Grant Thornton Honorary Auditors

FINANCE COMMITTEE

Alex Bernstein
Bernard Terry
Cllr Mrs S V Shaw
John Parsons
Mrs Rayna Dean
David Fairclough
Lynda Farran
Paul A Lee
Braham Murray

DEVELOPMENT COMMITTEE

Paul A Lee Chairman
Christopher Attrill
Barrie Bernstein
Mrs Rayna Dean
James Dunlop
Richard Fildes
Tom Finnigan
Peter Folkman
David Kaye
Ted McMahon
Paul Mitchell
Tim O'Brien
John Parsons
Philip Ramsbottom
Bernard Terry

ARTISTIC DIRECTORS

Artistic Directors
Gregory Hersov
James Maxwell
Braham Murray
Casper Wrede
Associate Artistic Director and
Casting Director
Sophie Marshall
Associate Director
Nicholas Hytner
Associate Director (Movement)
Fergus Early
Associate Director (Music)
Chris Monks

Honorary Artistic Director
Richard Negri

Secretary to the Artistic Directors
Shirley Lipman
Secretary to the Casting Director
Wendy Spon

ADMINISTRATION

Administrator
Lynda Farran
Staff Contracts and
Special Projects Manager
Denise Wood
Secretary
Helen Byrne

BOX OFFICE

Box Office Manager
Ean Burgon
Deputy Box Office Manager
Ann Williamson
Group Bookings Organiser
Julia Grimshaw
Assistants
Christine Chaplin
Carol Devine
Dawn Fawcett
Carmel Lonergan
Sally Noakes

CLEANERS

Head
Doreen Wright
Deputy Head
Marjorie Lazarus
Cleaners
Theresa Bennett
Gillian Bradshaw
Linda Cuddy
Jim Hartley
Diane Jones
Ann Livesey
Sheila Perry
Ann Marie Stanley

COSTUME

Costume Supervisor
Ginnie O'Brien
Assistant Costume Supervisor
Sophie Doncaster
Cutter
Jane Gonin
Cutter's Assistants
Debbie Attle
Marie Dunaway
Tailor
Robert Rainsford
Wardrobe Mistresses
Ann Darlington
Amanda Sawdon
Head Dresser
Enid Geldard
YTS Trainees
Georgina Shaw
Rachel Jones

CRAFT CENTRE

Craft Centre Manager
Morag Shaw
Senior Assistant
Geli Sargent
Assistants
Irene Gruber
Shel Sargent
Promotions Assistant
Rosie Cooper

DEVELOPMENT

Development Officers
Charlotte Bowen
Sue Lawton
Secretary
Ellie Gray

EDUCATION

Education Director
John Butterly

FINANCE

Financial Controller
David Fairclough
Deputy Financial Controller
Christopher Bolstridge
Assistant to Financial Controller
Robert Laird
Cashier
Sandra Hughes
Purchase Ledger Clerk
Lesley Farthing
Secretary
Elaine Ridyard

FRIENDS ORGANISATION

Friends Organiser
Sue Lawton
Props & Costume Hire
Gill Bates

FRONT OF HOUSE

Theatre Manager
Irene Muir
Front of House Manager
Lynne Yates
Relief Front of House Manager
Jill Bridgman
Exhibitions
Christine Bola
Head Ushers
Peter Adshead
Angela Gorman
Wendy Miller
Philip Robertshaw

122

Claire Robinson
Martin Seymour

GREEN ROOM

Supervisors
Monica Carlin
Nuala Reilly
Assistant
Yvonne Stott

LIGHTING

Chief Electrician
Vincent Herbert
Deputy
Taras Kochan
Assistants
Mike Adams

LITERARY DEPARTMENT

Literary Manager
Alan Pollock
Writer in Residence
Gabriel Gbadamosi (Mobil Bursary)
Secretary
Wendy Spon

PRODUCTION

Production Controller
Philip Lord
Production Assistant
Sue Burke
Props Buyer
David Millard
Stage Director
Bob Cummings
First Technician
Jeff Salmon
Technicians
Nick Kyle
Jeremy Hodgson
Maintenance
Rodney Bostock
Driver/Handyman
Steve Aston

PROPS AND SETTINGS

Head of Construction
Rob Stirling
Head of Props
Mike Hubbard
Prop Makers
David Bloodworth
Michael McLoughlin
Stephen Bedford
Loren Hickson
Ged Mayo

PUBLICITY

Marketing & Publicity Director
Lynne Walker
Publicity Officer
Karen Forster
Distribution Assistant
Yvonne Robinson
Secretary
Sandra Gregson

SECURITY & STAGEDOOR

Day
Jeff Follows
Anthony Whittaker
Eric Anderson
Evening
Jim Doyle
Jason Sankey
General Assistant
Ben Adams

Stage Door Receptionist
Maureen Pooler
Stage Doormen
John Cundall
Tony Mellam
Harold Slater

SOUND

Sound Man
Philip Clifford
Deputy
Rosalind Elliman
Assistant
Tim McCormick

STAGE MANAGEMENT

Company Manager
Ann Harrison-Baxter
Stage Managers
Gill Allen
Helen Thursby
Deputy Stage Managers
Rachael Artingstall
Fiona Francombe
Assistant Stage Managers
Kim Ford
Cathy Sluggett

TOURING

Tour Manager
Keith Halsall

WIGS

Head of Production Wigs
Barbara Taylor
Assistant
Gina Kane

WILLSHAWS THEATRE
BOOKSHOP

Manager
Andrew Forster
Assistants
Betty Haworth
Sally Howles
Julie Jones
Julie Swain

123

The Royal Exchange Theatre Company Ltd,
St Ann's Square, Manchester M2 7DH

Administration/Stage Door	**061-833 9333**
Box Office	**061-833 9833**
Group Booking	**061-833 0483**
Catering	**061-833 9682**
Information (Publicity Dept)	**061-833 9938**

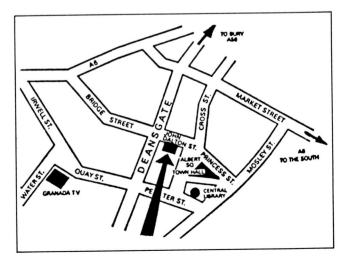

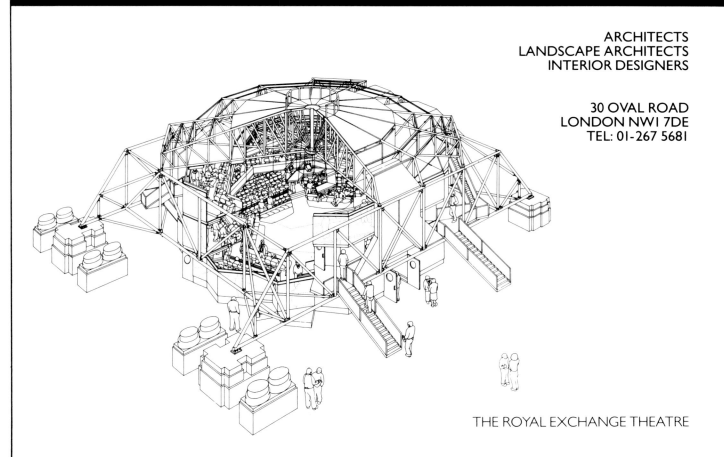

A giant performance in the North-West.

ICL is this country's leading supplier of computers and information systems. Many of our achievements have emanated from our investment in the North-West.

At West Gorton we have a purpose-built site for the design and development of mainframe computer systems. The operation has strong links with the academic community. The liaison with Manchester University has been a particularly fruitful example of industry and education working together.

In central Manchester we operate one of the most comprehensive sales, service and support operations in the United Kingdom.

ICL designs, develops and manufactures its highly successful Series 39 range of mainframe systems entirely in the North-West utilising the most advanced computer-controlled assembly line in Europe.

To further demonstrate our commitment to the North-West, a new £1 million extension has just been completed at West Gorton and an additional £1.3 million is being spent on new production facilities at our manufacturing plant in Ashton.

This kind of investment typifies our confidence in the North-West and is part of a record of achievement that leads to one inescapable conclusion.

There is no better or stronger IT company to do business with.

We should be talking to each other

A MEMBER OF THE STC PLC GROUP

POSTCODES
STRIKE THE RIGHT NOTE
AT

Royal Exchange Theatre	M2 7DH
Library Theatre	M2 5PD
Forum Theatre	M22 5RT
Bolton Octagon	BL1 1SB
Oldham Coliseum	OL1 3SW

Royal Mail postcodes
061-837 2590

Congratulations from

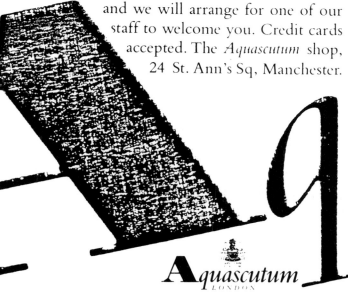

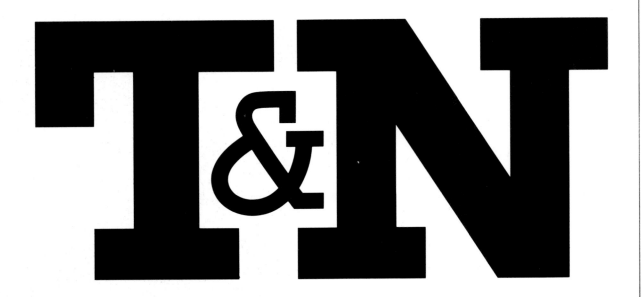

Inter Theatre

Theatre & Literature Courses

Theatregoing Bus • Residential Schools

Courses in Manchester

Membership

You get a regular Newsletter, priority bookings and discounts on courses. You get special theatre visits and opportunities to meet actors, directors and other members of the theatrical profession. You may join as few or as many events as you wish.

InterTheatre Artistic Director Robin Allan 10 Dale Road, New Mills, Stockport SK12 4NW. 0663 42809

The Centre of

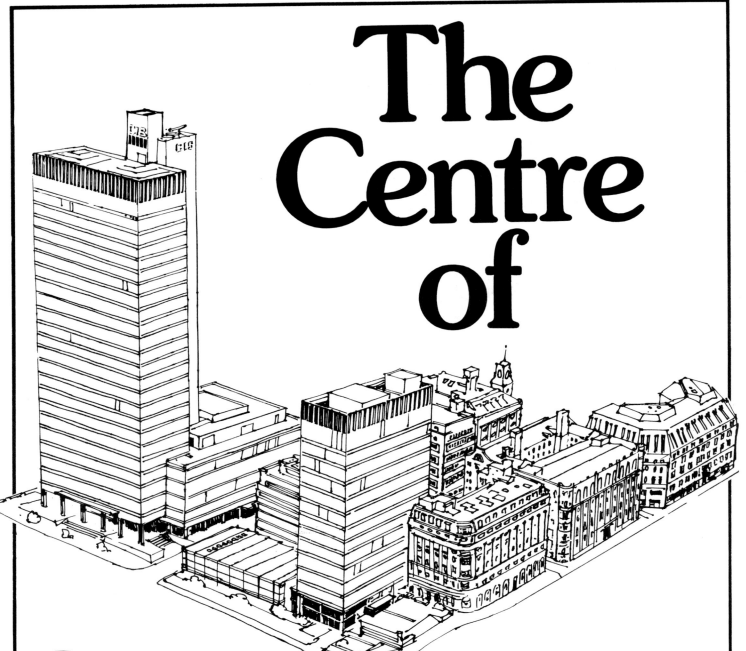

Co-operation

The Co-operative Wholesale Society, Co-operative Bank, Co-operative Insurance Society and Co-operative Retail Services, together form the heart of the Co-op, in the centre of Manchester

Every day of the year CWS farms, factories, warehouses and financial institutions provide goods and services worth many millions of pounds to Co-op societies and individual citizens throughout Britain.

Co-operative Wholesale Society Ltd., P.O. Box 53, New Century House, Manchester M60 4ES.

co op People who care

Nickerson
FUEL OILS LIMITED
LUBRICANTS LIMITED

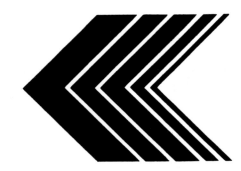

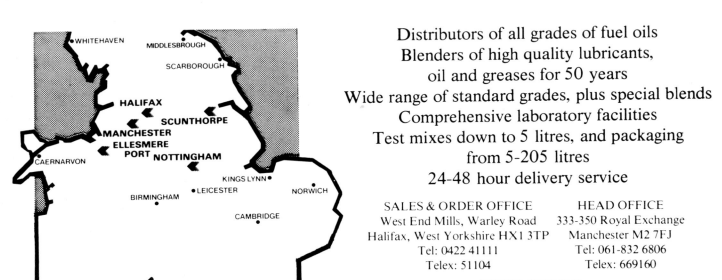

Distributors of all grades of fuel oils
Blenders of high quality lubricants,
oil and greases for 50 years
Wide range of standard grades, plus special blends
Comprehensive laboratory facilities
Test mixes down to 5 litres, and packaging
from 5-205 litres
24-48 hour delivery service

SALES & ORDER OFFICE	HEAD OFFICE
West End Mills, Warley Road	333-350 Royal Exchange
Halifax, West Yorkshire HX1 3TP	Manchester M2 7FJ
Tel: 0422 41111	Tel: 061-832 6806
Telex: 51104	Telex: 669160

OTHER OFFICES
Ellesmere Port
Nottingham
Scunthorpe

When you need service
We deliver

**Nickerson Lubricants Limited and Nickerson Fuel Oils Limited
are both part of Nickerson Investments Limited**

FRIENDS OF THE ROYAL EXCHANGE *Theatre*

Are you getting the most out of THE ROYAL EXCHANGE THEATRE If you're not a FRIEND the answer is NO!

FIND out more about Royal Exchange productions.

RECEIVE generous discounts at several major stores, restaurants and in our excellent Craft centre.

INCREASE your contact with the Company

ENJOY the many and varied events organised for members.

NURTURE your interest in the Royal Exchange by helping us in you spare time, back stage, front-of-house and in our costume hire department.

DON'T delay fill in the application form below and join us at the next set of events.

SEND with payment and a stamped addressed envelope to Sue Lawton, Royal Exchange Theatre, St. Ann's Square, Manchester M2 7DH

MEMBERSHIP FEE Single £6.00 Joint £10.00 Student £4.00 Company £40.00

....

Name ....

Address ....

....

....

Post Code ....

Tel. No. home .... work ....

I wish to pay by Access/Barclaycard/Diners Club

Signature ....

cash/cheque £ .... please make cheques payable to the Royal Exchange Theatre Company Ltd.

That magic moment is now captured on a Royal Exchange Theatre postcard available at Willshaws Theatre Bookshop

Also:
Sweatshirts
T-shirts
Posters
Keyrings
Pens, etc

Royal Exchange Theatre Gift Vouchers are available in units of £1, £5 and £10. They can be exchanged for theatre tickets from the Box Office and for goods at Willshaws Theatre Bookshop and the Craft Centre.

BOX OFFICE: 061-833 9833

For a clearer picture
of the State of the Arts